Red Sky, Black Death

A Soviet Woman Pilot's Memoir of the Eastern Front

RED SKY, BLACK DEATH

A SOVIET WOMAN PILOT'S MEMOIR OF THE EASTERN FRONT

ANNA TIMOFEYEVA-YEGOROVA

TRANSLATED BY
MARGARITA PONOMARYOVA & KIM GREEN

EDITED BY KIM GREEN

Bloomington, Indiana, 2009

SLAVICA

Cover design by Austin Gray.

Maps in the back cover pocket are from the collection of the University of North Texas Libraries.

Photos following page 104 are from the personal collection of Anna Yegorova.

Library of Congress Cataloging-in-Publication Data

Timofeeva-Egorova, A. A. (Anna Aleksandrovna)
   [Ia--"Bereza"--Kak slyshite menia? English]
   Red sky, black death : a Soviet woman pilot's memoir of the Eastern
   Front / Anna Timofeyeva-Yegorova ; translated by Margarita
   Ponomaryova & Kim Green ; edited by Kim Green.
      p. cm.
   Includes bibliographical references.
   ISBN 978-0-89357-355-3
   1. Timofeeva-Egorova, A. A. (Anna Aleksandrovna) 2. World War, 1939-
1945--Aerial operations, Soviet. 3. World War, 1939-1945--Personal narratives,
Soviet. 4. Fighter pilots--Soviet Union--Biography. 5. Women air pilots--Soviet
Union--Biography. 6. Geroi Sovetskogo Soiuza--Biography. 7. World War,
1939-1945--Participation, Female. *. Title.
   D792.S65T56313 2009
   940.54'4947092--dc22
   [B]
                                    2009000761

Slavica Publishers   [Tel.] 1-812-856-4186
Indiana University   [Toll-free] 1-877-SLAVICA
2611 E. 10th St.   [Fax] 1-812-856-4187
Bloomington, IN 47408-2603   [Email] slavica@indiana.edu
USA   [www] http://www.slavica.com/

I dedicate this book to those who have perished and those who have survived, and to those who passed from our midst after the war, my dearest regimental comrades of the 805th Attack Aviation Regiment of Berlin, awarded the Order of Suvorov. Please forgive me if I have forgotten or missed anything, or if I have failed to mention anyone.

A. Timofeyeva
Moscow, 1992

... There are women in Russian villages
With calm, self-possessed faces,
With beautiful strength in their movements,
With the gait and the look of tsarinas,...

They follow the same path as all our people,
But the filth of poverty doesn't stick to them.

A blooming beauty, a marvel to all the world.
Rosy-cheeked, tall, and slender,
Beautiful in any clothing, deft at any work.

Even on horseback, you couldn't catch her in a game.
In trouble, she will not falter—she'll save you.
She would curb a galloping horse,
She would walk into a burning hut!...

—Nikolai Alexeyevich Nekrasov (1821–78)

Contents

Foreword

Woman has always played a role in war. She has defended her home and children from invading forces, nursed wounded soldiers at the front, and disguised as a male soldier, she has fought bravely in the trenches. She has spied for her country, participated in armed resistance as a partisan, a sniper, an infantryman, a combat pilot. In the history of war, woman has played patriot, killer, and savior.

The most controversial role woman has played throughout history in war is that of warrior. Often driven by a desire for adventure, a love of country, and a need to break from their narrow, conventional roles in society, women have volunteered to fight alongside their countrymen, often disguised as men. In the American Revolution Deborah Sampson enlisted in Colonel Henry Jackson's Fourth Massachusetts Regiment under the name of Robert Shirtliff. Fanny Campbell, disguised as a second officer on the British merchant brigantine *Constance*, sailed to Cuba to rescue her imprisoned husband and ten other jailed Americans. In the American Civil War hundreds of women fought in the Union Army disguised as men, and the number was higher for women of the Confederacy. Loreta Janeta Velazquez took on the male persona of Lieutenant Harry T. Buford and fought against the Yankees, recounting the experiences in her memoir *The Woman in Battle*.

Earlier, in 1806, Nadezhda Durova, disguised as a boy, ran away from home to fight in the Russian wars against Napoleon, where she experienced nine years of combat and was personally decorated for heroism by Tsar Alexander I. One hundred years later, in 1917, Maria Bochkareva would lead Russia's first all-female battalion in defense of the ill-fated Provisional Government.

History is peppered with the exploits of women on the battlefield. The experiences of women, however vivid, often appear only as footnotes or are explained away by historians as exceptional or insignificant. Throughout the centuries women have expressed a desire to not only care for soldiers wounded in battle, as has been their traditional role, but to be soldiers themselves. In the twentieth century with the advent of aviation, women proved that they could fly as well as men, and the early women pioneers of flight paved the way for women to become military pilots.

As women's confidence grew in the air, they saw for themselves an important role alongside their male counterparts when war threatened their country. World War I signified the first armed conflict to utilize air power. Despite their skill and experience in the cockpit, women were not allowed by their governments to fly in combat. Although they did fly in different capacities throughout the war, it would not be until two decades later when women would be permitted to pilot military aircraft in wartime.

On June 22, 1941 the German *blitzkrieg* invaded the Soviet Union in the form of Hitler's Operation Barbarossa. Six months later in the early morning hours of December 7, 1941, the Japanese attacked the American naval base at Pearl Harbor, thus inciting the United States to join its European allies in World War II. As a result of these two events, thousands of Soviet and American men and women, fueled by patriotism, eagerly volunteered for the armed forces.

That same year American aviatrix Jacqueline Cochran and Soviet pilot Marina Raskova would inspire firsts in both their countries. Cochran convinced President Franklin D. Roosevelt that women should fly military aircraft as ferrying pilots and organized the Women Airforce Service Pilots (WASP) program. Raskova, with Stalin's blessing, formed the world's first all-female air regiments which would carry out combat missions along the Eastern Front.

To understand the significance of these American and Soviet women pilots' accomplishments in World War II, it is necessary to look back in history at women's early involvement in the area of aviation. Whether they disguised themselves as men or fought as women, the history of war is interspersed with the accounts of female soldiers. While women have proved themselves useful in war, they often appear a dangerous threat to the social order after it. War provided new opportunities for women to break down the gender barrier—if only temporarily. Even after proving their capabilities to their country, the Soviet women pilots found themselves in the awkward position of being cautioned to discount their experiences. When Stalin praised the work of women in the war on November 6, 1944, he did not mention that they had fought in combat. After the war Soviet President Kalinin warned his country's female veterans, "Do not speak of the services you rendered."

Since the days of the early balloon flights in the eighteenth century women have been involved in all aspects of aviation and have piloted everything from balloons to space vehicles. For women aviators, the country of origin for many firsts was France. Madame Elisabeth Thible became the first woman to fly in an untethered balloon as a passenger, watched by the King of Sweden in May 1784. According to accounts, Madame Thible flew a mile high, elegantly attired in a lace-trimmed dress and a feathered hat. Although she did not repeat the experience, she apparently enjoyed it so much that she burst into song.

In 1805 Madeleine Sophie Blanchard, wife of the famous balloonist Jean Pierre Blanchard, became the first woman aeronaut in her own right. She gained such a reputation in her lifetime that Napoleon made her Official Aeronaut of the Empire. She was killed in July 1817 during an aerial fireworks display at the Tivoli Gardens in Paris when her balloon caught on fire and she fell onto a roof and died of a broken neck.

In Châlons, France on October 22, 1909, Raymonde de Laroche became the first woman in the world to drive a heavier-than-air machine into the air alone. Five months later she was issued license No. 36 by the Aero Club of France, joining the growing number of men licensed in Europe and the United States. Other women pilots were soon to be added to the list, including Harriet Quimby in the United States and Lydia Zvereva in Russia in 1911, becoming the first licensed women pilots in their respective countries. The next year Quimby would go on to become the first woman to fly solo across the English Channel.

Although aviation developed more slowly in Russia than in the West, there were a small number of women who flew in the Imperial period. Born into a military family in St. Petersburg in 1890 and educated at the Tsar Nicholas I Institute for Girls, Lydia Zvereva proved that she was just as skilled on the ground as a mechanic as she was in the sky as a pilot. She would use this talent many times when her male mechanic could not figure out the problem with her airplane. After receiving her pilot's license on August 22, 1911 at the Russian Aviation Association Flying School at Gatchina, Zvereva entered several flying contests, but found to her dismay that many of the men did not welcome female pilots. The Aero Club demanded such a high security deposit for the race at Tsarskoe Selo that she had to bow out. As her reputation grew as a skilled flyer, she became the object of sabotage when a competitor put iron filings in the motor of her Farman airplane.

During an air show in May 1914 Zvereva became the first woman pilot in the world to perform a loop in an airplane. When war broke out that same year she continued to produce planes in the airplane manufacturing plant in Riga and St. Petersburg that she had started with her husband and former flight instructor, Vladimir V. Slyusarenko. Zvereva died on May 1, 1916 from typhoid fever and was buried in Alexander Nevsky Monastery while an aerial formation flew over the cemetery in her honor.

The second Russian woman to earn a pilot's license was Eudocie V. Anatra, who on October 3, 1911, received certificate No. 54 at Gatchina airfield. She opened a flying school in 1912, and one of her best-known students was Eugenie Shakhovskaya, a princess born in St. Petersburg in 1889, and the third woman to take to the skies. Flying was becoming more acceptable for women now, and Shakhovskaya's aristocratic background freed her from worry about respectability. On August 16, 1912 she received her pilot's license in Berlin. That same year when war broke out in Italy, Shakhovskaya proposed to fly as an aerial reconnaissance pilot for the Italian government, but the Italians refused her offer. Despite the refusal, Shakhovskaya did not give up her desire to fly for the war effort, and was later hailed as the "first military airwoman" in the world when she became an air scout for the Russian Army in the First World War. Princess Shakhovskaya reportedly obtained the tsar's permission to serve as a reconnaissance pilot, although she did not hold military rank or participate in combat.

Lyubov Golanchikova, a former dancer-singer known as Molly Moret, became a popular pilot in Russia after she broke the altitude record at Johannisthal airfield near Berlin on November 21, 1912 with a flight of 2,200 meters. Well known for her skill in exhibition flying, it is reported that Lyuba, as she was later called, is believed to have gone on to fly for the Red Air Fleet when the Russian Revolution began in 1917. She reportedly flew several missions for the revolutionary forces during the civil war, but details are sketchy.

Nadezhda Degtereva, who is said to have disguised herself as a boy and entered military air service in 1914, also flew reconnaissance missions. It was not until after she was wounded while flying over enemy lines on the Austrian front in Galicia that her true sex was discovered. Her valor earned her a promotion to the rank of sergeant and the Cross of Saint George, Fourth Class. Degtereva holds the distinction of being the first woman pilot to be wounded in combat. Princess Sophie Alexandrovna Dolgorukaya is also reported to have flown for the Air Service in 1917 after Alexander Kerensky, the leader of the Provisional Government in Russia, opened military service to women.

The first American woman to make a solo flight was Blanche Stuart Scott on September 2, 1910, but according to Ann Hodgman and Rudy Djabbaroff in their book *Sky Stars: The History of Women in Aviation*, it may have been unintentional. According to the authors, Scott was sitting in the plane while her instructor, famed aviator and airplane designer Glenn Curtiss, gave her a lesson. As she began to practice driving the plane back and forth across the field, a "sudden gust of wind lifted the plane into the air." Because the engine was on at the time and the plane was light, Scott was soon forty feet in the air. She managed to maintain her composure and landed the aircraft safely.

Bessica Faith Raiche was also learning how to fly at the same time as Scott. Two weeks after Scott soloed so did Raiche. Because Scott's flight may have been caused by a trick of the wind, it was Raiche who was given the distinction by the Aeronautical Society on October 13, 1910, as being the "first woman aviator of America." Her failing health later forced Raiche to give up flying, and she went on to study medicine and became a practicing physician.

Despite women's early successes in aviation, it was difficult for them to find jobs other than in exhibition flying performing for crowds. The public viewed women flyers more as a novelty than serious pilots. Opportunities to teach flying or work for the government as aviators were still a distant dream for most women. The advent of World War I saw the birth of air power and American women began to offer their services to a reluctant nation.

As many women did at the outbreak of the war, pilot Ruth Law wanted to get involved. Like most female flyers during this period, she accumulated her flight hours performing in air shows around the country. Law offered herself to the United States government as a fighter. "I could drive a machine with a gun and gunner and go into actual battle," she said at the time. "That's what I'd like to do more than anything—get right into the fight!" Not surprisingly her offer was turned down. Law went on to fly for the benefit of the Red Cross and Liberty Bond drives, setting a new women's altitude record of 14,700 feet. In November 1917 she sent a petition to the War Department requesting that she be allowed to fly military aircraft for the war effort. Again Law was turned down. She was allowed however to do recruiting work for the Army and Navy, and for that work she was given an Army officer's uniform.

Since the Soviet Union had the distinction of being the first country in the world to proclaim legal equality for women in 1917, the military flying schools and Osoaviakhim (the Society for Cooperation in Defense and Aviation-Chemical Development) could not legally refuse entry to qualified women. It was through Osoaviakhim, a paramilitary organization, that most Soviet women received flight training. Founded in 1927 to train teenagers and young adults in quasi-military skills such as defense and chemical warfare, marksmanship, and parachuting, by the 1930s it began developing a network of air clubs to provide flight training in light aircraft. The Soviet government emphasized the importance of aviation and air travel, which was seen as the most promising means of transportation, especially since the vast expanses of Soviet territory were still not linked by roads or railroads.

Officially young Soviet women were encouraged to participate in all facets of Osoaviakhim training. However, many women encountered obstacles when attempting to get into flight training. Marina Chechneva (who subsequently became a night bomber pilot and a Hero of the Soviet Union in the Second World War) described the manner in which her male flying club instructor discouraged her from seeking a career as a pilot as being typical of the time:

> Quite a few women were studying at the air club; however, the attitude of many of the instructors towards them was, to put it mildly, less than enthusiastic. The instructors took women in their groups unwillingly. That was clear. Women were only beginning to enter aviation. Not everyone believed that we would be able to work in this field on an equal basis with men. The example of famous women pilots did not convince the skeptics. "Aviation is not a woman's affair," they declared repeatedly, and tried in every way possible to dissuade young women from joining the air club.

Nevertheless many Soviet women persevered and learned to fly. By 1941, 100 to 150 air clubs had been established; one out of every three or four pilots was a woman. The purpose for the training (for the men anyway) was to prepare them for either active or reserve military duty. The men who received flight training at the air clubs were registered in the military reserve forces, but women were not. No provisions were made for women pilots to play a military role — at least not yet.

Arguably the most celebrated woman pilot in American history was Amelia Earhart. Although her flying career lasted less than ten years, her accomplishments and personality beguiled a nation and helped to extend the possibilities of women in aviation. A setter of many aviation records, she is probably best known for being the first woman to pilot a transatlantic flight, the first solo crossing for a woman, and the fastest crossing by anyone. In 1937 Earhart and her navigator Fred Noonan set out on a round the world flight at the Equator that had never been done before. It was on this flight that she and Noonan disappeared. The United States organized the largest air and sea search in its history (at that time), combing an area of 265,000 square miles for sixteen days, but no trace of the pilots or their plane was ever found. Earhart remarked just before her final flight: "I want to do it because I want to do it. Women must try to do things as men have tried. When they fail, their failure must be a challenge to others."

In 1929 the first national air race for women took place in Santa Monica, California. Nineteen women took part in the race, including Amelia Earhart. The first Women's Air Derby became known as the "Powder Puff Derby." The derby made the women who flew in it realize how much they could benefit from organizing themselves. Four pilots — Margery Brown, Fay Gillis, Frances Harrell, and Neva Paris — sat down together and wrote a letter that they sent to all licensed women pilots in the United States. On November 2, 1929, twenty-six women gathered at Curtiss Airport in New York to make plans for forming the world's first all-women aviation organization. It was Amelia Earhart who suggested the organization be named for the number of charter members who joined it. This idea was immediately accepted. Earhart was made president of the new group, and after all the members were counted, the organization became the "Ninety-Nines." The group remains in existence today with more than 5,500 active members in 35 countries.

In the 1930s an American by the name of Jacqueline Cochran began to be known for her achievements as a pilot. Cochran would go on to form the Women Airforce Service Pilots (WASP) program a decade later, which would give American women the unprecedented opportunity to fly military aircraft during World War II. Born into poverty with a tremendous drive to succeed, she started out in the cosmetics business. Thinking that learning how to fly might help promote her new company, Cochran (with the financial backing of her millionaire husband Floyd Odlum) earned her pilot's license after only two-and-a-half weeks. In her 1954 autobiography *Stars at Noon*, Cochran described her first flying lesson in 1932: "I showed up at Roosevelt Field, Long Island, at the flying school," she wrote. "At that moment, when I paid for my first lesson, a beauty operator ceased to exist and an aviator was born."

In December Cochran set a new national transcontinental record—beating Howard Hughes' earlier one—by racing from New York City to Miami in only four hours and twelve minutes. The flight was a dangerous one, but taking risks became Cochran's hallmark. That same year the International League of Aviators voted Cochran the world's outstanding pilot, an award that she would win for three consecutive years.

In March 1939 Cochran was awarded her second Harmon Trophy, the highest award given to any aviator in America. The day before the Harmon Award was announced, she had broken a women's altitude record by climbing to 33,000 feet above sea level. Over the next few months Cochran broke two women's and two national speed records, and one intercity record—between Burbank and San Francisco. On each of her record-breaking flights, sustained only with a half-filled bottle of Coca-Cola (a full one would explode at high altitudes) and a fistful of lollypops for "dry mouth," she tested new types of oxygen masks, engine superchargers, sparkplugs and airplane fuel and wing designs which would appear in the airplanes soon to become America's air arsenal.

That same year the Civil Aeronautics Administration began a program of pilot cadet training in American colleges and many young women eagerly signed up for flying lessons. In 1941, however, women were dropped to make room for more men. Cochran sensed early in the war, however, that women would be needed as pilots, and she eagerly sought out the opportunity to bring female aviators into the war effort. She recalled in her autobiography: "The pressure on our man power during World War II and the increasing use of war power made it certain that eventually there would be a need for women pilots. All my war work up until the time General Arnold called me home from England (where she was assisting with the Air Transport Auxiliary) had been in preparation for this time of need."

Thousands of miles away another accomplished flyer was preparing to organize a group of young female pilots to fly in defense of Soviet Russia. Marina Raskova, one of the most venerated and best-loved women aviators of the USSR, is largely unknown in the West. Raskova was admired for her achievements in aviation in the same way Amelia Earhart was in the United States.

Founder of the world's first all-female air regiments during World War II, Raskova, who rose to the rank of major, would become the first woman navigator in the Soviet Union and commanding officer of the 587th Dive Bomber Regiment, subsequently renamed the 125th M. M. Raskova *Borisov* Guards Dive Bomber Regiment after her death in 1943. One of the first women to earn the coveted title Hero of the Soviet Union, Raskova served as a role model for her fellow aviators, male and female, for not only her tremendous skill and personal courage, but her ability to make decisions and lead her regiment under severe and often very difficult circumstances.

Like Cochran, Raskova did not set out early in her life to become a pilot. She aspired to be an opera singer, but a middle-ear infection at the age of fifteen pushed her life down another path. Raskova chose instead to study chemistry and engineering, and later mastered the theory of air navigation. She became the first woman in the USSR to earn the diploma of professional air navigator, going on to become an instructor at N. Ye. Zhukovsky Air Force Engineering Academy in Moscow.

As an instructor Raskova taught military navigation to male officers, who although initially skeptical of her knowledge and abilities, would later admit that they were now convinced, based on her performance, of women's capabilities in aviation. The Academy rewarded Raskova by sending her to the Central Flying Club at Tushino, near Moscow, for flying lessons, which she completed in August 1935. After her training Raskova became an instrument flying instructor and taught advanced navigation for command personnel.

By the mid-1930s Raskova became involved in a greater number of important aviation-related events, and in August 1935 she took part in her first independent flight as a pilot. In July 1936, Raskova began probationary navigator training in the 23rd Heavy Air Brigade. In the meantime she continued instructing at the Academy. In June 1937 Raskova participated as navigator in an air race from Moscow to Sevastopol and back to Moscow, flying the same plane as in the 1935 flight but this time with additional fuel tanks. She was the fourth to arrive in Sevastopol and the sixth to return to Moscow, completing the journey within twenty-four hours. That same year Raskova met pilot Valentina Grizodubova, who proposed to her that they fly together in a Yak-12 to establish a long distance record. On October 24, 1937 they set a new women's record when they covered approximately 1,443 kilometers from Moscow to Aktyubinsk, Kazakhstan.

On July 2, 1938 Raskova again established a new women's long distance record when she flew (as navigator) with pilot Polina Osipenko and co-pilot Vera Lomako in an MP-1 non-stop from the Black Sea to the White Sea, having taken off in Sevastopol and landed in the vicinity of Arkhangelsk on Lake Kholmovskoye. The route lay across four different air masses: tropical, continental, polar, and arctic, and required tremendous skills by the crew. The aviators set an international women's straight-line distance record when they flew 5,947 kilometers. As a result of this record-setting flight, senior lieutenants Osipenko and Lomako as well as lieutenant Raskova (who became a career officer in 1938) were each awarded the Order of Lenin.

Not long after this flight, Grizodubova, with Stalin's support, arranged for an aircraft to be assigned to them for their proposed flight to the Far East (with Osipenko as co-pilot). It was an ANT-37 (a converted long-range DB-2 bomber) nicknamed *Rodina* ("Motherland") by Grizodubova. In addition to flight training, the three women practiced firing rifles and pistols. The flight was delayed after Raskova developed appendicitis, and in September 1938 a state commission cancelled the flight due to the lateness in the year and anticipated bad weather. Stalin, however, overruled the decision and the *Rodina* took off on September 24, 1938 at 8:16 a.m.

During the course of this mission, overcast skies completely obscured all visual landmarks, leaving radio signals as the only means of orientation. When the radio station ceased transmitting, there was nothing to do but continue on, eventually running out of fuel. Raskova's crew position in the nose of the aircraft was hazardous for a crash landing, so she was ordered to parachute from the plane over the *taiga*, a dense, swampy, forested area of Siberia. Raskova landed in the swamp and it was not until ten days later that she finally came upon her aircraft and was reunited with Osipenko and Grizodubova. The story of Raskova's flight was widely publicized, and her courage and stamina caught the imagination of the Soviet people.

Raskova spent several months recovering from the injuries to her legs she sustained as a result of the historic flight. Not only had Raskova proven her courage but she was also intelligent and beautiful, and at the age of twenty-six she was a national celebrity, a recipient of the second Order of Lenin, as well as the Gold Star of Hero of the Soviet Union. Raskova, along with Grizodubova and Osipenko, became the first women to receive the country's highest honor, and the only women to receive it before the war. The flyers were elevated to the equivalent status of American movie idols in the USSR and they received significant attention from the press. Stalin toasted the pilots in a banquet held in their honor at the Kremlin in a speech about the ancient times of matriarchy in Russia. He concluded by saying, "today these three women have avenged the heavy centuries of the oppression of women."

Raskova would come to inspire hundreds of young women to fly for the Soviet Union when the time came to defend it. In Reina Pennington's book *Wings, Women and War: Soviet Airwomen in World War II Combat*, pilot Yevgeniya Zhigulenko recalled Raskova before the war: "Marina Raskova was an exceptional person. A famous pilot and Hero of the Soviet Union, she was still a simple, kind woman. She helped many young women who wanted to fly." Raskova became the idol of many, including Soviet fighter ace Liliya Litvyak, who would become the first woman in history to shoot down an enemy aircraft. She reportedly kept pictures of Raskova in her notebook. The aircrew of the *Rodina* met for the last time on March 8, 1939 at the Pilots' Club on International Women's Day. Osipenko would be killed only two months later in a plane crash. Stalin himself would be one of the pallbearers.

When Germany invaded the Soviet Union on June 22, 1941, Raskova, who was working as a civil defense volunteer at the time, began receiving hundreds of letters from women pilots eager to utilize their flying skills in the war. In October, after getting the full support of Stalin, Raskova set in motion a voluntary recruitment of women flyers and the Aviation Group 122 was born. Three women combat aviation regiments would be formed under its auspices: the 586th Fighter Aviation Regiment (Yak-1 fighters), 587th Dive Bomber Aviation Regiment (Pe-2 bombers), which would be renamed the

125th Guards Dive Bomber Aviation Regiment after Raskova's death, and the 588th Night Bomber Aviation Regiment (U-2 biplanes, renamed Po-2 in 1944). In February 1943 the 588th would be renamed the 46th *Taman* Guards Night Bomber Regiment in recognition of its outstanding achievements in combat.

A little over one thousand women flew a combined total of more than thirty thousand combat sorties, producing at least thirty Heroes of the Soviet Union. Included in their ranks were two fighter aces. More than thirty women pilots are believed to have been killed in action.

The 46th was the only one of the three original regiments that remained exclusively female throughout the war (the other two regiments incorporated some men.) The regiment flew a total of 24,000 combat missions and was the most decorated of the women's regiments with twenty-three of its members being awarded the Gold Star of the Soviet Union (by 1990), five of them posthumously. The women pilots were nicknamed *Nachthexen* (Night Witches) by their German counterparts, who came to fear their successful aerial tactics in the wooden Po-2 planes they flew on night missions.

Soviet women pilots, navigators, and gunners also served in male regiments during the war. Women flew in dive-bomber, reconnaissance, and ground attack regiments, while others like Liliya Litvyak and Katya Budanova flew in the 296th Fighter Regiment, later renamed the 73rd Guards Fighter Regiment. Needless to say the female pilots had a tougher time integrating into the male regiments than they did in Raskova's regiments. The women pilots had to work hard to overcome the prejudices of the male aircrews that were openly hostile to the idea of women flying in combat. It did not take long, however, for the airwomen to earn their comrades' respect in flight.

In the United States the women's air program formed by Jacqueline Cochran proved a success, despite its losses. Of the 1,074 American pilots who graduated as Women Airforce Service Pilots (WASP) from 1942–44, thirty-eight were killed in service. Stationed at 120 Army air bases throughout the United States, the aviators flew more than sixty million miles in every type of aircraft and on every type of mission the Army Air Force had except combat. On December 20, 1944, the WASP program was officially disbanded, and it would not be until November 23, 1977 when the women flyers would be officially recognized as veterans.

The women military pilots of the Second World War proved to the world that women could not only accept the challenge, but also make the ultimate sacrifice during one of history's darkest hours. These female warriors answered their countries' call to duty and paved the way for future generations of women in aviation.

Anna Timofeyeva-Yegorova's courageous life story will at once astound and humble the reader. One will come away from the experience of reading her memoir with a greater appreciation for the Soviet experience and the immense sacrifices made by our allies in the Great Patriotic War. If a person still exists on this planet that harbors any doubt that a woman can distinguish herself in aerial combat, I challenge him to read on.

Amy Goodpaster Strebe
Author, *Flying for Her Country:*
The American and Soviet Women Military Pilots of World War II

Translators' Note

In translating this text for a general audience, we have attempted to clarify in footnotes anything that wouldn't necessarily be common knowledge to a non-Russian reader, such as historical events and figures, geographical names, and cultural elements. For flavor, we have left certain Russian words and phrases in the original when they refer to well-known Russian-specific concepts, with explanatory notes.

Some of these footnotes exist to shed light on the "unofficial" story of the "Great Patriotic War" (which is how Russians refer to *their* World War II). While these may occasionally contradict Ms. Yegorova, they are in no way meant to discredit her, but to uncover the truth behind the propaganda and evasions promulgated by the Soviet government in the war years and for decades afterward. In some cases, these evasions have been so effective that a reliable historical account remains subject to some speculation to this day. We have relied on several excellent historical texts for help. For a full list of sources and recommended reading, see the pages following the translators' note.

Russian names can be especially confusing for outsiders. Please note that Russians have a first name, patronymic, and a family name, with endings corresponding to gender, used in different combinations according to relationship to the speaker. For example, Anna Alexandrovna Yegorova (the patronymic means "daughter of Alexander") might be called the more formal "Anna Alexandrovna" or "Comrade Yegorova" by a subordinate, or one of many diminutive nicknames (such as "Anya," "Annushka," or "Nyurochka") by a close friend or relative. Masculine endings vary from feminine ones in the patronymic and family names (e.g. Vasily Alexandrovich Yegorov, or "Vasya" for short).

The political language of the Soviet era can be particularly difficult to fathom for a non-native speaker. Russians often referred to Soviet institutions by common abbreviations, frequently created by uniting first syllables. For example, *zampolit* (a type of military commissar) stood for *zamestitel komandira po **polit**rabotye,* or "deputy commander of political work." We have left only the most familiar and widely used of these in their original form.

Officialspeak, with its penchant for overblown rhetoric, can also seem oddly fervent and sanctimonious to the Western ear, sometimes naively so. In some cases, we have toned down the more extravagant patriotic embellishments for the sake of readability and to eliminate repetitions, but often, we've left them, to give a sense of the tone of that era.

In rendering proper names, we have usually used transliterations that would most closely approximate the pronunciation of the word rather than adhering to any specific linguistic system. We have seldom anglicized proper names, except when the name or place is well-known in English, such as "Moscow" or "Peter the Great." We've attempted to render any non-Russian foreign names in their original spelling rather than a phonetic equivalent. For place names, we've chosen what seem to be the most popularly used and accepted spellings.

Lastly, we have taken slight license in editing Ms. Yegorova's memoir (with her permission), occasionally deleting or changing the order of sections or chapters for the sake of readability and narrative flow, and sometimes eliminating passages which digress from the main story or seem redundant. We have made every effort to retain both the facts and the essence of her life story, using a literal translation whenever possible.

Bibliography and Recommended Reading
(Editor's Note)

In preparing the many historical footnotes for this text, I've often found it quite difficult to arrive at a succinct and simple version of the "facts" of events and the politics and motives surrounding them. A number of excellent histories of the Soviet era and of World War II on the Eastern Front provided this context from different (and sometimes contradictory) perspectives.

Alexander Werth's classic war history, *Russia at War: 1941–1945*, remains one of the most comprehensive works, and a very readable "human" one at that. As a Russian-born (naturalized English citizen) London *Sunday Times* and BBC correspondent in the Soviet Union during the war, Werth was one of the few "Westerners" who could provide eyewitness accounts of the war on the Eastern Front. As he points out, "One of my chief qualifications for writing this story ... is that I was there."

I also found the texts below helpful as military and political histories of the war years:

Beevor, Antony. *Stalingrad*. London: Viking, 1998.

Clark, Alan. *Barbarossa: The Russian-German Conflict, 1941–45*. New York: W. Morrow, 1965.

Erickson, John. *The Road to Stalingrad*. London: Weidenfeld and Nicolson, 1975.

Glantz, David M., and Jonathan House. *When Titans Clashed: How the Red Army Stopped Hitler*. Lawrence: University Press of Kansas, 1995.

Hardesty, Von. *Red Phoenix: The Rise of Soviet Air Power 1941–1945*. Washington, DC: Smithsonian Institution Press, 1982.

Overy, Richard. *Russia's War*. London: Allen Lane, 1998.

Salisbury, Harrison E. *The 900 Days: The Siege of Leningrad*. New York: Avon Books, 1969.

The following histories also proved helpful:

Conquest, Robert. *The Harvest of Sorrow: Soviet Collectivization and the Terror-Famine*. New York: Oxford University Press, 1986.

Davies, Norman. *Rising '44: The Battle for Warsaw*. London: Macmillan, 2003.

Sebag Montefiore, Simon. *Stalin: The Court of the Red Tsar*. London: Weidenfeld and Nicolson, 2004.

Service, Robert. *Stalin: A Biography*. Cambridge: Cambridge University Press, 2005.

Service, Robert. *A History of Modern Russia*. Cambridge: Cambridge University Press, 2003.

For more information about Soviet women soldiers and airwomen, see the following:

Cottam, Kazimiera J. *Women in Air War: The Eastern Front of World War II*. Nepean, Ont.: New Military Pub., 1997.

Cottam, Kazimiera J. *Women in War and Resistance: Selected Biographies of Soviet Women Soldiers*. Nepean, Ont.: New Military Pub., 1998.

Noggle, Anne. *A Dance with Death: Soviet Airwomen in World War II*. College Station: Texas A&M University Press, 1994.

Pennington, Reina. *Wings, Women, & War: Soviet Airwomen in World War II Combat*. Lawrence: University Press of Kansas, 2001.

Strebe, Amy Goodpaster. *Flying for Her Country: The American and Soviet Women Military Pilots of World War II*. Washington, D.C: Potomac Books, Inc, 2009.

For help sorting out cultural references and identifying obscure Soviet historical figures, I owe a debt to Eloise M. Boyle and Genevra Gerhardt's *The Russian Context* and to the *Sovetskii Entsiklopedicheskii Slovar'*, a dictionary of Soviet terms, institutions, and prominent people.

One of the most enjoyable aspects of this research was reading the following two recently-released works: Catherine Merridale's excellent *Ivan's War: Life and Death in the Red Army, 1939–1945* tells the story of that colossal struggle through the eyes of ordinary Soviet soldiers and seeks to uncover the truth of their experiences somewhere beneath the Soviet mythology of the unwavering patriotic hero; *A Writer at War: Vasily Grossman with the Red Army, 1941–1945*, edited and translated by Antony Beevor and Luba Vinogradova with superb explanatory notes, finally makes available the diaries of Vasily Grossman, the popular Soviet wartime journalist and novelist. In both texts, first-hand accounts of the "Great Patriotic War" prove both fascinating and enlightening and offer useful context to Anna Yegorova's memoir.

Of course, most rewarding of all were the glorious hours spent at table hearing Ms. Yegorova's spellbinding reminiscences, and also asking countless questions of my marvelous Russian friend and tutor Inna Sanovich and her husband, Viktor Kopelevich, whose knowledge and memory are a bibliography in their own right.

Chronology

Oct. 1941– Jan. 1942	Battle of Moscow
Dec. 7, 1941	Japanese bomb Pearl Harbor.
Dec. 11, 1941	Hitler declares war on U.S.A.

1942

May	Second Battle of Kharkov: Russian offensive at Kharkov fails disastrously, resulting in encirclement of Soviet forces. A Messerschmitt sets Yegorova's plane on fire, forcing her down in the Kharkov sector.
Jun. 28	Operation Blau: German Army Group South launches summer offensive. (In July, Hitler orders the attack to be split into two simultaneous thrusts—one south toward the Caucasus and one eastward to Stalingrad.)
Jul. 28	Hitler issues Order 227: "Not A Step Backwards!"
Aug. 23	Germans advance to the Volga, just north of Stalingrad.
Early Nov.	During Yegorova's last mission in the U-2, she crashes in the Alagir region (Northern Caucasus) while under pursuit by Nazi fighters.
Nov. 22	Red Army encircles more than 300,000 German troops at Stalingrad.

1943

Jan. or Feb.	Yegorova transfers to 805th Attack Aviation Regiment / 230th Attack Aviation Division / 4th Air Army.
Feb. 2	Germans surrender at Stalingrad.
Mar.	Yegorova and the 805th join the Northern Caucasus Front at Taman.
Apr.–May	Height of the air war in the Kuban (Northern Caucasus); Yegorova's regiment flies many missions over the Taman and Kerch Peninsulas.
Jul.–Nov.	Major Red Army advances in Northern Caucasus, Donbass, and Ukraine.
Jul. 5	Battle of Kursk begins.

Sept. 16	Red Army liberates Novorossisk ("Hero City" on the Black Sea).
Oct. 7	Taman Peninsula cleared of German troops.
Nov. 6	Russians retake Kiev.

1944

Jan. 27	Leningrad blockade is broken.
May	Russians liberate Sebastopol and clear Crimea of Germans.
May or Jun.	Yegorova's regiment joins 197th Attack Air Div. / 16th Air Army / 1st Belorussian Front.
Jun. 6	D-Day: Western Allies invade Normandy.
Jul.	Russians liberate Maidanek concentration camp, near Lublin. (Yegorova tours the camp with a delegation from her regiment.)
Jul. 31	Red Army offensive reaches the Vistula, just south of Warsaw, and is stopped by fierce German resistance.
Aug. 1	Warsaw Uprising begins.
Aug. 20	Yegorova's Il-2 is shot down near Warsaw.
Aug. 25	Allies liberate Paris.

1945

Jan. 17	Soviets capture Warsaw.
Jan. 31	Red Army liberates Küstrin camp (where Yegorova is interned).
Feb. 4–11	Yalta Conference—meeting of the "Big Three" (Churchill, Roosevelt, and Stalin).
Apr. 21	Russians enter Berlin outskirts.
Apr. 25	Soviet troops meet Western Allied forces at Torgau, on the Elbe.
Apr. 30	Hitler commits suicide.
May 2	Berlin capitulates to Soviet General Chuikov.
May 7	Germany signs unconditional surrender.
May 8	"V.E." Day

May 9	"Victory Day" in the U.S.S.R.
Aug. 6	U.S.A. drops atom bomb on Hiroshima.
Aug. 8	U.S.S.R. declares war on Japan.
Aug. 9	U.S.A. drops atom bomb on Nagasaki.
Sept. 2	Japan signs surrender agreement.

1

A Deception of Sunlight and Mist

I remember our send-off at Kazan Station as a festival of vivid sunlight, though it was actually a dreary, overcast day. My friends' smiles, laughter, and jokes so dazzled me that my head spun with giddy elation. I felt so full of joy that I could hardly see, and I leaned against the railing of the train car, my vision blurring through half-closed eyes.

I have made my choice! I'm going to be a military pilot! I thought. No more would I divide my heart between this pursuit and that. *Flying is who I am,* I whispered to myself.

As soon as we arrived in Ulyanovsk,[1] I hurried to a high, steep bluff along the Volga River, a place we called *Venets*.[2] A breathtaking view of the vast Russian steppe stretched out before me, an unimaginable expanse. Here was the great, fertile Mother Volga, for centuries blessing Russia's heartland with mighty *bogatyri*.[3]

Here she was, crusted with new December ice. To my amazement, a sudden blaze of color lit up the deep blue sky. A rainbow had thrown a multi-colored yoke over the Volga, and I burst out laughing at the miracle of it. A rainbow in winter! The euphoria I'd felt back in Moscow at Kazan Station came rushing back to me like waves along the shore. The horizon seemed to me swathed in a rosy mist. Surely this was a good omen.

Indeed, it seemed luck had shone on me. I'd passed my exams, had somehow made it past the Medical Commission's exhaustive inquisition, and was enrolled as a flying school cadet.

My new uniform seemed to me the best clothes I'd ever worn — the men's pants and shirt with blue-striped patches, the soldiers' foot-wrappings and boots — even though it was all far too big for me.

I loved my life at the school: waking to the strains of reveille, the physical training and marching, the martial songs in the evening before taps, the constant studying. Everything was going splendidly.

---

[1] A port city about 550 miles (885 km) east of Moscow, on the Volga's right bank. Formerly called Simbirsk, the town was renamed in 1924 for Lenin (pseudonym of Vladimir I. Ulyanov), who was born there.

[2] Literally, "The Crown."

[3] Medieval warrior-heroes of Russian folklore and defenders of Holy Russian soil; celebrated in songs, artworks, and epic poems called *byliny*. Each *bogatyr* (the most famous being Ilya Muromets) is known for certain traits of strength and character.

And suddenly… I still recall that day, like the most vivid of nightmares…

"Cadet Yegorova!" came the order. "You are summoned to the superintendent of the flying school."

I reported immediately to his office. A group of officers seated there greeted me with stern hostility and withering glares. I stood at attention and waited.

"Do you have a brother?"

"I have five," I answered.

"Yegorov, Vasily Alexandrovich?"

"Yes, he's my older brother."

"Why did you conceal the fact that your brother is an enemy of the people?"

"He's no traitor. He's a communist!" I shot back angrily. I wanted to say more, but my mouth and throat had gone dry. The words trailed off in a parched whisper.

My heart pounded in my ears. I no longer saw nor heard the officers at the table in front of me. All I could think of was my brother, who was in trouble. This was the first I'd heard of it.

"We are expelling you from the school."

In a daze I left the office, the door closing behind me with finality. I hardly remember retreating to my quarters and changing out of my uniform.

I found myself again gazing over the Volga, this time from a low-lying bank on the outskirts of town. The overcast sky seemed to mock me. I felt as though the heavens themselves had cast me out. The rainbow had been nothing but artifice—a pretty, treacherous liar and an ill augury.

I thrust my fists into my pockets, finding my passport, Komsomol[4] card, and a slip of paper emblazoned in red with the symbol of the Moscow Metro—a certificate of thanks for the construction of the city's first subway line. These were all the things I owned.

In anguish, I made up my mind to visit my mother in the village where I grew up. Mama would understand my troubles.

---

[4] A syllabic abbreviation word for *Kommunistichesky Soyuz Molodyozhi*, or "Communist Union of Youth"; the youth wing of the Communist Party. Members ranged in age from fourteen to around twenty-eight. Children aged nine to fourteen joined the Pioneers organization, and younger children joined the Little Octobrists. Formed in 1918 from groups of young people who had participated in the Revolution, Komsomol's aim was to educate Soviet youth in Communist ideology and prepare them for membership in the Communist Party. Komsomol and CP membership conferred certain benefits, including improved educational and employment opportunities.

Unfortunately, I had not a single kopek for a one-way ticket home. So I headed to the city Komsomol committee headquarters. As it turned out, it would be a very long time before I saw home again.

2
Land of Our Fathers

The call of childhood and home never seems to fade. Long after other recollections grow dim, the profoundest memories of youth remain—a golden time, and an unforgettable page in life's book.

I recall our lavish Russian hospitality, how on patron saints' day festivals, we welcomed not only our families but friends from near and far, just as our forefathers had done for generations.

Continuing a centuries-old tradition, Mother always brewed beer for festival days in our village. We grew hops in the vegetable garden. In the autumn, we harvested it and stored it for beer-making. We hung barley over the stove in large sacks until it sprouted and became malt. Mother brewed the malt on the stove in a cast-iron pot to make mash, then added hops and yeast. After the mixture fermented, she strained it into kegs. Two or three days later, the beer was ready. Anybody who came by our house was treated to home-brewed beer in large mugs or dippers. It was so sweet and delicious that even the children were allowed to have a sip.

Our tiny village Volodovo, tucked away in the forests between Ostashkovo and ancient Torzhok,[1] had only one street and around forty-five peasant homesteads. That's where we lived, went to school, worked, celebrated, and inhaled the fragrant aromas of our fields and meadows.

For centuries, my ancestors sowed flax on our land. When it bloomed, you could scarcely tear your eyes from the undulating, deep-blue sea of flowers, and when it ripened, the fields turned golden.

We drank crystal-clear water right from the Vyeshna and Pyeschanka springs and plucked black currants along winding banks of the Yaremenko River. In the summer, we gathered mushrooms and berries in the fields and copses of Galanikha and Mikinikha, in the nature preserve, and on Sidorovy Hill. When the snows came, we skied and tobogganed from Moloshnaya and Sopkiye hills and played all sorts of games. When early spring dried the ground at Moloshnaya Hill, adults and children played lapta[2] together. On long winter evenings, men mended bridles and harnesses, women spun flax and embroidered, and children organized dances.

---

[1] An ancient town 40 miles (64 km) northwest of Tver, in Tver oblast (region), northwest of Moscow.

[2] A Russian game similar to baseball.

On clear days, we children would run to a nearby hill called Shish to admire the distant crosses perched atop Torzhok's many churches.

According to an old saying, Torzhok's origins lie "shrouded in the darkness of centuries." Hugging a bank of the Tvertsa, a Volga tributary, streams of merchants and goods from the north and south converged on the town, bearing fur and cloth, salt and weapons, honey and pelts from all over. Into the world Torzhok sent barges loaded with grain from the many granaries that lined her streets and riverbanks, and an ancient gold embroidery art that came to us overriver in ancient times, perhaps from Byzantium or Assyria or even Babylon.

After I finished all the classes at the village's primary school, Mama decided to take me to Torzhok and enroll me in one of the gold-embroidery schools there. I was below the minimum age, but Mama persuaded the principal to accept me on probation.

The school fascinated me—the hordes of little girls, the haughty, grand ladies lecturing all about the embroidery trade. In the evenings, they led us to a spacious hall where we gathered around a piano. An old lady wearing pince-nez sat down and played while we sang in unison, "And mine always, and mine everywhere, and my woodchuck with meee..."

What on earth is a woodchuck? I remember thinking, as I fell asleep that night.

A week later I asked the principal to send me home. I understood at once, even with my childish mind, that I would never be able to sit still for whole days over fine needlework. I had no talent for it; it wasn't my calling.

But if I wasn't to be a Torzhok gold-embroidery seamstress, what was I to do? Torzhok had no secondary school. So my older brother Vasily decided to bring me with him to Moscow so I could go to school.

3
Moscow

I clearly recall my first steps in the grand city of Moscow. My brother Vasya[1] pulled me along with one hand and carried my belongings with the other as we hurried through the bustling streets. I stopped short, frozen to the ground, stunned by all the terrible noise and bustle—the horse-drawn cart-wheels clattering along cobblestone streets, the tram bells and train whistles—and awed by the three magnificent train stations of Kalanchevskaya Square.[2]

Kazan Station especially caught my fancy, with its soaring tower that actually had clocks on it! I had never in all my dreams seen such tall and beautiful buildings, surpassing even the churches of Torzhok. And so many trams, so many people hurrying to and fro—in all my twelve years, I'd never witnessed anything like it.

"Where are they all running to?" I asked Vasya.

Vasya glanced at me, smiling, and said, "To their business."

In surprise, I wondered, *What business do they have? Here I am with no business at all.*

Riding the tram terrified me, especially when an oncoming tram clattered by furiously right next to us. I seized Vasya with both hands, screwing my eyes shut tightly.

"Sukharevsky Market!" announced the conductor.

My brother nudged me. "Look to the right. Do you see that tall building with the clock, in the middle of the street?"

"Yes."

"That's Sukharevskaya Tower.[3] Moscow's water supply used to come from there, in a tank on the top floors."

"But why is it called Sukharevskaya?" I asked him timidly.

"It's history!" said Vasya, laughing. "Everyone should know the history of his own country. It's just as important as studying math and our Russian language.

---

[1] A nickname for "Vasily."

[2] After 1932 called Komsomolskaya Square, the busy square is known informally as "Three Station Square" because of the three railway stations there—Leningrad, Yaroslavl, and Kazan.

[3] Formerly one of Moscow's best-known landmarks, it was destroyed by Soviet authorities in 1934.

"Do you know anything about Peter the Great and his *streltsy*?"[4] he asked.

"Of course not. How chould I know anything about tsars and *streltsy*?"

"Well, there was once a very good tsar named Peter—"

"There are no good tsars!" I broke in.

"OK, fair enough. As for your question, Sukharevskaya Tower was named in honor of a strelyets colonel named Sukharev. He was the only commander whose regiment remained loyal to Tsar Peter during the *streltsy* uprising."

"And why is there a street market here now?" I demanded.

"Have you heard of the War of 1812?"

"Isn't that when the French burned Moscow?"[5]

"Well, sort of..." my brother continued, patiently answering my fusillade of questions. "Anyway, after the great fire and the French retreat, Muscovites started coming home and searching for their plundered property. The Governor-General issued a decree stating that any returning citizen finding loot in Moscow became its rightful owner and that on Sundays people could sell those goods in the square opposite Sukharevskaya Tower."

Every so often the conductor called out another strange and fascinating tram-stop name above the din:

"SA-MO-*TYE*-YE-KAAA!"

"KARETNY *RYA-AD*!"

---

[4] Plural of *strelyets* (literally, "musketeer"), a member of a military corps created by Ivan IV (Ivan the Terrible) in the 16th century. By the late 1600s, the *streltsy* had become a conservative, elite military caste with many special privileges. In 1682, a ten-year-old future tsar named Peter saw his uncles and others murdered by mutinous *streltsy* in the Moscow Uprising of 1682, which left him bitter. In 1698 several thousand *streltsy*, suspicious of Peter's modernizing influence, rebelled against Tsar Peter (Peter the Great), giving him his opportunity for revenge. He defeated the uprising, and tortured and executed a number of the rebels. He disbanded the Moscow *streltsy* regiments and exiled the men and their families.

[5] Although this was widely believed in Russia for many years, Napoleon's troops didn't burn Moscow—they wanted it intact. In *Moscow 1812: Napoleon's Fatal March*, historian Adam Zamoyski contends that the military governor of Moscow ordered his police superintendent to set fire to anything the French could use as the Russian army abandoned the city after the epic Battle of Borodino (70 miles west of Moscow) of September 7. Zamoyski quotes Napoleon's description of the great conflagration: "It was the most grand, the most sublime, and the most terrific sight the world ever beheld!" The fires destroyed around two-thirds of Moscow—a hollow victory for Napoleon. This, along with Tsar Alexander's refusal to negotiate for peace, ultimately obliged the Grande Armée to withdraw from the city and begin their disastrous retreat westward. Of an estimated 500-600,000 Grande Armée troops who assembled along the Neiman River for the Russian campaign, fewer than 100,000 returned home that winter.

We changed trams twice, Vasily all the while informing me about the city. It seemed to me that all the passengers listened, rapt as I, to his stories. I glowed with pride for my older brother, so smart!

"*KRA-A-A*-SNAYA *PRE-E*-SNYA!" shouted the conductor, drawing out the syllables.

"We're here," said Vasily.

On the way to Kurbatovskaya Street, where Vasily lived with his family, he told me about the events of the 1905 Revolution, about how the workers of the Krasnaya Presnya district built barricades in the streets and heroically fought the tsar's troops and gendarmes. He pointed out a street called "Shmitovsky Passage," named for a Moscow University student and furniture factory owner named Nikolai Shmidt. During the December uprising, his factory became a fortress for the worker-revolutionaries, and he, a staunch fighter. After Tsar Nicholas suppressed the revolt, Shmidt was imprisoned and executed at Butyrskaya Prison.

My brother continued pointing out interesting sights and telling stories, but I barely listened. My eyes welled with tears, blotting out all the sights and sounds around me. I felt sorry for poor Shmidt, the martyred worker. I recalled my quiet village, Volodovo, and the girlfriends I'd played with there. I began to cry even harder.

Vasily stopped at a street vendor, one of those "Mosselprom" stands that we seemed to pass at every step. He bought me a stick of candy in a bright red wrapper with fancy tassels, but it didn't console me. Then he started asking about home, Mother, and our brothers.

"After Papa died," I began, sniffling and smearing tears all over my face, "Mama started getting sick a lot, and crying and even praying to God! She made us go to church and pray before dinner. Zina and Kostya were sneaky—they would look at Mama instead of the icon when they crossed themselves. But I couldn't fool her, and I wouldn't look at the icon."

"And why wouldn't you look at the icon?" Vasya teased.

"I am a Pioneer, 'Godfather!'" I teased. "Can't you see my Pioneer scarf?"

Vasya took a good, long look at me. I was, indeed, wearing a faded red scarf, which poked out from beneath the collar of my shabby, patched overcoat. On my feet I wore mid-calf boots with rubber soles, sewn by Mama's brother, Misha. A scarf covered my head, and two long pigtails tied with rag bows stuck out of it.

"Our sister Manya made my Pioneer scarf out of her old red blouse, 'Godfather'!" I declared proudly.

"OK, but will you please stop calling me 'Godfather'? I'm a communist, for heaven's sake, and a deputy of the Moscow Soviet[6]," said Vasya, as we approached the house.

---

[6] Literally, "council." The soviets were part of a hierarchy of local, regional, and national governing bodies in the Soviet Union. Delegates at all levels were nominally

✯ ✯ ✯

I felt very comfortable at my brother's home, especially when his one-year-old son Yuri reached for me with his tiny, warm hands. The little boy wouldn't let me out of his sight, morning and night. If I disappeared, he would let out a wail that woke the whole apartment.

I didn't go to school that year because I had arrived two months too late. Instead, I cared for little Yuri, took him for walks in the apartment's courtyard with the neighbors' children, helped with the housework, and went to the store to buy bread.

Once I went to Malaya Gruzinskaya Street to buy kerosene with my girl-friend Tomka, who lived on the floor below us. But instead of heading straight for the store, we found ourselves at the hairdresser's. We had our braids chopped off and our hair styled in the latest fashion, called the "Charleston," with a small curl plastered to the sides of our foreheads.

We left the hairdresser and gaped at each other, then burst into tears. We ran to the drugstore and bought an *arshin*[7] of gauze to bind up our foolish heads so as not to frighten our families. We bought two two-pound cans of kerosene with what was left of the money.

We dragged our heels on the way home, walking more slowly and quietly with every step. By the time we'd reached the stairs to Tomka's apartment, we'd nearly lost our nerve altogether. I rang the bell and then shot up the stairs, skipping every other step. Soon I could hear Tomka's howls rising into the stairwell.

It took ages for me to reach the landing in front of our apartment, and I stood in front of the door for what seemed an eternity. Finally, I knocked, with a resigned *Come what may!* and rang the bell.

---

elected, but the elections were closely controlled by the Communist Party, and ballots generally contained only one name.

Striking workers created the first workers' soviets during the Revolution of 1905. The revolution was suppressed, but in 1917, after Tsar Nicholas II's abdication, factory workers elected the Petrograd Soviet of Workers' and Soldiers' Deputies, which then turned over authority to the official Provisional Government. Soviets elected by workers, soldiers, and peasants began emerging all over Russia—an attempt at establishing a sort of grassroots direct democracy. When Lenin returned to Russia, he announced his opposition to the "imperialist" Provisional Government and his support for the soviets, which to his thinking were a practical manifestation of the people's will—a "dictatorship of the proletariat." His slogan, "All Power to the Soviets!" his policies of land nationalization, government control of industry, and extracting the nation from World War I, and his demands for "peace, land, and bread" won him popular support.

When the Bolsheviks seized power from the Provisional Government in October, the regional soviets began to cement their power throughout the new Soviet nation. The soviet became the official organ of government, from the village to the national All-Russian Congress of Soviets, which was the highest unit of government.

[7] An old Russian unit of length, equivalent to about 28 inches (71 cm).

Vasya's wife Katya opened the door, saw my bandaged head, and started wailing.

"Little Nyurochka,[8] what's the matter? I should have gone to get the kerosene myself!" she cried, and began slowly unwinding the gauze from my head, so as not to hurt me. She stood, stunned, gaping at my shorn head.

"No, I'm not going to whip you, miserable girl! Let your brother teach you a lesson when he gets home. Until then, sit down at the table and do twenty math problems from the textbook I bought you." Katya picked up little Yurka, snatched the can of kerosene, and left. A puddle of kerosene spread across the floor.

I wiped up the spill and sat down to work on the math problems. Our neighbor in the communal apartment peered into the room to ask about the strong kerosene smell. "Ach!" she sighed, as she caught a glimpse of the barber's handiwork in all its splendor. "Where are your braids, Nyurochka?"

"I left them at the hairdresser's, Auntie."

The neighbor woman found some scissors and cut off the absurd ringlet, combing the short hairs into a tiny bang. "That's much better," she said, and left. I resumed my sums.

That night, before my brother came home from the factory, Katya took me down to Tomka's apartment.

"Wait here at the Frolovs' while I prepare Vasya for the big surprise," Katya told me.

She prepared him all right. When I got back to the apartment, my brother glared at me angrily, grabbed me by the ear, and started yanking on it painfully, all the while scolding me:

"You good-for-nothing, willful girl! You should have been shaved with a razor!"

Little Yurka came to my rescue. The minute he saw his favorite being punished and heard my violent sobs, he let out a shrill cry, slid down from the divan, rose onto his still shaky infant's legs, and took his very first steps, to my side to defend me!

Peace in the household was restored. At dinner, Katya even said, "Vasya, look! The bangs are becoming to Anna."

In the winter, a thick sheet of ice, perfect for skating, covered our courtyard. We drew figures on the ice with hand-made wooden skates tied to our felt boots with string. We went to the circus, where grandfather Durov performed. And Vasya took me to the Bolshoi Theater. I'll never forget seeing Borodin's opera "Prince Igor" there. I didn't understand the words or the music, but I remember the "Polovtsian Dances" and Prince Igor's soaring aria as if I saw them only yesterday.

I had occasion to hear that aria again, in German captivity. Seeing my broken and battered condition, an Italian prisoner named Antonio sang it for

---

[8] An affectionate diminutive for "Anna."

me to lift my spirits, until the Nazis came for him. A firing squad executed him.

Many years later, when my second son was born, I named him Igor, after the fabled Russian prince.

These are the powerful impressions and recollections from my Moscow winter, at the dawning of my adolescence, that still flutter through my consciousness like glistening snowflakes out of a black night sky.

4
Volodovo

In the summer, Yuri and I were sent back to the village.

As soon as Mama discovered that her grandson had not been christened, she resolved to rectify this unforgivable sin. Behind Vasya and Katya's backs, she christened him in the village church, renaming him "Yegor."

When my brother and his wife came to visit, they soon learned what Mama had done. "We've been under Soviet power for twelve years now," Vasya raged at her. "You are living in the past!"

But Katya viewed the whole thing as a big joke. She laughed heartily and kept begging Mama to tell her about the christening over and over again— how Yuri didn't want to climb out of the font, how he splashed water everywhere and giggled all through the proceedings.

When Vasya's family returned to Moscow, Mama refused to let me go with them. "I don't want her twiddling her thumbs in Moscow. Let her go to the fifth grade here. Five kilometers is a long walk, but she can handle it. I heard Lomonosov walked all the way to Moscow from Arkhangelsk in search of knowledge."

"That's right," said Vasya. "Besides, I used to walk to primary school four kilometers away from our village, in all kinds of weather."

"The elders say that Volodovo had a school and a teacher to educate the peasant children, in the old days before the tsar freed the serfs," Mama added, looking pointedly at Vasya.

"What tsar?"

"Alexander the Second. Haven't you seen the cast-iron bust in the barn? That's Alexander the Emancipator," said Mama.

"That's news to me."

"My uncle, Father Gavril, told me we used to have a teacher here in 1859 who was also a tailor and a shepherd," Mama told us. "The school had eight girls and eleven boys. We had twenty homesteads in the village, all farmers.

"Thank God we at least have the comprehensive school in Novo," she went on. "They just opened it. You'll go there," she told me.

And so it was decided. But Mama wasn't finished. "Our village was in the Baranyegorsky Parish then," she recalled. "The parish had such a lovely church, with a high bell tower. That bell was so loud, you could hear it even in our village, calling us to Mass. But Soviet power destroyed all that.

"We had a village elder. We settled all our problems together, at village meetings. We didn't have to go running to the regional authorities ten miles away for every little thing, like we do today. It's always the same thing: whenever you go, they're at lunch, on break, in a meeting, or they're just 'not in today.' So you trudge ten miles back home through the mud with nothing to show for your pains," she held forth.

"Are you saying you lived better before the October Revolution?" Vasya demanded.

"Absolutely," Mama shot back. "There was order. If you sinned, you went to church and confessed, and your soul rested easier. If you had a complaint, you went to the village elder, a few doors down. He settled disputes fairly because he was one of us. He knew our village, and we knew him. He wouldn't stand for these false accusations!"

"Enough, Mama!" I interrupted. "How can you keep glorifying pre-revolutionary times? Look around! What have we inherited from those days? The past has given us nothing but poverty and ruins. Socialism is a new start for us!"

"Oh, my little daughter! You don't know how it was! The Great War, then the Revolution, the Civil War—it's brought us only destruction, tears, and bloodshed. After the Revolution, the commissars[1] tore everything to pieces and spread their blasphemy—"

"Stop it, Mama!" I cut in, breathlessly. "Let's not fight about it anymore."

That year I entered the fifth grade in the new school in the village of Novo. Seven of us from Volodovo walked ten kilometers round-trip every day, in all kinds of weather—bitter cold, downpours, in mud and snow up to our knees. When I advanced to the sixth grade, only two students remained: Nastya Raskazova and I.

Because we were second-shift pupils, we came home from school very late. In the autumn, the trip was especially difficult because of the early darkness and the muddy, treacherous road. We preferred walking through the fields to entering the woods. We'd sing songs all along the way until we approached the dark forest, where we fell silent. We imagined that some fearsome beast would seize us if we took even a step into the dense blackness. Sometimes we'd catch a glimpse of a wolf's eyes glittering in the dark.

Nastya and I started coming home later and later from school. Konstantin Yevgenevich Belavsky, our physics and math teacher, kept us after classes to do extra math problems that he dreamed up for us. He shared our feelings of triumph when we came up with creative solutions to the problems. His eyes lit up like stars when he checked our notebooks, expressing sincere delight at our mathematical talents. "Just bite into one more nut," he would tell us,

---

[1] A title associated with various Communist Party officials, both in the military and the civil administration, whose job was to supervise the political education and loyalty of Soviet subjects.

offering us one last problem that he claimed he couldn't quite figure out. It was his zeal and encouragement that first awakened in us the stirrings of independent thought.

Sometimes we constructed rudimentary equipment for physics and chemistry experiments and made toys, decorations, and ornaments for our classrooms and lecture hall. Our Russian language and literature teacher rehearsed plays with us, which we staged for the whole school and in the neighboring villages—Zamoshye, Pryamukhino, Velemozhye, Tavruyevo, Obabkovo, Baranya Hill, and many more.

I still remember our history teacher, Anna Dmitriyevna, with a mixture of gratitude and awe. She would glide into our classroom, her hair neatly combed back into a bun, dressed in her "uniform," a stark white blouse and black skirt, with her deep blue eyes sparkling as she addressed us: "Children, today we're going to talk about the history of our home region!" And we would listen, captivated by the marvelous tales she spun. We glowed with pride for our motherland. Our little villages suddenly seemed to us impossibly ancient and mysterious, haunted by generations of fallen heroes.

We learned that the names of villages in our region evoked the dark days of tyranny under the Tatar-Mongol hordes. A major battle against the horde raged near the villages Tavruyevo and Obabkovo, named for the Tatar commanders who were killed and buried there. That's where the horde's army was crushed and turned back from its march on Novgorod. We wrote and staged a play about it in history class.

Anna Dmitriyevna also took us on excursions to the famous Pryamukhino estate, founded during Peter the First's reign. Mikhail Bakunin,[2] the famous revolutionary philosopher and poet, was born there in 1814. His name is inscribed on an obelisk in Alexander Garden, by the Kremlin Wall.

---

[2] Mikhail Alexandrovich Bakunin (1814–76). Anarchist and revolutionary theorist Bakunin believed that governments and organized religions should be abolished and advocated revolution as a means of doing so. An energetic, charismatic speaker and activist, he became involved in popular uprisings in Western Europe and spoke out against Russia's oppression of the Polish people—for which he spent six years in the Peter and Paul Fortress in St. Petersburg.

He famously broke with his contemporary, Karl Marx, about the necessity of a "dictatorship of the proletariat," writing in *Statism and Anarchy*, "They say that this state yoke, this dictatorship, is a necessary transitional device for achieving the total liberation of the people… Thus, for the masses to be liberated they must first be enslaved… We reply that no dictatorship can have any other objective than to perpetuate itself, and that it can engender and nurture only slavery in the people who endure it. Liberty can be created only by liberty…"

5
Dizzy with Success

One day, a young man came to our class and introduced himself as the secretary of the Kamennaya Regional Komsomol Committee. He told us about the program and charter of the Communist Youth Union and then asked, "Who wants to be a Komsomol? Raise your hands." A roomful of arms went up.

A week later, the man reappeared and solemnly presented the new Komsomols with membership cards. One by one, we approached a table covered with a bright red cloth and recited the oath—to serve faithfully on the front lines as builders and defenders of our motherland—as we blushed and stammered before the assembled crowd.

We proudly wore our khaki soldier's blouses tied with a wide sword-belt, our red membership badges gleaming. We'd earned the money for the uniforms ourselves, loading and unloading train cargo at Kuvshinovo Station.

In addition to our regular work, we were now expected to perform special Komsomol assignments. Nastya Raskazova and I joined a Komsomol agitprop brigade assigned to recruit peasants to form collective farms at the Novo Village Soviet.[1] We went on our first assignment, to Zhegini village, with an agent from the Regional Executive Committee, the chairman of the village soviet,[2] and the principal of our school.

The village peasants crowded into a spacious *izba*[3] furnished with rows of wooden benches. Two glowing kerosene lamps hung from the ceiling. Bluish clouds of thick smoke curled above our heads as the men puffed on home-grown tobacco.

The Regional Executive Committee agent, in his sixth identical speech of the day, extolled the advantages of collective farming over working individ-

---

[1] In 1929–32, the Soviet government began a massive program of "collectivization" and "dekulakization" (see footnote next page) among peasants in Soviet territory. Private property was seized and peasants forced to join collective farms. That policy, along with impossibly harsh grain requisions by the central government, resulted in famine and millions of deaths by starvation in 1932–33.

[2] Robert Conquest in *The Harvest of Sorrow* writes, "The village Soviet was in principle elected on universal adult suffrage, but from the start it had been controlled by the authorities as the 'rural arm of the dictatorship of the proletariat.'"

[3] A traditional wooden peasant hut.

ual plots. He explained that with a tractor you could work ten *desyatinas*[4] of land in a single day, when it would take the whole spring or autumn with an old wooden plow.

"We're sick of your stories," someone shouted. "Where is this 'tractor' of yours?"

"Join the collective farm, and you'll get one."

When our school principal took the floor, the whole back row began shouting at him. "And have you joined this collective farm?"

"No, I am a teacher! I teach your children!"

"Oh, I *see*. You're on a salary. But how are we supposed to feed our families if we give everything we have to the collective farm?" the *izba* roared. "And what about these Komsomol girls? Did they join?"

I thought about the confrontation I'd had with Mama that morning when I brought up the topic. She wouldn't have anything to do with any collective farm. "Join it if you like," she said. "But don't bother me with it. I'm not giving away my last cow to some 'communal homestead.'"

The Zhegini meeting raged on. The chairman argued and cajoled the assembled crowd to join, but no one volunteered. Finally, a scrawny peasant wearing a tattered sheepskin coat and patched felt boots approached the table and announced, "I've got nothing to lose. Write my name down!"

By morning more than twenty families had signed up. But two weeks later, when the authorities came to "collectivize" everyone's cows and chickens, the collective farm dissolved. Around this time, Stalin's editorial, "Dizzy with Success"[5] appeared in *Pravda*, and masses of peasants took their names off the lists.

Meanwhile, they started arresting our so-called *kulaki*[6] and *podkulachniki*[7] and deporting them. Where on earth did they find wealthy peasants in our

---

[4] A *desyatina* is equal to 2.7 acres.

[5] Responding to mass unrest in the countryside (and pressure from some "moderate" Politburo members), Stalin published this famous article in *Pravda* on March 2, 1930 in which he reproached local officials for abusing their power and for "excesses" in forcing the supposedly voluntary collectivization of peasant holdings (although the officials were merely implementing Stalin's directives): "How could such blockheaded exercises in 'socialization' have arisen in our midst ... which in fact bring grist to the mill of our class enemies?... Certain of our comrades became dizzy with success, and for a moment lost the capacity of clear thinking...." This apparent tactical retreat shifted responsibility for the crisis to local activists, but it was only a temporary, and quite insincere, bit of posturing. Stalin had in no way reversed his policy of collectivization. After a brief period in which millions of peasants withdrew from collective farms, Stalin continued the collectivization and grain seizures campaign in earnest later that year, with disastrous results.

[6] Literally, "fists." Before the revolution referring to a wealthy peasant who used hired labor or lent money (with the connotation of an exploiter or usurer), the term came to be applied far more loosely in the Soviet era, often meaning simply a "class enemy" or

Tver villages? All those "wealthy" peasants always went hungry after Christmas.

The laziest, poorest peasants ascended to posts in the "Poor Peasants' Committees," which conducted late-night show trials of kulaks at our school in Novo. Sometimes they exiled people to God knows where without even a trial or investigation.

The committee declared my friend Nastya's father, Vasily Raskazov, a *kulak* because he had a cow, a horse, and two sheep on his farm. Mama, who owned only one cow, was pronounced a *podkulachnik* because she defended Vasily. Nastya and I were expelled from the Komsomol for failure to execute our mission and for connections to *kulaks*. With a heavy heart, I laid my Komsomol card on the table before our local Party activist, Tolka Guryanov.

A number of villagers voiced their objections to our expulsion, but Guryanov ignored them and read lengthy passages from Karl Marx's *Das Kapital*. I stood there with my head drooping, unable to comprehend what was happening.

I stayed up all night writing a long letter to the regional committee, begging them to allow me to rejoin the Komsomol and to punish Tolka Guryanov for expelling me.

By graduation, they had restored my membership.

At the ceremony, Nastya and I dressed in our finest "down-feathers and dust," as they say in the village: black leather skirts, white blouses with sailors' collars, and rubber slippers. At the party we sang, recited poetry, and danced the "Yablochko."[8]

Along with our certificates, we received recommendations for further study—Nastya to an agricultural school and I to a teachers' institute.

---

anyone who resisted collectivization. In December of 1929, Stalin called for the "liquidation of the kulaks as a class" and began deporting (and sometimes executing) millions of the most productive farmers. One village soviet chairman claimed in 1930 (quoted by Robert Conquest in *The Harvest of Sorrow*), "we create kulaks as we see fit."

[7] One who supports or assists *kulaks*; literally "sub-*kulak*."

[8] Literally, "little apple"—a traditional Russian sailor's dance popular in the Soviet era, to the tune of a well-known folk song.

6
Underground

The newspapers issued a call to action, summoning us all to take part in the Five-Year Plan.[1] Our school's graduates scattered all over, aspiring to do their part to industrialize the nation. We wanted to work hard and study.

That summer, my brother Vasily came to visit with his family. He helped Mama cut hay for the cow and prepare the farm for winter. He kept telling us all about Moscow, all the new construction there, and a new railroad they were building underground—a "metropolitan."

"What's it for?" asked Mama.

"So people can get to work faster," Vasya informed us. "Many developed countries have had subways since the middle of the last century! London's 'Underground,' as they call it, was opened in 1863 with steam-trains. New York, in 1868, Paris in 1900…"

We were certainly impressed with Vasya's knowledge. But most of all, the idea of a Moscow metropolitan enthralled us. We'd never even heard the word before! I secretly promised myself that I would go with Vasya to Moscow and find a way to work on this strange underground railway.

When I announced my plan to Mama, she wailed in protest. "I've spent my whole life raising you children, and now that I'm old and lonely, you go flying away out of the nest!"

Vasya urged her to let me go, pointing out that in Moscow I could continue my studies. With that, we left for the city.

As soon as I got to Moscow, I headed straight for the district Komsomol committee. I entered the building timidly, unsure of which door was the right one.

"What are you looking for, young lady?" asked a man in worker's overalls.

"I want to work on the Metrostroy!"[2] I announced.

"You're a Komsomol?"

"Yes!"

---

[1] The Soviet government implemented the first Five-Year Plan (1928–32) to transform (and tightly control) the national economy through rapid industrialization. It set production goals in mines and factories, eliminated private companies, and exported seized grain abroad to purchase modern machinery. "Laggards are beaten," said Stalin in 1931 (quoted by Robert Service in *A History of Modern Russia*).

[2] A syllabic abbreviation word for "Metropolitan Construction."

"Fill out this application," he said, then asked a girl who was walking by, "Where should we send her?"

"What are her qualifications?" the girl asked him.

"None yet," he answered for me.

"Then send her to the Metrostroy training school."

Standing in the corridor, the man wrote the address of the school on a slip of paper. "Take tram number 27 to the end of the line, then ask the way," he explained.

When I arrived, the selection committee told me they desperately needed steel framework fitters. I had no idea what one was, but I answered firmly: "OK! I'll be a steel framework fitter!"

Fifteen-thousand Komsomols and 3,500 communists, all in workers' overalls, helmets, and "metrowalkers" (as we called our special rubber boots), stood at the vanguard of the grand Metro-building effort. By 1935, in just three years, we finished the first Metro line.

As shock workers, we drove ourselves hard, and the work was difficult. We weren't accustomed to hard labor, and at first our hands and backs ached. But no one lost heart.

We girls didn't want to fall behind the boys. Every time the doctors told us we couldn't work underground, we found ways to get permission anyway. When they categorically forbade us, we sent three girl-delegates to petition Mikhail Ivanovich Kalinin[3] himself.

"Why won't you let us work in the caisson?" asked the young Komsomols.

"As I understand it," he said, "caisson workers descend into a hermetically sealed chamber and pump pressurized air in to force ground water out of the rock. Yes? And how on earth can a delicate female body endure such things? No, we can't have girls in the caisson. You won't be able to have babies."

"We absolutely *will* have babies, Mikhail Ivanovich! We'll have babies *and* build the Moscow Metro!" The Komsomol Metro-workers persisted until the All-Union Elder said yes.

The newspaper *Metrostroy Shock-Workers* printed a story about the first female caisson worker: "When on July 29, 1933, Sofya Kienya pulled on the stiff worker's overalls and awkwardly headed toward the mineshaft, it was all quite extraordinary and frightening to her. She later confessed that her eye-

---

[3] Mikhail Ivanovich Kalinin (1875–1946). Titular head of the Soviet state from 1919–46. His official title varied; from 1924–38 it was "Chairman of the All-Union Central Executive Committee." One of the more popular Soviet leaders, he was informally called the "All-Union Elder." Thousands of workers, soldiers, peasants, and even children addressed letters to "Dear Grandfather Kalinin" (instead of to Stalin) with their complaints, suggestions, and petitions. During the purges, many letters pled for amnesty for exiled prisoners.

brows ached and she felt a heaviness in her ears. But she withstood the pressure of the caisson."

Sofya Kienya became a legend, and not just among the Metrostroy. She combined mental toughness and exacting mining skills with femininity and kindness. The All-Union Elder himself awarded her the Order of the Red Banner of Labor, newspapers printed photographs of the fair-haired beauty from a poor Belorussian village, and poets wrote verses about her. She was our beacon.

At the Metrostroy school, we studied four hours of theory and four hours of practical classes a day. We admired how our instructor Nefyodov deftly handled the wire-cutters. We could barely manage them.

I moved into the school dormitory—a cluster of huts—to be closer to my classes.

Each hut had four big rooms with three rows of beds and nightstands and a large table in the center covered with an oilcloth. We did our homework and drank tea around the big table and ate light snacks of bread and boiled water with sugar through the day.

I still smile when I remember the day my friend Tosya Ostrovskaya and I tried to sell our tea rations at the market. We'd received vouchers to buy boots, but we didn't have enough money for them, so we decided to do "business." We stood shivering in the market, me holding two packets of tea and Tosya in the role of barker.

A *muzhik*[4] approached us and started disparaging the quality of our tea, trying to bring the price down. I couldn't abide such slander, and I blurted out, "You know tea like a pig knows oranges!"

He exploded with rage and shouted, "Police! Police!"

We fled the market at top speed, not slowing down until we reached Timiryazevsky Park. We'd lost one tea bag during our hasty retreat, and we decided to give the other one to Tosya's grandmother. She chided us and made us promise never to try to make money that way again.

Bit by bit we learned to read detailed schematics, use wire cutters, and heat the thin wires for binding. We passed our practical exam in the "Red Gates" tunnel and thus became steel-fitters.

---

[4] Russian male peasant.

7
Red Gates

I still become cross when anyone suggests that there's any metro station in all of Moscow more spectacular than my "Red Gates."[1] After all, the station won a Grand Prix for architectural design at the 1938 World's Fair in Paris. Everything is on a massive, monumental scale: broad cornices supported by powerful marble columns; gleaming-white arched ceiling between deep-red pillars; floor tiled with red and white squares. Even now, whenever I pass through that station, it strikes me as the most beautiful of them all. I sometimes get off the blue-line express train at Red Gates, and when no one is looking, I stroke the cold red marble pylons that bring to mind my Komsomol youth.

At first, descending into the deep mine terrified me. Although we lowered beams and equipment mechanically, we miners had to climb forty or fifty meters down a long, icy ladder to get to work. I'll never forget that slippery, precipitous ladder, how it plummeted into the darkness of a narrow shaft, tight as a gunbarrel. Passing each other on it was treacherous. We had to take our gloves off just to hold onto the slick rungs. Light from our tiny lamps disappeared into the mine's dense haze, and sometimes we accidentally stepped on another miner's fingers as we climbed down in the dark. But the deeper we descended, the warmer and lighter the tunnel became.

Mine cars bore loads of rock continuously toward the surface. The shaftman's job was to keep these wagons moving, to wheel them into the cage and send them up. Dressed in an enormous rubber jacket, boots, and wide-brimmed hat, the shaftman looked like a giant, as he (or she—one couldn't tell!) expertly handled the overloaded mine cars.

Once the cage was safely on its way up, our shaftman would sometimes whip off the huge rubber hat, letting the small cap underneath slide to the back of her head, and smooth back a fall of lush golden curls.

"Zina! Are we going to the movies tonight?" came the usual question, from a laughing young man who was rolling a wagon toward the blonde shaftman.

"No! I've got to study tonight," she retorted, rebuffing his constant flirtations. Then she'd pack her curls into the wide hat, pull on her gloves, and drag the empty mine car back down into the mine.

---

[1] In Russian, *Krasnye Vorota*—named for the Red Gates triumphal arch which was near the present-day site of the metro station and torn down by Soviet authorities in 1928.

We novice steel workers shouldered the girders, bending from their weight as we trudged along in tandem toward the tunnel, where the frames would be bound together with wire and encased in concrete. I fantasized about throwing down the heavy beam and stretching my back out straight again. But we carried the heavy loads in silence, until someone started to sing: "In the valleys, in the hills…"

Suddenly, a violent tremor, a brilliant flash of light, then blackness. Awful screams emanated from the dark, just before the surge of electricity hit.

I awoke above ground, in the mine yard. I was being carried toward an ambulance. I broke away in fear and ran behind some piles of gravel…

I stayed at Botkinskaya Hospital for two weeks. When I returned to the mine, I found out that our comrade Andrey Dikiy had died when he became caught in an exposed electrical wire. His death stunned us all, but the letter from his father that arrived soon afterward upset everyone even more.

> *Dear Son!*
>
> *We got the cash you sent. You are a good son to care so much for your old parents.*
>
> *Please forgive us for opposing you and not giving you our blessing when you wanted to leave home.*
>
> *Sonny! We didn't know your address before, but now I'm coming to see you for a whole week. Thanks to you, now I have the money for the ticket. I'm bringing homemade sausage and salo.[2] Mom can't come with me because she is sick…*

When we read the letter, the girls burst into tears, while the boys deliberated, then called a Komsomol meeting.

Here are the minutes of the meeting:

> *Resolved: I. To organize a commission of five persons to greet the father of our comrade, Komsomol Dikiy, Andrey, who perished in the line of duty.*
>
> *II. To faithfully maintain the gravesite of Andrey Dikiy; to fence the site and erect a tombstone, supplied by the Metrostroy marble factory and engraved with his name.*

We did everything we could to commemorate our fallen comrade. It seemed the only consolation for the boy's grieving father.

The mining commission wouldn't allow me to work after the shock, instead offering me a permit to stay at a recreation and rest home. I declined,

---

[2] Salted pork fat, a Ukrainian delicacy.

deciding instead to visit Mama in the village. I didn't write to tell her I was coming. So when I stepped off the train at Kuvshinovo Station, I gaped with surprise to see her waiting for me in the station with my sister Maria.

"How did you know I was coming?" I asked Maria.

"Mama dreamed that you were going to come," Maria explained. "She woke me early this morning and told me, 'We're going to meet Annushka. She's coming today.' You know Mama. She ordered me like a commander to do as she said. In her heart she's a prophet, as she's so fond of telling us."

"Why are you so skinny, my little daughter?" Mama asked. "You look pale."

"I started to feel sick on the train. You know, all the swaying and zigzagging..." I lied. I didn't want to worry her.

"Of course, God bless you," said Mama.

We climbed into the wagon and headed toward Volodovo. The haymaking season had just started, and the grasses had burst into brilliant bloom.

The next morning, Mama woke me before dawn. We walked through fields of high grass toward a forest. The sun had just risen, and the birds shook off sleep and began to chatter noisily. When we got to the meadow, Mama spread an old coat under a spruce tree, laid a bundle of food on it, and sharpened two scythes. "Stand behind me, Daughter," she said, and began to mow.

At first, my scythe kept getting caught in the soil or the bushes, but I gradually improved. When the sun rose higher, Mama made me rest in the cool shade under a spruce tree. What bliss it was, stretching out on the freshly-mowed grass! My arms and legs ached from the work. But it was a happy fatigue, and I slipped into a sumptuous nap. I felt elated to be stretched out on that cozy, warm spot of ground, my native soil—the "Non-Black Earth Zone,"[3] as certain dry administrators called it. But I called it home.

I awoke to see Mama sitting next to me, a birch-bark sack of wild strawberries in her hands. Lying on a white linen cloth were two loaves of bread, two eggs, and a bottle of milk. I couldn't recall eating anything so delicious in my whole life.

My holiday flew by, and soon I returned to the mine. In September, I enrolled in the Metrostroy workers' training facility. We usually worked a six-hour shift, but sometimes we stayed for two shifts in a row, with little regard for our health.

Once we stayed through the night shift, after working all day, to finish the framework in the tunnel arch. Our arms ached terribly after holding the

---

[3] The "Black Earth Zone" consisted of primarily steppe land in southern Russia and Ukraine, with its fertile, dark soil and large farms. Northern Russia, called the "Non-Black Earth Region," was (and still is) more heavily forested and had poorer soil, with smaller clearings devoted to agriculture.

wire cutters above our heads all day. The tunnel was hot and stuffy, and we started to get sleepy as morning approached. One boy had even curled up on the scaffolding stairs and fallen asleep.

Suddenly, almost deliberately it seemed, the chief of our mine appeared underground accompanied by a people's commissar. They stopped in front of the sleeping boy.

"Why are there children in the mine?" the commissar demanded menacingly.

"He's a Komsomol," explained the mine chief.

"Send him to the surface immediately!"

But for an open revolt among the Komsomol workers, we might have been banished from the Moscow Metro altogether that day. However, we weren't going to give up our hard-won right to work in the mines so easily. Most of us had falsified our ages when we applied for the Metrostroy. In the future, we knew, we would have to take greater care in evading the commissar's eye.

We young people had such fighting spirit back then. We were always trying to learn something and improve ourselves. Tosya and I constantly competed for readiness badges—"Ready for Defense Work," "Ready for Medical Defense Work," and even "Voroshilovsky Marksman." We joined a choir and went roller skating at Sokolniki Park. Tosya was good at it, but I always scraped up my knees and elbows. Stubbornly, I kept peeling myself up off the asphalt until I eventually learned to skate.

Such was the atmosphere in the mines that we hurried to work every day with happiness in our hearts. What a joy it was to feel useful and needed! As we chipped away at the frozen earth with picks and shovels, we felt fortunate to do such work and to know that after we were gone, we would leave our homeland something beautiful, built with our own two hands.

8
From the Mine to the Sky

One day an announcement about a meeting of the Metrostroy Aeroclub appeared at the mine cafeteria. All the newspapers had trumpeted the recent appeal by the Ninth Komsomol Congress: "Komsomols—to the planes!"

Our in-house newsletter, the *Metrostroy Shock Worker*, reported that the Metrostroy Aeroclub had acquired four U-2 planes, three gliders, and a plot of land for an aerodrome not far from the Maliye Vyazmy station. The article invited prospective airplane and glider pilots and parachutists to help clear land for the airfield and build hangars.

I had always, in my most furtive imaginings, dreamt of flying, like one dreams of a captivating, but ever-unattainable distant land. So when I read the announcement in the cafeteria, I gathered my courage and headed for the advertised address—Kuibyshev, 3.

I found the place, but I was too nervous to go inside. I read every word of the posters, announcements, and wall-newspapers in the corridor, but I still couldn't summon the nerve to approach the door I so wanted to enter—the one marked "Selection Committee."

"Who are you waiting for, young lady?" asked a man in a military pilot's uniform.

I didn't see his face. I fixated instead upon the gold-embroidered badge on his sleeve—the emblem of the Soviet Air Force. That image remains burned into my memory to this day, for it was the same insignia that, years later, the pilots interned at the Küstrin POW camp gave me as a gift. They wove a small purse out of the straw they slept on, embroidered the Air Force emblem (a propeller) on it with my initials, A.Ye, and slipped it to me secretly.

I struggled to answer the Air Force officer, stammering that I hoped to enroll in the aeroclub's flight school and had even filled out an application.

"You'll need more than just an application," he said. "You'll need a recommendation from the mine and the Komsomol organization, permission from the medical board, and birth and education certificates. Once you collect all those, take them over to the Credentials Committee. They'll make the final decision."

After thanking the pilot, I flew into the street with renewed zeal. I rushed straight to the Red Gates mine, my feet barely touching the ground.

The Komsomol Committee approved my admission to the club, but the brigade foreman objected. "What do you want to do that for, Yegorova?" he demanded morosely. "You'd be better off enrolling in an institute. Let men do the flying."

"What's she playing at?" chimed in Tosya Ostrovskaya. "She's overreaching, trying to be a pilot, sickly as she is. She still hasn't recovered from the accident!"

This, from Tosya, my closest friend in the world! We slept side by side in the dormitory, worked in the same brigade, and studied together at the Metrostroy school. We even shared clothing—what was mine was hers. One day she would wear the skirt and blouse and I'd wear the dress, and the next day we'd switch.

Antonina Sergeyevna Ostrovskaya dreamt of becoming a doctor. I hadn't decided yet about my future, and that's the one thing we always argued about. She hoped I'd study medicine with her. In that, she didn't get her wish. But we did both make it to the front when the war came—she as a surgeon, and I as a pilot.

On this occasion, our brigade foreman settled our dispute. "She's wiry. She can handle it. Let her enlist," he declared, and, to my surprise, gave me a recommendation!

I still had to pass two medical board examinations. I had serious doubts. Rumors of a labyrinthine system of tests flew around the aeroclub. I imagined some fearsome panel of devious doctors throwing pitfalls and barriers into the paths of unwitting would-be pilots. But to my relief, it wasn't like that at all. Ordinary doctors sat in ordinary rooms, tapped and prodded us, spun us on special stools, and checked our inner ears. Anyone who had no significant defects, they pronounced "fit."

Everything went well for me, and the doctors unanimously declared me "healthy"—to me, the most wonderful word in the entire Russian language.

I then had to go before the Credentials Committee. All manner of people—some grey-haired and some young, a few wearing military uniforms and others in civilian coats—sat across a massive oak table and determined who was worthy of ascending into the sky. Certificates, character assessments, and recommendations lay in a heap on the table—dry, meaningless documents to pore through and examine, when a few questions and a little thought could tell a lot more about a person's aptitude, it seemed to me.

After my night shift, I showered, had breakfast at the mine cafeteria, and headed to the Credentials Committee hearing at the new aeroclub offices, located in a converted church on Yakovlevsky Street near the Kursk Railway Station.

It took them a long time to call me in, so I cat-napped on the corner of a wooden couch. When I heard my last name called, I sprang up and dashed into the room, still half-asleep. I was to present myself to the committee at full attention, but instead I mumbled feebly, " I am Anya Yegorova, from the Twenty-First Mine ..."

The entire Credentials Committee burst out laughing. Then they hit me with a barrage of questions, about my parents, brothers, and sisters, my work, my Komsomol assignments, and about international affairs and geography.

"Determine the latitude and longitude of Moscow," asked someone from the committee. I went up to the wall-map and ran my finger nervously up and down along the meridians, left and right across the lines of latitude, finally answering after a long while. Again, the committee roared with laughter. Apparently, I had confused latitude with longitude.

"She's just embarrassed," cut in the Komsomol representative. "She's a shock-worker."

"Well, if you're a shock-worker," the pilot asked in a mocking tone, "then pray tell us, girl, in which group do you, in fact, wish to enlist?"

I understood then that if I were not to become a joke, I would have to stop mumbling, pull myself together, and speak to them with a clear, confident voice. I wouldn't get a second chance. I took a deep breath and declared, "I want to be a pilot!"

"We-ellll! She's a bright one after all, it seems, and the Komsomol representative assured us she was just shy. She's aiming for the flying group right away!"

"She's too young," another voice from the table growled. "She'll have to wait a year."

Too young for the gold embroidery school, too young for the mines, and now this! And I had even padded my age by two years.

"You can join the glider group," the committee pronounced.

"And what, exactly, is a glider?" I asked.

"You don't know? How strange! It's a flying machine. How do I explain? It's a plane without an engine."

"But, you see, I need to fly a real airplane with a real engine!" I insisted, leaning right up against the table and speaking directly to the pilot.

"This year, you'll fly a glider. If you like it, you can transfer to the flying group later on. Next!"

All winter we studied flying theory. Somehow I managed to balance work with my studies at the Metrostroy school and the aeroclub and even to go to the movies and to dances with Tosya now and then. An operetta company sponsored our mine and often gave us tickets to musical performances. We always tried to get tickets whenever our idol Mikhail Kachalov was performing, and we'd sit as close as we could to the stage, bewitched by his velvet voice.

In early spring, we started our practical training at the village of Kolo-menskoye,[1] where the serf Nikitka built himself wings and leapt from a high bell tower.[2] We launched our US-4 gliders from a steep bank of the Moscow River. The method was, of course, extremely primitive. A student would climb into the cockpit, while the other cadets clambered down the slope and hauled the glider's shock-absorber cord back, drawing it tight. When they re-leased it, the glider would catapult into the air, as if propelled from a sling-shot, and glide for two to three minutes.

Every day that summer, after my night shift at the mine, I made my way to the high bank at Kolomenskoye to stretch the shock absorber cord again and again and take my turn at soaring.

By autumn, the satisfying aromas of wet paint and varnish permeated the metro tunnel. The delicious smells of decorating and of good work nearly done filled our hearts with satisfaction. An excited, festive mood seized us as we strolled along the nearly finished station platform. Someone had already cleared away all the construction rubbish and coated the floor with veneer and rubberoid.

That's how the renowned cleanliness of the Moscow Metro was born— from the painstaking care of the metro-constructors themselves. We strode cautiously along the concrete platform floor as if it were a delicate parquet mirror, afraid of dropping a single speck of dust from our rubber boots.

Still, the walls stood bare, as the architects and engineers unloaded boxes of electrical equipment and sketched out the finishing touches. The shift fore-man led us to an unfinished wall with barrows of cement and boxes of tile stacked alongside.

"Here stands a thing of beauty! But she needs vestments. Shall we dress her before lunch?" he cried.

"Of course we'll dress her!"

"Then I'll see to it that you get all the cement you need, with no interrup-tions. Agreed?"

Thrilled to see our beloved project through from start to finish, we steel frame-fitters took to the new craft, learning to install facing and other finish-work. We completed the wall ahead of schedule, and each received a coupon

---

[1] The former country estate of the tsars, first mentioned as early as the 14th century. Some 16th-century structures remain, including the Church of St. George bell tower. Located in a four square-kilometer park in the southern part of Moscow.

[2] According to Russian legend, a serf named Nikitka, owned by a boyar named Lupotov, fashioned a set of wings and sought to fly away to the settlement of Alex androvsky in the presence of Tsar Ivan the Terrible and an assembled crowd. After the serf's successful flight, the Tsar decreed that "A man is not a bird… Those who affix wooden wings to themselves do so in opposition to nature's will…" The myth holds that Ivan IV then beheaded the aviator, fed his body to pigs, and burned his invention, which the Tsar declared was made with "demonic assistance."

for lunch at the mine cafeteria. After lunch, we installed slabs of red marble and polished the pylons to a rich gleam.

In October of 1934, a bright red two-carriage train made its first trial run through the station. How we rejoiced! With choruses of "Hurrah!" and songs, we hugged each other, danced on the platform, and ran after the clattering train.

In May of 1935, the Moscow Metro opened for passengers. The Moscow Komsomol organization won the Order of Lenin for shock-labor in the mines.

The mines were a marvelous school for me and other young Metrostroy workers, teaching us courage and toughness, tempering our characters for the years to come.

9
A Partisan Character

"Enough of this digging in the dirt!" my brother announced one day. "It's time for you to think about the future. Use your head! You need to enroll in an institute. I've already arranged for you to work in the editorial offices of the newspaper *Labor*. The job's nothing to rave about, but you'll always be around intelligent and educated people.

"Maybe they'll influence your combative 'partisan' character!" he declared and hauled me off to the newspaper's editorial offices at the Palace of Labor.

The work was interesting, but I missed our devoted Komsomol-Metrostroy collective. After suffering through four months at *Labor*, I fled back underground to work on construction of the second metro line, in the "Dynamo" mine. This time I repaired heavy equipment and volunteered in the mine's library, studying with the flying group in the evenings. By then I'd finished the Metrostroy workers' secondary school and my glider training, earning a glider-instructor rating.

That spring, we began ground instruction at the aeroclub. We studied aerodynamics, theory of flight, navigation, and meteorology from the "Manual of Flight" and the systems and operation of the U-2 aircraft.[1] Every Sunday we boarded the steam train at the Belorussian Station for an hour-and-a-half trip to the town of Vyazma, then walked a kilometer through the woods, along a riverbank to our aerodrome.

Near the village of Maliye Vyazmy, the broad clearing, with its new hangars, offices, and dormitories we ourselves had built lay enfolded by woodlands, quietly awaiting us. We Komsomol-Metrostroy had followed our hearts to serve our motherland in the mines and now hoped to ascend into her boundless skies.

We studied from a thin blue manual entitled "Red Army-Air Force School Flight Training Course." Our instructors reminded us constantly that this text

---

[1] Designed in 1927, the Polikarpov U-2 open-cockpit biplane (renamed the Po-2 in 1944 after its engineer Polikarpov's death) was created as a light trainer and used as a night bomber and liaison aircraft during WWII. Highly maneuverable and forgiving to fly, the wood-and-fabric craft could take off and land on short fields and could actually use its slow speed to good advantage against faster German fighters. However, it was a rather undesirable combat aircraft because it had no radios or armor, lacked the necessary instruments for flying in poor visibility, and was easily set on fire.

was written in pilots' blood. Our predecessors' mistakes supplied us with a wealth of practical advice:

"Constantly strive to cultivate in yourself the following: military discipline, both on the ground and in the air; an organized and cultured demeanor in work and daily life; constant attentiveness, even with small things; precision, accuracy, and speed in action; and especially, a calculated habit of industry and initiative in carrying out your duties."

Some sections of this extraordinary book we even learned by heart, reading and re-reading them before each flight and carrying the words with us aloft, like this bit of philosophy:

"Never lose heart in the face of temporary failures. On the contrary, when you fail, be persistent and strong-willed, and work even harder to overcome your difficulties. When you succeed, don't let your head swell with pride. Never allow yourself to become lax or to slacken your attention, and don't ridicule your comrades. Remember that a pilot must approach each detail of a flight with seriousness and wariness, regardless of his abilities and experience. Violating this rule inevitably leads to mistakes and accidents, while observing it ensures accident-free, high-quality work."

After we took our first exam with the mechanic on aircraft powerplant and systems, we each in turn climbed into the cockpit, sitting in tandem behind the instructor. We practiced how to move the control stick and rudder pedals during takeoffs, turns, and three-point landings. The instructor patiently demonstrated what the horizon would look like in different flight attitudes, while the other students muscled the tail this way and that to simulate climbs, descents, and turns for the cadet inside.

With all our ground-school exams turned in, we were at last ready for our first flight, scheduled for the following Sunday. Our anticipation made the week crawl by.

During the week, I worked in a mine caulkers' brigade, caulking tubing joints for a hydroisolation tunnel. Our work was difficult and could be quite physically damaging. The cafeteria lady always delivered milk right to where we worked and made us drink as much as we could. My arms stayed numb from holding the caulking hammer above my head and from the constant stream of water leaking down my sleeve.

I blended cement, molten glass, and sand and filled tunnel joints with the mixture. It was simple enough work, but my thick gloves made the task awkward and difficult. So I finally took them off and packed the solution into the spaces between the tubing's uneven, cast-iron sides with my bare hands.

When I washed up after the shift, the dirt rinsed away to reveal skinless palms, raw and painful. A wave of anxiety flashed across my mind: How would I be able to fly like this? I rushed to the medical unit.

The doctor gasped. "What have you done, you stupid girl?" she exclaimed.

"Will they be healed by Sunday?" I asked, breathlessly. "I have to fly!"

"You can forget about flying," the doctor growled as she smeared an ointment on my sore hands and bandaged them. She handed me a doctor's note for work and forbade me to remove the bandages or to get them wet.

I went to work the next day anyway, but filling the joints was impossible, even wearing gloves, so I decided to haul sand and cement in buckets instead. I carried them over my bent elbows, like a lady's purse, to keep from harming my injured hands.

I passed a group from the tunnelers' brigade, arguing loudly over the deafening clamor of pneumatic and caulking hammers, the hiss of hoses, the clatter of trolleys. When they saw me, they somehow managed to shout over the construction noise. "Anya, An-ya! Tell us, how do you pronounce it, '*Oh*-per-a' or 'o-per-*ah*'?"

Two robust-looking lads, red-faced from arguing, stood there gripping their enormous wrenches and looking earnestly to me to resolve the conflict. I stepped between them, just in case, and said in a conciliatory manner, "We should be talking about the operetta, instead. After all, the operetta theater is our patron! But as for opera… What can I say about opera?" I stalled, thinking fast. "In French, it would be 'o-per-*ah*,' and in Russian, it's '*oh*-per-a.'"

They quieted down after that, casting sympathetic glances at my bandaged hands. "Anya, why don't we ever see you at the dances?" they asked.

"I don't have time," I said. "I'm studying at the aeroclub flight school."

"Really? Have you already flown?" the miners asked simultaneously.

"Of course," I lied, blushing and hurrying back to my section.

"Yegorova, what's the matter with your hands?" the shift foreman demanded when I returned. "Why are you carrying the bucket on your hip like that?"

"It's more comfortable this way," I evaded, speeding my steps.

The foreman forbade me to work any more, but I convinced him that I could still help the brigade, even just a little, to fulfill the daily plan. He relented.

After two weeks, my hands had healed, and I headed straight for the aerodrome. We were now to fly daily at the aeroclub, so I requested a shift change from foreman Zaloyev.

"I won't allow it!" he shouted. "You have no right!"

How handsome he was! It was as if I were seeing him for the first time.

His huge black eyes with flecks of blue flashed with fire from under their long, thick eyelashes. His eyebrows rose like two wings, and his black curls poked out from under the miners' helmet. On such a tall and graceful figure, even the hideous workers' overall was becoming.

I scrutinized him as he raged back and forth, yelling something in his native Ossetian language, brandishing his caulking hammer. For a moment I wondered if the hot-blooded Caucasian foreman might strike me with the hammer. But after a bit Zaloyev calmed down and said, in a placating tone: "Don't be angry with me. I wish you only the best. Give up flying! It'll only kill you. Stay here. We'll finish the station, then you can enroll in day classes at an institute and study whatever you like," he argued. "But right now, Anya, we must work!"

"No, Georgi." I said. "Thank you for your advice, but I won't give up flying!"

After the shift, we boarded the train for Maliye Vyazmy, wild with excitement about our rendezvous with the sky. The atmosphere on our rail carriage was noisy and festive. A beautiful fair-haired girl from the aeroclub named Anna Polyeva, wearing a navy-blue velveteen dress with red buttons and a blue silk kerchief to match her eyes, led songs. The hour-and-a-half trip flew by. In no time we found ourselves walking to the aerodrome.

The undulating plowed fields and forest had gone mad with greenery in the weeks we had been away. Along the streams and pathways on the way to the airfield grew dense thickets of hazel, blossoming cherry trees, and alder hung with golden catkins. Viktor Kutov ducked into the bushes and picked a bouquet of flowers for me. I accepted his gift, even though I was still a bit annoyed with him after an argument we'd had.

Here's what happened: when the government issued an appeal to young women to explore the Far East for settlement, I yearned to answer it. I requested a discharge from work and even stopped attending classes at the aeroclub for a time.

The personnel department sent me to the chairman of the Miners' Committee, an old veteran miner we all respected deeply, even loved. We went to him with our joys and misfortunes, as if he were our father.

When I gave him the application for my dismissal, he put on his spectacles and read the application. He sat quietly for a while, thinking, then looked closely at me and said after a long while, "I never saw this application. You may go."

Two "delegates" from the aeroclub came by that evening—a cadet named Tugushi and Viktor Kutov.

"Why haven't you been to class?"

"I'm going to the Far East," I answered.

"But why?" demanded Tugushi. "Our Komsomol construction project isn't any less important than the Far East."

"Maybe you're hoping to go East and get married," chimed in Viktor. "There's no need to go that far away. Marry me instead!" he added, excitedly.

I muttered some phrases right out of our political education classes—that I was answering the patriotic appeal to serve, the call of the Party, and the dictates of my heart.

"And why are they only calling for girls? Is it easier for girls to explore the taiga?"

Secretly, I agreed with everything they said, but I couldn't admit it. I stubbornly opposed their every argument. But the next day, I tore up my dismissal application and returned that evening to classes at the aeroclub.

Now I was holding the bouquet of cherry blossoms from Viktor in my arms. I began breaking off tiny petals one-by-one, but instead of the usual "he loves me, he loves me not," I whispered to myself, "I will fly, I won't fly..."

The last petal dropped—"I *will* fly," it assured me. With that, a burden seemed to lift, and I suddenly felt I could rush headlong into my future, un-burdened, happy, and free.

10
First Flight

Everything was glorious that morning—sun, sky, and earth, so springy beneath my feet. It seemed I could spread my arms like wings and take flight.

For what in this world is more extraordinary than flying?

This is what I remember: the airfield teeming with bluebells, our airplanes lined up in a row, and us opposite them, wearing our new blue flying overalls, Osoaviakhim[1] helmets, and goggles. The flight chief made his report to the aeroclub superintendent while we stood motionless. A gentle wind caressed our faces, and we breathed easily and freely. How marvelous it was to live in the world's bright light! What joy we felt, as though youth could never end, nor life itself.

"To the planes!" came the superintendent's order.

Cadet Tugushi climbed into the rear cockpit behind our instructor, Georgi Miroyevsky. We all envied our comrade terribly for his good fortune—for being the first to taste the sky.

"Staaaaart your engine!" the superintendent commanded.

"Switches off!" pronounced the instructor. To the mechanic standing by the propeller, he ordered, "Fill engine!"

"Filling!" cried the mechanic, pulling the propeller through to prime the cylinders.

"Start engine!"

"Starting!"

"Clear prop!"

"Clear prop!" repeated the mechanic, giving the propeller blade a forceful yank. As the engine turned slowly through one compression, he stepped briskly to the side.

The propeller rotated, and the engine coughed, spat a tiny puff of smoke, and roared to life. The instructor spread his arms to signal the mechanic to remove the chocks from under the wheels, and the airplane began taxiing gracefully to the runway.

---

[1] *Osoaviakhim* is a shortened form of (more simply stated) "The Society for the Defense, Aviation, and Chemical Industries." Organized nationally in 1927 as a paramilitary group to prepare people for civil defense roles, the organization encouraged thousands of young volunteers to train as pilots and for other military specialties (such as marksmanship, parachuting, and first aid) in the years before the war. It had millions of members, a third of whom were women.

Together with the slipcovers and instrument bags, we sat in the "quad-rant"—the spot on the airfield designated for waiting cadets and equip-ment—fixing our eyes on the plane as it circled the aerodrome a few times and landed.

We rushed to meet it, but the mechanic blocked our way. "Just Yego-rova!" he barked. I grabbed hold of the wing and loped along, trying to keep up with the plane. The instructor shouted, "Next!" without shutting down the engine. We encircled Tugushi and bombarded him with questions.

"Was it good?

"Great!" he answered, grinning with all his teeth.

"It wasn't scary?" I asked.

"Not at all."

"What did you see?"

Tugushi pondered for a moment, then said, "The instructor's head, the tachometer, and the instructor's face in the mirror."

"That's it?"

"Not too much else," Tugushi answered earnestly, as we burst out laughing.

My turn came next. "May I?" I asked the instructor. Miroyevsky nodded his approval. I climbed into the rear cabin, buckled in, and connected the intercom cord, slowly and deliberately, so as not to betray my nervousness.

"Ready?" he asked impatiently, watching me in the mirror.

"Ready!" I shouted, over the drone of the engine.

Through the intercom, the instructor briefed me. On this flight, he would do everything himself. I would hold the controls very lightly to learn how they operated.

"Pay attention to how I lift off and turn the airplane," he instructed, then added at last, "Let's take off!"

Once we were in the air, only the instructor spoke. "We took off south-west. To the right is Golitsino and Bolshiye Vyazmy. On the left, the train sta-tion at Maliye Vyazmy. Let's make the first turn."

He had my full attention. I tried to memorize everything I saw below me and the movements of the controls at the same time.

"Below us is the station at Maliye Vyazmy. Now here's the second turn. Notice my movements!" he repeated.

As we flew over a plowed field, the airplane lurched abruptly. I let go of the controls and grabbed the dashboard with both hands, but the instructor didn't seem to notice. "Altitude three hundred meters, flying straight and level," he announced. "Take the controls!"

I certainly wasn't expecting that. But I began manipulating the rudder pedals, the control stick, and the throttle. Right away the plane began to list to one side and the other, the nose rising and falling through the horizon, like a horse driven by an incompetent rider.

It reminded me of our horse Lidochka, back in Volodovo. We'd bought her cheap, not knowing her character. She was no lover of work, often simply lying down when she was harnessed to the cart, not getting up until she got hungry. She also took delight in throwing riders when they least expected it.

One day I was supposed to ride her to the meadow. I climbed on her back and set off without incident. Hardly had I eased the reins when she dashed off at a gallop, ignoring my cries of "Whoooooa!" I held onto her mane for my life and screamed for help as she raced toward the woods. I finally decided to jump off, but my foot caught in the reins. Lidochka dragged me quite a distance before she stopped.

That's just how my first flight was. The unruly machine would not yield to my clumsy, inept hands. It seemed like an eternity before the instructor took back the controls. He immediately subdued the aircraft as despair washed over me. *That's it. No more flying for me,* I thought. *I'm incapable. What a coward!*

The only thing I wanted then was that no one should know of my disgrace. I couldn't even manage to fly a plane straight and level! My dreams of becoming a pilot came tumbling down around me.

But Miroyevsky continued to talk me through the next turn, as if nothing had happened. He directed my attention to the landing "T" mark, explaining that we would try to fly a course parallel to it. After making the third turn, the instructor throttled back and began a descent, approaching the fourth and final turn. I held the controls ever so lightly, so as not to interfere with his movements. He cut power, put the airplane into a glide, then flared and made a three-point landing.

"That's it," came the voice over the headset. "We've landed! Now let's head back to the parking area." I interpreted his words to mean what I already knew: I was finished as a pilot. I would be dismissed as hopeless. Miroyevsky taxied back, shut down the engine, and climbed out of the cockpit. I unbuckled my seat belt, awkwardly clambered out onto the wing, and jumped down.

"I am ready to hear your criticisms," I said softly, hanging my head low.

"What's the matter with you, Yegorova? You're not about to cry, are you?'

"I'll never be able to d-d-do this!" I wailed.

"And who learns anything all at once?" he laughed. "Moscow wasn't built in a day, either."

11
I Am a Pilot

The first Sunday in June dawned as bright and warm as a midsummer day. At sunrise, intricate palaces of towering white clouds loomed all along the horizon. But by the time we were ready to fly, they had melted away, leaving us a perfect day for flying. Only a mischievous breeze disturbed the stillness, but even it blew just the right amount.

As always, the aerodrome woke early. As the sun's disc peeked across the treetops, our tall, lanky instructor Miroyevsky already strolled silently along our formation. He inspected our flight suits with a critical eye, as if we were soldiers at attention. When he finished, he pronounced affably in his beautiful, unusually low voice, "Yegorova will fly with me first, if there's no objection."

I certainly didn't object. I stepped out of formation, attempting to radiate an air of readiness.

"May I take my seat?"

"Sit."

I adroitly leapt onto the wing and clambered into the back seat.

"Taxi out!"

The obedient U-2 waddled from side to side like a duck, along the stiff grass to the runway.

"You control the plane yourself today," announced Miroyevsky.

"I control the plane," I repeated.

It was an ordinary flight lesson, like any other that spring. We took off, made several circuits, landed, and taxied back. Then the instructor changed places with the commander of the flight group.

Again, we took off, circled, and landed. And to my surprise, the chief of flying personnel, V. I. Lebedev, appeared by the runway at just that moment.

The flight group commander had already unfastened his seatbelt and thrown one leg out of the cockpit, but when I did the same, he signaled me to stay in my seat. Miroyevsky approached with a grin on his kind, oblong face. *Everything's OK*, the smile said. *I'm pleased.*

Meanwhile, the chief of flying personnel was already striding up to the aircraft, pulling on leather gloves and fastening his helmet along the way. Chief Lebedev was a simple and warm-hearted man who never lost his temper, never yelled at or humiliated his subordinates, always criticized us tactfully, and offered useful advice. In his lectures, he instilled in us the idea that our time in the sky taught us not just to be competent airmen but also molded our characters and forever changed our perspective on life.

Lebedev was a marvelous pilot, as well. He had supposedly earned a medal from China for outstanding training of Chinese pilots at a flight school in the town of Urumchi. How accomplished he must be, we thought, to have trained illiterate Chinese pilots who spoke not a word of Russian and had never seen an airplane in their lives! Each of us hoped for the chance to take a flight check with him.

A bold, thrilling idea flashed through my mind: *Could I be soloing today?* But I immediately felt ashamed of the idea. *That's ridiculous!* I thought. After all, none of the other students had soloed yet.

Still, I knew, something was about to happen. Lebedev climbed in the front cabin. "Make a circular flight pattern," came Lebedev's voice through the intercom. "Altitude three hundred meters. Make a three-point landing near the 'T' within the landing zone." I repeated the order and requested clearance to taxi.

"Cleared for taxi and takeoff!" Lebedev said, placing his hands deliberately outside the cockpit, to show me that I alone would control the plane. That didn't alarm me too much, since I had been operating the controls by myself for quite a while now. The instructor was always there, but only to supervise. Still, it was reassuring to know that if something happened, he could help me.

I smoothly opened the throttle and took off. I performed a "box" pattern just as I'd been taught, then put the airplane into a glide. Over the runway, I leveled off at the proper altitude and pulled back ever so gradually on the stick until the plane landed on three wheels right by the landing "T."

"Taxi back!" ordered the chief.

When I shut down the engine, Lebedev told me to stay in the cockpit, then went over to Miroyevsky to tell him something. The instructor yelled for someone to load a sandbag into the front cockpit. They usually did this to maintain the airplane's proper center of gravity when students made solo flights. Sure enough, the instructor turned to me and said, "You're going to fly solo now. Fly a pattern just like you did with the chief of flying personnel."

My mouth immediately went dry, my palms slick with sweat. I suddenly wished to thank Miroyevsky for teaching me to fly and for choosing me to solo first in the group. I wanted to find just the right words to express my gratitude and esteem for him, but instead, I only sniffled and pulled the goggles down over my eyes.

How many months had I longed to hear the simple phrase "fly solo" — words that indicated the utmost faith in a young pilot. I had dreamed of them, of the many possible ways I might one day hear them, and now, they had finally come! I hardly noticed Miroyevsky and a technician buckling the sandbag into the front seat.

"This sack is for Yegorova! So that she won't get bored. This will replace me," said Miroyevsky, then turned to me. "Airwoman Yegorova, have confidence! Everything will be fine. Just stay calm."

"Contact!"

"Clear propeller!"

Again, the propeller began counting its revolutions, and again, the plane lurched forward. I concentrated my full attention on the instruments. Instructor Miroyevsky walked with me to the takeoff position, holding onto the wing. A surge of confidence seemed to flow from his firm, able hands, through the aircraft body, and into me.

Control stick, throttle, magneto switch: I had touched and twisted them hundreds of times, had flown complicated maneuvers in the airplane, but always under the supervision of my older comrade. Now the aircraft answered to me alone. I felt a strange transformation within me. Only a few seconds before, this responsibility seemed fearsome and oppressive. But as I turned the U-2 into the start position, I felt the weight lift from my shoulders.

My heart beat steadily, my breathing light and easy, my mind clear. Memory took over, as I briskly repeated the rote procedures my hands had learned so well. My flights with the instructor stood me in good stead. I was utterly composed and purposeful.

The airplane gathered speed and tore itself from the earth. I was flying!

Are there many people who truly know how it feels to fly? "Millions," you say? So many planes carrying people from city to city, from one continent to another. But how can you compare an open-cockpit trainer to the tightly sealed cabin of a passenger liner? Flying in a jet airliner is like riding a bus. It has walls, windows, ceiling. You can walk around in comfort, totally unaware of the air outside, the temperature, the weather. But to ride through the air in a pressurized tube is only the illusion of flight. It's not really flying.

It's another matter altogether in a tiny training airplane like the U-2. You give yourself over entirely to the air—head, arms, shoulders. Dip your palm into the waves of air streaming by, and you can feel its harsh, icy thickness. Look around you. There's nobody anywhere near, as if you were alone in the universe. It's just the sky, you, and the airplane, compliant to your human will. It carries you higher and higher, toward the sun and stars, obeying your every command. You are its master.

Happiness overwhelmed me. I wanted to sing, to cry out into the heavens that I was a pilot! I, a simple Russian girl, a Moscow Metrostroy worker, could command an airplane!

Although this marvelous feeling seemed to last an eternity, in fact, I had only circled the aerodrome once. The next thing I knew, the U-2 was running along the grass. Miroyevsky stood near the landing "T." He put his thumb in the air and waved a white flag. After a moment, I realized he was signaling me to take off and make another pattern. That meant I had done everything right! On the second flight, my joy knew no bounds. I began singing and screaming, and my feet danced on the pedals. I scarcely noticed that I was approaching the fourth turn.

I concentrated on landing the airplane as precisely as possible, and I succeeded—the U-2 touched down right on the "T." Our Master Sergeant Khatuntsev met the airplane. With one hand he gripped the wing, giving me a thumbs-up sign with the other. In retaliation for his always making me scrub the airplane's tail, I stuck out my tongue at him and revved the engine. The plane taxied faster, forcing Vanya to run hard to keep up with me. How happy I was in those moments! How my heart rejoiced! It seemed to me that there couldn't be a happier person in all the world.

I taxied to parking and shut down the engine. The cadets swarmed around the aircraft, peppering me with questions and congratulating me, but I rushed straight to our supervisors to make my report.

"Excellent, Yegorova. Keep up the good work," said Lebedev, firmly gripping my hand.

After the flights, Master Sergeant Khatuntsev again "entrusted" me with washing the plane's tail section, but this time I didn't get angry with him. Quite the contrary; on that day, I took pail, rag, and soapy water to the U-2's empennage with gusto.

12
Trousseau

By the end of July, we had all soloed. The command invited us to spend our vacation from the mine at the aerodrome camp. Our Metrostroy Komsomol "god" Zhenya—the Komsomol committee secretary—encouraged us in this.

"We live in harsh and menacing times," he raged, appealing to the assembled youths to join Osoaviakhim and learn military specialties. "The clouds of war threaten us from the West. Imperialism, borne up by the gathering storm of Fascism, prepares to launch its aggression against our Soviet nation!"

Many young men and women from the Metrostroy heeded that call. A smith named Alyosha Ryazanov flew gliders at the mine's aeroclub and went on to defend the skies of Moscow, Stalingrad, Kuban[1], and the Baltic region as a fighter pilot. An aeroclub cadet named Luka Muravitsky distinguished himself as a fighter pilot over Leningrad and was awarded the Hero of the Soviet Union in the first months of the war. He rammed his Yak into an enemy bomber, cutting off its tail with his propeller. Before each mission, he painted the words "For Anna" on his airplane's fuselage in memory of his beloved Anna Poleva, who had worked in his Metrostroy brigade. She perished before the war in a parachuting accident while training to become an airborne soldier.

Yes, we women prepared to defend our motherland, too. In April of 1942, the State Defense Committee issued a decree on drafting women into the armed services— initially into the Liaison Corps, and later into the Air Force.

That decree lagged behind the realities of war. By 1942, a young Metrostroy woman named Motya, who took Morse Code courses before the war, had already been severely wounded while transmitting radio reports deep behind enemy lines in Lithuania. She lay near death for ten days in a bomb crater, encircled by Fascists, with only a flask of water to keep her alive. Years later, the "Lily of the Valley," the call sign under which she transmitted, won the Hero of the Soviet Union award.

---

[1] A region of the northern Caucasus, in southern Russia, surrounding the Kuban River—a 560-mile-long river that flows from the Caucasus Mountains into the Sea of Azov on the northern coast of the Taman Peninsula.

When asked how she had endured, Motya would always smile and say, "Why, I'm Russian, after all!" and recite Nekrasov's[2] famous verses about the Russian woman:

She would stop a galloping horse,
She would walk into a burning hut…

And so in the years before war came to the Soviet lands, we prepared ourselves: we worked, studied, and learned to defend our motherland.

Our daily routine at the aeroclub camp echoed the structure of a military base: reveille, calisthenics, tidying up our tents, then breakfast, on days when our flights were in the afternoon. But when we flew first shift, we rose before daybreak and took off at dawn.

Soon we moved through the box-pattern work and on to the most interesting part of training—aerobatic flight maneuvers. Again, we pored through the "Manual of Flight," which told us that the objective of aerobatic flight was to demonstrate to the pilot the full range of an aircraft's flight envelope. This would allow him to master to perfection any maneuver of which the plane is capable—a vital skill for combat flying.

For our first aerobatic "flight," Instructor Miroyevsky demonstrated aerobatic flight maneuvers to us with a model airplane. He showed us the aircraft's motion in all three axes and told us where to look, what we should see out the window, and how to position the controls.

"Yegorova," he said. "Describe the "loop" maneuver."

"A loop," I answered, "is a closed circle in the vertical plane."

"Excellent. You may sit down," said Miroyevsky encouragingly. "Now, Petukhov, what is a spin?"

Ivan Petukhov slowly rose to his full height, dropping his hands stiffly to the seams of his flight suit and said, "A spin is a rapid descent accompanied by a steep, spiraling rotation. It can arise when a plane loses speed, or 'stalls.'"

Ivan was born to a peasant family near Volokolamsk and always did everything scrupulously, in a proud and dignified manner. He was a master of all things mechanical. He and a friend had assembled a working truck from spare parts so that our aerodrome would have a real fuel truck instead of hauling gasoline around on a cart.

---

[2] Nikolai Alexeyevich Nekrasov (1821–78). A radical intellectual and editor of eminent literary journals, Nekrasov is best known for his poetry describing social injustice and the suffering of the Russian peasant. The excerpt is from an 1863 narrative poem called "Red-Nosed Frost" about a widowed peasant woman who freezes to death while chopping wood.

"All flight students must practice spins," Ivan continued, "to learn how to recover from an inadvertent spin, which can result from any flight maneuver performed incorrectly."

"Tugushi! What do you know about the barrel roll?" demanded Miroyevsky.

"It is a double revolution over the wing in the horizontal plane," the words tumbled out in a single breath. "But the U-2 airplane cannot accomplish a barrel roll because of its low speed."

Flying had changed Tugushi for the better. His early flights had not gone well. The instructor was always reprimanding him for fixating on the instruments instead of looking outside. "Why are you flying blind?" Miroyevsky would rage. "You're going to kill us both!"

When Tugushi flew badly, he would mope around with his head drooping. Even his black eyes seemed to dim to a dull brown. But then he had somehow caught up to us, and now he was radiant. He wore a crisp white shirt and tie to the aerodrome every day, his grey Osoaviakhim flight suit painstakingly ironed, his shoes polished to a brilliant luster. We joked that aerodrome dirt would not stick to him. Among ourselves, we nicknamed him the Georgian prince.

"Kutov! How do you perform an Immelman turn?" inquired the instructor.

Viktor Kutov demonstrated the maneuver. The brown-eyed young man with facial skin as soft as a girl's worked at the Metrostroy marble factory and attended classes in the evening. He loved to read, and he wrote poetry and collected books. He often bought two copies of the same book—one for him, one for me. I didn't have any space to store books, so I donated them to the mine's library after I read them.

Sometimes I would find Viktor's poems, handwritten on slips of paper, between the pages of the books he gave me. When no one was nearby, I gently took the verses out, read and re-read them, and folded them into my purse. Then I hid them all carefully in a secret box I kept in the dormitory.

After we finished the theory classes, we were allowed to work on aerobatics in the flight training practice area. All those pretty aeronautical theory terms like "turn," "loop," and "spin" became real to us as we struggled to master the maneuvers they represented. Everywhere I went, Viktor Kutov and Tugushi were my constant satellites. They always vied to sit at my table at the cafeteria.

I felt a deep affection for Viktor. I couldn't say the same about Tugushi. He followed me everywhere, endlessly trying to please and flatter me: "Anna, you fly as if you were born in the cockpit. I envy you. You didn't get a single criticism on your first solo flight. You handle the airplane as if it were a tamed horse! The thing won't obey me for anything."

I kept quiet. After all, I couldn't say what I was thinking: if only those praises came from Viktor.

Every day opened up new horizons for us. We were buoyant. Everywhere you could hear elated cadets sharing stories:

"You know, I was doing a loop today, and I nearly went into a spin!"

"Your turns look like pancakes instead of normal turns!"

"Vitya went into quite a dive today!"

One day we marched back from the launch area, singing our favorite song:

Ever higher, and higher, and higher
We aim our birds into the sky…

Suddenly, one of the cadets interrupted: "Look, everybody! What's that red thing in the females' tent?"

The song went silent. Everyone stared into the open flaps of our tent, where we glimpsed a flash of bright red. As we drew closer, we saw my bunk covered with a luxurious red quilt. My mother sat on a stool next to it.

"Look, guys—it's a trousseau for Anya!" someone said, and everybody roared with laughter.

The sergeant allowed me to break formation. I hurriedly greeted my mother, then blurted, "Why did you bring me a quilt? So everyone would make fun of me?"

"Daughter dear, I thought you must be cold sleeping under that soldier's blanket. My heart sensed it!"

"No one here, including me, is the least bit cold! Please take the quilt away so everyone doesn't laugh at me!"

Just then, my instructor walked in and introduced himself to my mother. He admired the quilt and told Mama that I was a good pilot, and that I would soon start learning how to parachute out of the aircraft.

At the beginning of the summer, I had mailed my salary home to Mother along with a letter telling her that I would spend my vacation at a summer camp. I had failed to mention what kind of camp it was. "What do you mean, flying?" Mama cried, rising weakly from her stool.

Miroyevsky turned to me, astonished. "Yegorova, why didn't you write your mother to tell her you were learning to fly?"

I didn't know what to say. My instructor explained to her as simply as he could what a forgiving and docile airplane the U-2 was. "Don't worry about your daughter," he said. "Our airplane is absolutely safe. It's just like a wagon, except a wagon is pulled by a horse, and the plane uses a motor with horsepower. And it's good that you brought that quilt. Everyone gets so cold at night. There's a forest and a river nearby…"

Mama calmed down a bit and turned to Miroyevsky confidentially. "Sonny, please look after her, would you? She's quite eccentric. First she made up her mind to work underground. Now she's up in the sky flying!"

"Of course, Mother. Don't worry. Everything will be fine."

That day Mama left for Moscow. The quilt stayed with me, but it occasionally disappeared for a night or two. One rainy day I found it in the men's tent, wrapped like a sleeping bag around a snoozing Luka Muravitsky.

13
Into the Abyss

In non-flying weather, we studied how a parachute worked, how to pack it, and the principles of bailing out. Our instructor Vladimir Antonenko made it all sound so simple, but the night before my first jump, I could barely sleep.

We had clear skies the next morning, so I strapped on my parachute, cinched up the lines, and hooked them to the flaps. The instructor checked my gear, and a nurse took my pulse.

My stomach churned with nervousness. I lumbered, bear-like, out to the plane, struggling with the restrictive parachute harness. I clambered awkwardly onto the wing and folded myself into the front seat.

The pilot took off and climbed to eight hundred meters. "Get ready!" he called.

"Ready," I answered.

I apprehensively climbed out onto the wing, gripping the strut, and looked down. It was terrifying! I desperately wanted to get back into the cockpit, and I probably would have, but just then the pilot closed the throttle and shouted, "Go!" and gave me a little nudge.

"Yes, sir!" I shouted back and leapt into the abyss.

I yanked the ring, but it seemed for a moment that the canopy wasn't going to open. Suddenly, I felt a violent shudder as the parachute dome unfolded above me. I sat back, suspended in the harness as if it were an armchair. Total stillness. Uncontrollable joy engulfed me, and I half-sang, half-shouted. The earth was very close now.

I drew up my legs, as we'd practiced, and rolled onto my right side. I stood up quickly, unfastened the parachute, and began deflating the canopy to repack it. The other cadets rushed excitedly to my aid. What a feeling! We were all ready to do it again.

After that jump, the earth felt different under my feet. It seemed somehow special, more solid perhaps. I began to acquire a certain confidence, a sense that I could do anything. Sergei Smirnov, one of our Metrostroy poets, captured the feeling perfectly:

Climbing out of the mine the first time,
I wiped the sweat from my brow.
And I suddenly felt beneath me
The earth, in all its beauty.
The feeling was a revelation,

And finally, I walked without hesitation
With long, masterful strides.

In the fall we finished our U-2 training coursework. All of us passed the theory and piloting exams given by the State Defense Committee, and the time came to bid farewell to the aerodrome and our instructors and comrades. It was a bittersweet moment—so happy to have earned our wings, we still felt sorry to say goodbye.

I returned to my former routine, working in the mine during the day and in the library, in the corner of the mine cafeteria, after my shift. In place of shelves, we stored books on buffet sideboards, and so I dished out spiritual sustenance—books—like a cafeteria cook.

A month later, we cadets gathered again, dressed in our finest, for our aeroclub graduation ceremony in a Moscow theater, on Malaya Bronnaya Street. The aeroclub superintendent spoke at the ceremony, informing us that the majority of cadets would be assigned to the military flight school to train as fighter pilots. At the end of his speech, he paused dramatically, then made one last announcement:

"There is one female vacancy at the Osoaviakhim Flying School in Ulyanovsk. We have decided to grant that spot to… Anna Yegorova!"

I nearly stopped breathing. It was a dream come true! My friends congratulated me during the intermission, but I still could not believe my good fortune. It didn't become real to me until I received the voucher and train tickets to Ulyanovsk.

14
False Accusation

I stood before the secretary of the city Komsomol committee, awaiting my fate. Expelled from the Ulyanovsk Flying School, banished from the sky, I felt my dreams of flying slipping away from me, as the secretary sat silently in front of me. He scratched his head, ran his fingers through his hair, and suddenly exclaimed, "I've figured it out, Yegorova! You'll go to work as a Pioneer leader at the NKVD[1] work-colony reform school for juvenile offenders. You'll be assigned there until next year's enrollment at the flight school. By that time, everything will have been straightened out, I am sure, and your brother will have been released. Then you can re-apply."

But Vasya wasn't exonerated that year. I dutifully worked and waited, struggling to make Pioneers of rebellious boys at the NKVD colony, until the program was cancelled. I then transferred to a military plant to work in the financial department, despite my protestations that I knew nothing about accounting. A very kind woman took me under her wing, taught me to calculate sums on an abacus, and protected and supported me as much as she could.

As soon as I heard that the flight school was admitting additional cadets, I sent an application to the admissions board. They rejected me in the preliminary interview: "Last time you concealed the fact that your brother was an enemy of the people, and again, you're trying to worm your way into the school. You won't sneak by us again. We are vigilant."

Again, I found myself on the train from Ulyanovsk to Moscow. Babies' cries and thick curls of smoke drifted up from the benches below me in the teeming common carriage. I lay in the upper berth, moaning with grief for my favorite brother and the death of my cherished dream.

---

[1] In 1917, Felix Dzerzhinsky created a secret police, security, and intelligence force called the "All-Russian Extraordinary Commission for Combating Counterrevolution and Sabotage (or "Cheka" for short). The Cheka had the power to arrest, torture, imprison, and execute Soviet citizens without a trial. The GPU and then the OGPU replaced the Cheka and expanded the agency's powers and its network of spies and forced labor camps. In 1938, the name was changed to the "People's Commissariat for Internal Affairs," or the NKVD, and it remained the Soviet Union's main instrument of terror and central control throughout the war.

"She's broken-hearted! She's been pining away all day, with nary a poppy's dewdrop to drink," came an old woman's muffled voice from a lower berth.

"Maybe she's sick," posited a balding man.

"*Love*-sick, probably," said a shrill voice, followed by a repugnant giggle.

I turned my face to the wall and covered my head with a coat. How could my brother be an "enemy of the people"? I wondered desperately. He *is* the people! We came from a family of sixteen children. Only eight of us survived. Father had to take whatever jobs he could find to feed the family. He worked as a carter, delivering fish from Ostashkov on Lake Seliger or buying cucumbers wholesale from Torzhok to sell. Some years he even went to Petrograd[2] to work at a dye factory. He froze in the trenches in the Imperialist War[3] and defended Soviet power with a rifle during the Civil War.[4] He came home a sick and broken man and died in 1925 at the age of forty-nine.

Vasya, the eldest, was eager to study. But when he finished primary school, the family decided he should become a tailor's apprentice. Father said, "Let's sell the sheep, Mother, and I'll take Vaska to 'Pieter.'[5] My brother-in-law Yegor can put in a good word for him with the owner. You'll see! He'll have a trade. What choice do we have? We can't afford to send him to school and feed and clothe him."

Father then turned to Vasya and said, "Sonny, if you don't want to become a tailor, I'll send you to Uncle Misha, Mother's brother, and he'll teach you to be a shoemaker. It's your choice." So Vasya decided to become a tailor.

When the October Revolution broke out, Vasya got hold of a rifle and joined a Red Guards detachment. Wounded and near death, he made his way to our Aunt Agrafena's. She immediately wrote a fearful letter to Mama, saying that God only knew whether Vasya would survive. Mama rushed to Vasya's side, nursed him, and brought him home, his head shaved bald, his frame skinny and ravaged.

Vasya didn't stay home long. He went to work for the railroad in Kuvshinovo, and soon the workers there promoted him to salesman in the railroad shop. With the country in ruins and so many people starving, this was an expression of their absolute faith in him. Eventually he was transferred to Rzhev, then to Moscow.

---

[2] St. Petersburg was known as Petrograd from 1914–24 and became Leningrad (1924–91) after Lenin's death.

[3] She is referring to World War I.

[4] In the Russian Civil War (roughly 1918–20), the Red Army defended the new regime against anti-Bolshevik forces, called the "Whites"—a disparate coalition of leftist and rightist Russians, nationalist non-Russian minorities, and foreign interventionists who opposed the Bolshevik seizure of power and Lenin's dissolution of the Constituent Assembly.

[5] An informal name for St. Petersburg.

Vasya lived like so many other workers of his generation: he worked, studied at night in the factory school, and became a communist. He graduated from the planning academy. The workers of Moscow Factory Number 5 elected Vasily as their deputy to the Moscow Soviet, and he was appointed chief of the planning section of the People's Commissariat of Domestic Trade.

How could a man like this be an enemy of the people? I thought, searching through the events of his life in my mind. It was slander. It was a false accusation!

I recalled how Mama used to pray on her knees before the iconostasis, at first pronouncing all her children's names, then asking for our health and sound minds, and always, at the end of the prayer repeating the words, "Protect them, Lord, from a false accusation!" As a child, I didn't understand what the words meant, but now their horrible import was laid bare for me. Mama's pleas to God hadn't saved Vasya after all.

How agonizingly slowly the train rolled into Moscow! But the closer I got, the more listless and apathetic I felt. Why was I here? Where would I go once I arrived?

Finally, Moscow—the city of my Komsomol youth, the place that had transformed a simple village girl's destiny and linked it inextricably to the sky.

A gloomy, overcast sky and rain greeted me in Moscow.

No one met me at the station. No one waited for me there.

I called Vasily's apartment from the station. His wife Katya answered. When she recognized my voice, she burst into tears and for a long while could not utter a word. Finally, she asked, "Where are you, Nyurochka?"

"At Kazan Station."

"Wait for me at the main entrance! I'll be right there."

I waited an hour, then two. Sudddenly, I saw her, barely recognizable with her worn clothes and downcast look. "Katya!?" I shouted in surprise.

She had been looking for me dressed in a smart military uniform, and I, for the proud beauty I remembered, with sumptuous black hair and glittering blue eyes. But these eyes shone with tears.

Katya seized my hand and pulled me into the depths of the station, to an unoccupied bench. She told me that Vasya had been tried by a *troika*[6] and sentenced to ten years confinement for espionage and ties to British spies. An article he had published in *The Economic Newspaper* had allegedly been copied by British intelligence. Vasya was accused of giving away state secrets.

---

[6] The word generally means a threesome of any kind, such as a sled drawn by three horses. In this context, it refers to an NKVD tribunal consisting of three people for the purpose of summary judgment and quick punishment of political prisoners, who had no right to legal defense. These special tribunals sentenced hundreds of thousands of people to death and exile during Stalin's purge of 1937–38.

"Ten years! For what?" Katya cried bitterly, her face streaming with tears. "Nyurochka darling, you mustn't call me or visit me. When you called, I just happened to drop by the apartment for a few minutes to pick up Yurka's things. We've been staying with friends, even though most of them are afraid of us these days. I'm afraid I'll be arrested too if I stay at home. What will happen to my son then?" she sobbed. I cried with her until we parted.

I had no idea where to go next. To Viktor's aviation unit? I didn't want him to see me like this. The aeroclub? No! The Metrostroy? No! I wouldn't tolerate being pitied, being reminded of the happiest time of my life and all my rash dreams. Those memories would taste of poison now. I'd go there later. Now, I'd just go wherever my gaze fell.

At the station, my eyes moved to the timetable, finding the train to my brother Alexey's house in Sebezh. I bought a ticket.

The train trudged along haltingly, stumbling to a stop at each tiny station. The wheels clattered out a melancholy beat: "*ev*-ery thing is *ter*-ri-ble… *ev*-ery thing is *ter*-ri-ble…"

I didn't find my brother in Sebezh. He had been transferred. I spent the night at his neighbor's house and set off for Alexey's new home early in the morning. I only had twelve rubles in my purse. I needed two rubles more to get to the small town where Lyosha had moved. *It doesn't matter*, I thought. *I'll walk the rest of the way.*

Again, I lay on an upper berth in the common carriage. To hold back my tears, I concentrated on the clack-clack of the train wheels, which whispered to me: *Where are you going… where are you going?…* After a time their "song" seemed to change: *Where is your will… where is your will?…*

Was I really so weak? If I did have any strength of will, surely I wouldn't be lying motionless and grief-stricken on this berth. Why didn't I fight for the right to fly? I recalled the words of Sasha Kosarev,[7] the much-loved Secretary of the Komsomol Central Committee who was declared an enemy of the people in 1938 and later executed: "Never give up on your dreams. Press ahead proudly and fearlessly…"

"Press ahead proudly and fearlessly," I repeated. Just then the train jerked to an awkward halt, as if it were granting me a chance to choose.

"Where are we?" I asked someone, hanging my head over the berth.

"Looks like Smolensk," a man answered.

"How long do we stop here?"

"About thirty minutes."

---

[7] Alexander Vasilyevich Kosarev (1903–39). As General Secretary of Komsomol begin-ning in 1929, he directed Stalin's purge of the Komsomol organization in the 1930s. According to Robert Conquest's *The Great Terror*, Stalin wished to redefine the youth organization's mission as "the necessity to seek out and recognize the enemy, who had then to be removed forcibly…." —which many thousands of Komsomol leaders indeed were. Kosarev himself was arrested in 1938, then tortured, tried, and executed in February 1939.

To the surprise of the other passengers, I jumped down from my berth, grabbed my coat and suitcase, and shot toward the exit. The man in the lower berth exchanged glances with a fellow-traveler and shook his head sympathetically. "Totally out of her wits," he said.

"Maybe she stole something," the fellow-traveler chimed in.

"Shame on you!" an old woman spat furiously. "Enough of these false accusations!"

15
Himself

The train pulled away. As it rattled past the traffic signals on the outskirts of Smolensk, I was already approaching the Komsomol Regional Committee building. The winter dawn had just begun to turn the white walls of the city's ancient houses a pale blue. The Komsomol office hadn't opened yet. I idled for a time by the locked door until the wintry air chilled me to the bone. I set off at a trot down the street, jogging as far as a poster stand, and then turned and ran back. I did this several times, until a pleasant warmth spread throughout my body.

The city slowly changed colors, from violet blue to a faint pink. I heard the rattle of the day's first streetcar and the drone of its first truck.

When the door finally opened, I rushed into the office with a group of eagerly waiting visitors. I stuck my head into one doorway after another, seeing no one.

"Where has the First Secretary gotten to?" I demanded of a frail-looking man with spectacles who was striding importantly down the corridor carrying a leather briefcase. He peered over his glasses at me in surprise, a mute question in his eyes: who on earth might need to talk to "Himself"? But then, he caught the look of stubbornness on my face and decided not to press the question. "The black door around the corner," he answered.

A short, plump secretary staunchly blocked the door to "Himself's" office. But something about me, perhaps my height or the look on my face, made her cede the way. I stepped jauntily across the threshold and, afraid that I'd be immediately ejected, blurted out in one breath, "I need work and a place to live, as soon as possible!"

A young man seated at an imposing-looking desk raised his head and fixed his bespectacled eyes on me with interest. "What's your problem, Comrade?"

"My problem can't wait," I answered, letting spill my whole story in a confused and agitated jumble. I told him everything: the metro, the aeroclub, the military flight school, my brother. The First Secretary listened in rapt silence, with concern in his eyes.

He seemed to understand me. A young girl, a Komsomol, who had mastered the complexities of aviation, was being denied her greatest love. He also knew as well as I did that war stood at our nation's doorstep. We Soviets were then fortifying our defenses, developing our industry, and rearming the military at a furious pace.

As "Himself" listened to my muddled tale, he began to wonder: why expel a qualified aviator for no reason, especially at a time then the nation desperately needed pilots, and Osoaviakhim's combat training program was strained to the limits?

"Do you have your papers with you?"

"Here they are," I said, handing him my passport, Komsomol card, my red Metrostroy certificate, and my graduation records from the aeroclub.

I sat on the divan and wept bitterly while "Himself" perused my documents and made phone calls, asking me questions in a sympathetic tone. Finally, he said, "Look, could you teach our boys to fly gliders?"

"Of course I could!"

"Excellent. Your papers are certainly in order."

My joy and relief stole my breath away.

"Well, Crybaby, let's go have lunch," said the Secretary sardonically.

"No, thank you!" I said, but he would have none of it. "Let's go," he said, and pulled me by the hand to the canteen.

After paying for lunch, he glanced at my empty wallet and lent me twenty-five rubles until my first paycheck. "So, you're interested in a job and a place to live?" he said with an air of amused triumph. "Well, while you were busy howling, I arranged for you to work as an accountant at the Smolensk flax factory. You'll like the factory collective. They're young, energetic people. Meanwhile, you'll start organizing the glider school.

"Go straight to the personnel department at the factory. I've already arranged everything. Once you get things settled there, go see the aeroclub commissar. I understand there's a training group there for cadets who have already mastered piloting skills.

"By the way, how many brothers do you have?" the Secretary added suddenly.

"Five."

"Well, you are rich in brothers. I have none. If they ask you to write a resume, don't waste too much paper on brothers. Got it?"

"Thank you for your advice!"

"Show them your documents at the aeroclub and insist on being enrolled in the training group. If you have any problems, don't hesitate to come and see me."

"Thank you!" I murmured, sniffling. I tore out like a bullet to the flax factory, feeling joyful and lucky to have encountered such kind people.

The factory accepted me as a bookkeeper that day and installed me in the workers' dormitory that evening. I enrolled in the aeroclub training group, and soon I was flying again.

16
Kokkinaki

How overjoyed I was to be once again hurrying to the aeroclub after work, where each day a waiting truck carried us to the aerodrome, far outside the city.

Late that autumn we passed the state theory and practical flight tests, but our group was then immediately disbanded, awaiting special orders.

I had lost all hope of re-enrolling in the military flight school. Besides me, five other women trained in our detachment, all native to Smolensk. I was a stranger there, the last in line, I reasoned dismally, and in despair I nearly gave up on the aeroclub altogether. I began studying for the entrance examinations to an aviation institute. If I couldn't continue training, I figured, at least I could be involved with aviation.

My brother Vasily had once urged me to study at an institute. I had written to him but received no reply. Where was he now? Somewhere far away, probably in the North, serving his time, denied the right to answer my letter. Six months ago I had bid farewell to him and to Moscow, the Metrostroy, the aeroclub, my comrades, and Viktor…

Mama wrote to tell me that a friend had helped her compose a petition to our countryman, Chairman Mikhail Ivanovich Kalinin. She waited and waited for an answer, then decided to go to Moscow herself. So Vasily's wife Katya and her son Yuri escorted Mama to see the All-Union Elder. After waiting in a long line, they were ushered in to see, to their disappointment, not the bearded Kalinin, but a minor assistant, who said simply, "Mikhail Ivanovich isn't considering such applications."

I continued working at the flax factory, studied with the glider cadets twice a week, and took preparatory courses to enroll in the institute.

On one of my evenings off, I sat down in a café and ordered a scoop of ice cream. "Yegorova!" someone yelled from behind me.

I turned toward the voice and saw the aeroclub commissar. He introduced his wife and daughter to me and invited me to join them. "Why haven't I seen you at the aeroclub much lately?" he asked.

I shared my doubts with him. "That's silly," he said. "Just yesterday we decided after a long debate to assign you the single female spot at the Kherson[1] Flight School.

"Me?"

---

[1] A port city in southern Ukraine on the Dnieper River near its mouth at the Black Sea.

"Yes, you, Kokkinaki!"[2] he said, turning to his wife. "You see, all the students call her 'Kokkinaki,' and so do I." Everyone laughed.

"You can call me that whenever you wish," I said. "I like it."

"You need to come to the aeroclub tomorrow to collect your orders and your dismissal from the factory, then get yourself to Kherson right away," he said. "Prepare yourself: you'll have to take entrance exams on academic subjects. The competition will be fierce."

Graduates of aeroclubs from all over the country converged on Kherson—from Moscow and Leningrad, Arkhangelsk and Baku, Komsomolsk-on-Amur and Minsk, Tashkent and Dushanbe. The navigation department accepted females, but the instructor-pilot section took only males.

Again, I passed through the admissions gauntlet: medical board, entrance exams, and credentials committee. Fortunately, the math exams were given by an old pedagogical professor who couldn't hear very well. We prompted each other, and everyone did quite well on the math section. But our ranks were thinning.

Following the kind Secretary's advice, I did not mention my oldest brother. When the school posted the lists of those accepted, I found my name: "Anna Yegorova—navigation school."

I felt none of the delirious joy I'd experienced in Ulyanovsk, but I ran to the post office all the same to send Mama a telegram. I hoped the news would give her happiness.

Now that I'm a mother, I know how she must have felt when she received my telegram. When my son told me he hoped to enroll in military flight school, I did everything I could to dissuade him. He seemed to agree at first, but then, two weeks later, he came to see me.

"Mama!" he said. "You gave me my love of flying, like milk from your breast. Since I was a baby, I have listened to stories about airplanes. I know how hard it was for you to become a pilot, but you did it, all by yourself. You've got to let me go, Mama. Please…"

And so I relented. But I secretly hoped he wouldn't be admitted. Then I got his telegram: "Admitted. Happy! Kiss you, Pyotr,"

But was I happy? Common sense aside, my maternal instinct wanted him to live and work nearby, closer to the nest, so I could watch over him and offer him a shoulder in hard times.

How must my mother have felt so many years ago when she received my telegram from Kherson? This is what she wrote back:

Hello, my dear!
I got your telegram. I am so happy for you. But I would be even happier if you didn't set your sights on the sky. Aren't there any good professions on the ground? Your friend Nastya Raskazova graduated from veterinary

[2] Brothers V. K. and K. K. Kokkinaki were famous Soviet test pilots and aviation record-breakers. (A. Yegorova's note)

school and now lives at home, cares for livestock on the collective farm, and doesn't worry her mother. But you, all my children, are so restless. You're always craving something more.

There's no news from Vasyenka. How my heart aches for him, Daughter! Is he still alive? I remember visiting him in Moscow. He was already some kind of director and a deputy or something-or-other. He wrapped his leather jacket around my shoulders and led me to the theater by the hand. There were mirrors all around, and I thought we were surrounded by people who looked like us! I wonder if you can intercede for him.

As for you: work hard, study. What else is there to do now that you've lost your heart to aviation? It comes so easily to you. If my children are happy, I am happy. When you're in trouble, I grieve, because I am your mother.

I have eight of you children, and I worry about each one. My fledglings have all flown from the nest! Even my youngest Kostya has gone off to the army. I charged him to serve loyally and faithfully. But when the train disappeared around the bend, I collapsed, unconscious, on the platform. I don't know what came over me...

Oh, Mama! How could I explain to you what flying meant to me? It was my life, my song, my love! Anyone who falls in love with the sky and finds his wings will never betray that love and will be true to it until the end of his days. And if it happens someday that he cannot fly, then he will still fly in his dreams.

The war with Finland[3] drastically curtailed our coursework. We hastily completed our studies and final exams. The school tailor couldn't finish our dress parade uniforms in time, so we graduated in our shabby old cadets' blouses and skirts.

---

[3] Known as the "Winter War" or the "Soviet-Finnish War." In autumn of 1939, the Soviet Union (after signing the non-aggression pact with Hitler which permitted the Soviets to "set right" certain frontiers) began negotiations with Finland, seeking a naval base at the port of Hangö and a strip of territory between the Gulf of Finland and Lake Ladoga, just northwest of Leningrad (to buffer the city's defenses), in exchange for a portion of Karelia further to the north. On November 30, the USSR attacked following an alleged border incident and began preparing a pro-Soviet "People's Government of Finland" which waited in the wings. Although Soviet troops vastly outnumbered the Finns, the Red Army (reeling from Stalin's devastating purge of the military) conducted the war incompetently and fared poorly against well-equipped Finnish troops and fortifications, suffering much heavier losses than their opponents. Still, the Soviets' greater numbers eventually overwhelmed the Finnish Army, and in March 1940, the Finns signed a peace treaty. Finland ceded the entire Karelian isthmus, the Hangö base, and some territories north of Lake Ladoga. But the cost to the Red Army—in casualties (an estimated 126,800 troops) and the army's reputation—was disastrous and led to a much-needed reorganization of the Soviet military.

17
Daughter, You'll Fall

I was sent to the town of Kalinin[1] to become the aeroclub's navigator. When I arrived, I discovered that the aeroclub already had a navigator but badly needed a flight instructor. I jumped at the chance—I had long been yearning to fly. I passed the flight check and began training cadets.

I was in charge of twelve restless young men of widely varying temperaments and backgrounds. But their love of aviation bound them together. They could hardly wait to get through their ground training and into the sky. I understood them well.

Commander of the flight unit, Senior Lieutenant Pyotr Chernigovets, often attended the lessons. A former fighter pilot in the Red Army, he was a born pilot with an excellent grasp of physics and math. He could explain complex aerodynamics formulas with ease. He respected the cadets, and they loved him for it. He helped me train my first fledgling students.

One day, a veteran instructor named Gavrilov crashed during a training flight. The impact threw his student from the cabin. The cadet immediately jumped up and dashed off wildly. The doctors examined him and exempted him from flying for five days, but on the sixth day he died.

All flights were cancelled. The cadets were despondent. Lieutenant Chernigovets called the unit together to discuss the incident.

"An airplane, as you know, is always an airplane" he began, "no matter how slow and docile it may be. You must call it 'Sir,' and give it the utmost respect, attention, and seriousness. Those who ignore these rules will be punished! Here we have an experienced instructor who placed too much faith in his student and who apparently ignored the rules of aerodynamics or simply didn't know them well. Here we see the result. In the final turn, as we all saw, the aircraft nosed up, lost speed, and fell into a spin. It didn't have enough altitude to recover from the spin and therefore crashed.

"The aviation profession," he continued, "may seem romantic. But it's dangerous, too. Still, we can't lose heart. We must get back to business."

He started describing various flight attitudes and drawing them right there in the sand of the airfield, all the while quizzing the cadets. The ice began to break.

---

[1] Now the city of Tver (called Kalinin from 1931 to 1990), located about 104 miles (167 km) northwest of Moscow.

For a flight instructor, sending a student on his first solo flight is at least as terrifying as his own first solo was. I remember the first student I sent out on his own, a cadet named Chernov. The unit commander had "okayed" him, but I wasn't so sure. I asked the squadron commander to fly with him first. They flew a circle flight, then landed. "Why are you wasting aircraft resources?" he shouted. "Let him go!"

In agitation, I fiddled with the white signal flag, just like the one Miroyevsky had once held for us. All eyes fell upon the student sitting in the cabin, his face fixed in a mask of total concentration, awaiting my order. I raised the white flag and abruptly whipped it in the direction of the runway.

Chernov taxied the airplane to the launch position. I wanted to shout some additional instructions after him, but the plane was already rocketing down the runway and tearing itself from the earth.

My eyes didn't leave that airplane for a second as I walked to the landing "T" to meet my charge.

Then came Cadet Sedov. I had no end of trouble with him. Skills that were easy for Chernov, Sedov mastered ever so slowly. Slowly, but surely, I later discovered. Only after I soloed all twelve of my cadets did I realize that Sedov had less flight time than anyone. I was so busy holding Chernov up as an example, at the same time sending Sedov back to the books for more ground training, that I didn't notice Chernov was simply burning more aviation fuel. In the end, Sedov became the surest and most graceful flyer of all my students.

When the State Commission turned up for a surprise flight check, I wasn't worried about my cadets. Only one of them received a "four"[2] in aerobatics flying, and the rest got an "outstanding."

On Aviation Day, the aerodrome held an air show. Spectators looked on from a roped-off area as the pilots demonstrated formation flight and glider soaring and performed aerobatics in the UT-2 trainer.

Finally, the announcer called my name. I took off, flew my aerobatics program, and was just taxiing back when someone told me, "Your mother is here."

Apparently, she'd read about the air show in the regional newspaper, taken a train to Kalinin, and shot straight to the aerodrome from the station. Packing a basket of goodies with her, she settled into the grass at the edge of the aerodrome and craned her neck to see just what all this nonsense was that went on in the sky. She sat quietly until she heard my name called.

When she saw the airplane making its wild rolls, loops, and spins, she ran toward the runway, screaming, "Daughter, you'll fall out!" She stood miserably in the middle of the aerodrome, spreading her lacy holiday apron wide to catch me if I fell.

---

[2] In the Russian grading system, ranging from 1 to 5, a 4 is considered good, and a 5, outstanding.

The patrol brought Mama to the staff headquarters. When the superintendent found out why she was so upset, he offered her a plane ride, but she would have no part of it.

After we instructors graduated our cadets, we were rewarded with a boat trip to Moscow to visit the Agricultural Exposition.[3] We floated along the Mother Volga, admiring the loveliness of her banks.

After we toured VSKhV, I went to see my brother's family on the Arbat. Katya worked at a knitting factory. Yurka was in school. We talked for hours. Vasya had somehow found an "opportunity" to send a message home. He wrote that he had been transported along the Yenisey[4] with a bargeful of common criminals. The "bandits" took every opportunity to ridicule, humiliate, and brutalize the political prisoners, even taking their clothes and food away from them. The guards saw nothing, or else pretended to see nothing.

The exiles disembarked at Igarka, where they were forced to march through the tundra on foot. More than half of them sickened and died along the way.

Moscow's second metro line was now running, and I stopped by to see my old "Dynamo" station. I admired the beautiful onyx-faced pillars, the benches in between with bas-relief images of athletes above. But I didn't feel compelled to stroke the cold stone there. This wasn't my beloved "Red Gates," whose marble I had polished with my own hands. And now, Metrostroy workers were busy carving out new underground palaces on the Kurskaya-Izmailovskaya line.

Nearly all of my comrades from the Metrostroy aeroclub had finished their flight training and now served in the Air Force. My "fiancé" Viktor Kutov had become a fighter pilot in an air regiment along the western border. He sent me verses in the mail and begged me to write him back, but I, as usual, never had time. When he graduated, he came to visit me at Kherson, hoping to take me away with him. But I wouldn't listen.

"I'll come to you when I finish school," I told Viktor.

"No you won't! I know you too well. I'll have to marry you by force!" he said.

"Go ahead and try!" I retorted angrily, and he left.

I walked back to the school miserably, weeping bitterly. If only I had known it was the last time I would ever see him.

After five days in Moscow, we returned to Kalinin and constant work, with no days off. All that pre-war winter we trained special recruitments of pilots right out of college or excused from their jobs. By spring most of them

---

[3] Originally established in 1939 as "VSKhV," or the "All-Union Agricultural Exposition," this exhibition later became known as "VDNKh," or the "Exhibition of Economic Achievements."

[4] One of the longest rivers in Asia, the Yenisey flows for more than 2,500 miles (4023 km) south to north through central Siberia.

had graduated, and we'd recommended them to intensive flight training programs.

Day after day we helped young men earn their wings, until...

18
Girls, It's War!

The June night seemed in no hurry to arrive, though the hour was quite late. My flights had dragged on far into the evening, and tired though I was, I couldn't go home yet. I still had to debrief my cadets and finish their logbook entries. I had scarcely sat down at my desk, when my friend Mashenka popped her head in the door.

"Don't stay too long, Anyuta! We're off to the forest early in the morning," she said and flitted away.

That's right, today's Saturday, I thought. After so many weeks with no weekends and no days off, we were due for a break. How wonderful that the girls had the idea for a picnic in the woods! The weather was absolutely made to order, and there was no shortage of enticing spots near Kalinin. We had only to board a tram, which would take us straight to a pine forest behind the "Proletarka" stop.

We took the first morning tram and filled it with laughter, jokes, and songs. We so seldom had the chance to get together and enjoy ourselves like regular young people.

"People in your position should be more serious," joked the tram driver. "You look down on the world from a great height."

Not today, we didn't. The minute we reached the forest, we ran whooping and screaming like wild beasts among the towering pines. We were starved for a bit of fresh air.

Nothing can compare to the marvelous Russian countryside. I wish you could see it for yourself, especially in the morning, when the curtain of mist lifts to present the day's opening act. You can't look upon it without marveling at the spectacle.

Our inseparable flock of four girls—Tamara Konstantinova, Katya Piskareva, Masha, and I—roosted on a blanket spread across the thick, sweet-smelling grass. What a delight it was to lie still, chattering about whatever popped into our minds and breathing in the pine-scented air. For the moment, peace prevailed. The virgin forest uttered not a sound, sunlight filtered through the branches, and dew sparkled on the grass like diamonds.

And then, suddenly, voices—unnaturally loud men's voices, arguing. I turned my head toward where our male comrades had been sitting. A man who hadn't come with us on the tram approached, his face darkened with alarm. His voice trembled as he said, "Girls, it's war! I just heard it on the radio in the village."

War. What a hateful, terrible word. It's like a sword, slashing the world into pieces. Joy and light flee into the past, and the future promises only suffering and despair. Seconds after the pilot uttered those thunderous words, the scene before us transformed. The colors of the forest morning faded, and the once tranquil silence twisted into something ominous.

In that quiet moment, each of us heard the inner voice of his conscience. Just yesterday, our lives were simple and ordinary. All that the world demanded of us was to fulfill our official duties conscientiously and attend to our personal lives. But today and onward demanded the greatest possible spiritual maturity. In that moment, we knew our characters would be tested to the utmost and revealed for whatever they truly were. Our value as human beings would be tried, as would our courage and our loyalty to the motherland.

It was instantly clear to us, standing there in the pine grove that Sunday morning, that our country must rise to mortal combat, and that we were blessed with a valuable and scarce gift that would soon be sorely needed. We knew in that moment that we would not stand aside when the time came. "It's time to go home," someone said.

Less than an hour later, we all ran into each other at the town military commissariat. "Attend to your own work, girls," the military commissar urged us when we asked to be sent to the front. "There'll be plenty of work to do in the rear."

After a month and a half of twiddling my thumbs at the aerodrome, far from the action, my patience ran out. Troubling reports from the initial days of the war spurred us to action, especially when we learned that the aeroclub would soon be evacuated far to the rear. So I bought a train ticket to Moscow. An aircraft technician named Musya saw me off at the station.

Her husband, a tankist, had been grievously wounded. He was slowly dying in one of the town's hospitals. Musya didn't cry, but her beautiful face looked drawn, and her dark brown, almond-shaped eyes had gone dull and expressionless beneath her long eyelashes. Another tankist, the husband of my Metrostroy aeroclub friend Tatiana Nikulina, lay missing an arm in a nearby ward. She left her little daughter with a neighbor in Moscow and came to see him. She sat with her broken husband day and night, nursing him and consoling him as well as she could.

"Be patient, dear Alyoshenka. It'll be all right!" Tatiana whispered, stroking his remaining hand. He lay silently, frowning, while she showered him with tender, hopeful words. "What am I going to do, Tanya?" Alexey said finally. "I want to teach these Fascist rats a lesson, but what can I do with one left hand?"

"You silly, ridiculous man. My uncle lost his leg in the civil war. He got a prosthetic leg and lived to fight another day! Tukhachevsky[1] himself awarded him a medal. Now he's the leading engineer at the plant, as you well know. And you with your 'What am I to do?'" she said, imitating him affectionately.

The war was already teaching its bitter, irrevocable lessons.

At the railway station, Musya kissed me and, placing a silver one-ruble coin in the breast pocket of my soldier's blouse, said softly, "It's a talisman. You'll return it to me once we rout the Fascists."

By some miracle, I managed to hold on to Musya's talisman throughout the war. But many years passed before I was able to return it to her. For years, she assumed I was dead until she saw my picture in the paper one day and called me. I remember standing at the gate, watching a familiar face approach from the bus station. At first, she asked if I knew an Anna Alexandrovna, and then, suddenly, the tears streamed down her face…

I waved goodbye to Musya and boarded the train. After I arrived at Leningrad Station in Moscow, I steered toward the Moscow Central Osoaviakhim Soviet. Camouflage shrouded the buildings on Three Station Square like a theatrical set. I was astonished to see white paper crosses[2] adorning the terminal windows and the oppressive absence of the normal bustle of travelers. People in soldier's blouses stepped briskly through the great station halls, and the booming sound of barked orders ricocheted off the stone walls. Hurrying across the square, I nearly smashed into some soldiers and the silver barrage balloon they were carrying. Massive anti-aircraft guns stood like long-legged storks on the roofs of multi-storied apartment buildings.

The scene was the same on the way to Tushino.[3] Anti-aircraft guns kept watch in parks, troops marched in columns, posters on the walls exhorted men to battle, and a pall of stern reserve blanketed the streets. Not only in the outskirts—the capital's central thoroughfares also bristled with anti-tank hedgehogs and growing chains of barricades.

Moscow was beginning to look like a front city. With each passing day, the city grew gloomier and grimmer. Levitan's[4] daily broadcasts delivered

---

[1] Mikhail Nikolayevich Tukhachevsky (1893–1937). After serving in World War I, Tukhachevsky gained renown as a Red Army officer during the Civil War, defeating Alexander Kolchak's White Army in Siberia and suppressing the Kronshtadt rebellion. As Deputy Commissar for Defense and later Marshal of the Soviet Union, Tukhachevsky advocated modernizing the Red Army into a tank-based force. In 1937, he was arrested and executed for allegedly conspiring with Germany but was rehabilitated in 1988.

[2] To contain glass shards in the event of a bomb blast.

[3] In that era, the site of an Osoaviakhim flight school, airfield, and aircraft factories, in the north of Moscow.

[4] Yuri Borisovich Levitan (1914–83). A radio announcer with possibly the most famous voice in the Soviet Union during the war years. He read Stalin's speeches and

increasingly alarming reports: "After stubborn and fierce battle, during the course of which…" The Sovinformbureau reports followed us everywhere: home, at work, in the street. We could scarcely believe them.

I remember sitting on the bus, my face pressed against the window, wondering why we were moving so slowly. I noticed with surprise a girl in a military uniform energetically waving a small red flag to clear the way for a huge column of Red Army soldiers. Such things would soon seem terribly ordinary.

When I presented myself to the colonel at Osoaviakhim, he quickly scanned my papers and pronounced, in a tired and hoarse voice, "Yegorova, what the devil do you want from me? What's happened in Kalinin? Are they out of fuel? Not enough planes? Please, get to the point quickly. Can't you see how many people are waiting?"

Indeed, the smoky room teemed with pilots of all ages. Some wore civilian clothing, others field uniforms as they chatted, discussed the latest news from the front, and waited for the Central Aeroclub powers-that-be to decide their fates.

I have only one personal question," I shouted over the din.

"Do you really think now is the time for personal questions?" he said.

"Forgive me, I didn't mean 'personal,'" I blushed. "I only wanted to ask that you send me to the front."

"Oh, 'only' that?" he shot back, unbuttoning his uniform collar. "Everybody's asking me the same thing over and over: 'to the front, to the front!'"

"And who, I ask you," his voice rose in frustration, and he looked around angrily, addressing not just me, but the whole waiting room. "Who, I ask you, is going to *train* the pilots for the front?" he shouted, then turned to me. "No, dear. Go back to Kalinin and do your job. Who's next?"

Instead of retreating, I moved closer to the colonel's desk. "My areoclub is evacuating to the rear," I said firmly. "I'm not going to the rear. I am asking you to send me to the front. I am a highly experienced pilot, and right now I'm more needed at the battlefield!"

"Look, Yegorova, he grumbled. "Let us decide where you are more needed." But he could tell I was immovable. He thought a minute, then tossed a paper in my direction, looked at me askance, and said, "OK, fine. Go ahead. We'll send you closer to the fire, to the aeroclub at Stalino, in the Donbass.[5] That's—"

---

chronicled the advances and retreats of the German army for millions of Soviet citizens during WWII.

[5] An industrial city in eastern Ukraine, Donetsk was called Stalino from 1924–61. "Donbass" is an abbreviation for **Donetsky Bassein,** or "Donets Basin," a coal-producing area of eastern Ukraine and southwestern Russia north of the Sea of Azov and west of the Donets River.

"Stalino!" I gasped. "But my brother... that's where he was arres—" I stuttered. After a moment I regained my composure and said firmly, "Of course. Write out the orders."

On the way to the railway station, I stopped by to see Vasya's family on the Arbat. Katya was out somewhere digging trenches. Yurka, just home from school, was ecstatic to see me. He bustled about looking for something to give me to eat, but the only food in the house was a bit of bread and a cube of sugar. He told me all about how his geography teacher in the sixth grade had volunteered for the front and how the school principal tried to do the same but hadn't been allowed to go.

"If I were him, I'd have run away to fight the Fascists a long time ago, but he's still waiting to get his papers, the idiot," said Yuri.

"Have you heard anything from your father?" I asked my nephew.

The boy immediately drooped his head, then rose silently, took a stack of papers from the writing table, and handed them to me.

"Here. Read it," the words tumbled out with scarcely a breath in between. "Yesterday a colonel stopped by. He said he and Papa had been together not too long ago, somewhere far away in the North. He said the night never ends there in winter, and in the summer, the sun doesn't set. Papa's building a beautiful city there, a city like Leningrad, and a big metallurgical plant. The colonel and many other former officers were sent to the front. He even managed to pay a visit to his family and to come see us. But he was very upset that Mama wasn't here when he stopped by our house."

I read the papers Yuri had given me. One was a letter from Vasya to his wife and son, and the other, an application to be sent to the front to defend the motherland from Fascist invaders.

"When Papa goes to the front," Yura confided, "I'm going to ask him to take me, too. If he won't, I'll go without him. Vitka Timokhin and I decided long ago to go to the front, except that Vitka's too short. I'm taller than anyone in my class, so they'll most likely let me in. It's too bad you're not going to the front, Auntie Anya, because I would love to go with you. I can always go back to school once we crush the Fascists!"

The air-raid siren blared late that night, but we decided not to go to the shelter. We stayed up all night talking. In the morning, I walked Yuri to school on my way to the station. I made him give me his word that he would not take a single step toward the front without talking to me first. He agreed, but only if I would promise to send for him at the front, if I managed to get there. Meanwhile, he would study hard at school and learn to use a rifle and machine gun. With that, we parted.

As for for the front, Yurka didn't keep his promise.

19
Closer to the Front

It was impossible to breathe in the packed train carriage. With no possibility of any solitude whatsoever, I made conversation with my neighbor, an elderly officer. We talked about recent events at the front. Was there any other topic in those days? I mostly did the asking, and he the answering, knowing far more than I about the situation. The only question he asked me was why I, a girl, was headed toward the front lines. I showed him my orders.

"Idiots," the officer gasped in surprise. "There is no Stalino aeroclub anymore. They're evacuating the entire city."

"That can't be!" I exclaimed.

My traveling companion sighed deeply. "Oh, but it can, my dear girl."

Indeed, I found not a soul at the aeroclub. Everyone had evacuated. A fierce wind from the steppe roared through the deserted buildings, banging doors open and shut and shattering windows like a mischievous ghost. I felt utterly lost. I had no idea what to do or to whom to turn.

I left the aeroclub and started to get my bearings back as I hurried toward the city center. I wanted to find some kind of functioning office or agency, or at least people, hopefully someone who could give me useful advice.

I had hardly walked a block before someone grabbed the sleeve of my uniform from behind me. "You're quite fast!" said a lively, youthful voice. "I could hardly catch you!"

"Was it worth the effort?" I shot back rudely and turned abruptly to face the stranger. I couldn't stand these street beggars pestering me. They seemed especially out of place in this nearly deserted city, so near the front.

"I mean you no harm," he said, in his young, soothing voice. "I saw you leave the aeroclub. I thought you must have some business there. By the way, I'm Pyotr Nechiporenko, a cadet at the flight school."

I took his hand guardedly. My suspicion didn't go unnoticed. "You don't believe me, do you? Look, here are my papers. I'm on my way to the military commissariat to be assigned to the front."

"To the front?" I echoed with newfound respect.

"That's right. But that's none of your business. Fighting is a man's job. I only chased you down because I spotted your pilot's blouse, and I wanted to tell you that a big-shot official is coming to the aeroclub tomorrow. Don't miss your chance."

"Tomorrow?… And what am I supposed to do all day today?"

"Go to the opera," the cadet said, smiling. "They're playing their farewell performance before everyone evacuates. *Carmen*. The theater is nearby in the city center. Do you want to walk together?"

I accompanied Pyotr as far as the military commissariat and wished him a safe and victorious return home. I envied him a little. He was on his way to war, to defend our motherland, while I was merely going to the opera.

At the theater, I watched the stage as if through a frosted glass pane. From the fifth row of the half-empty hall, the performance seemed foggy and indistinct. My thoughts hovered far away. Spain, toreadors, passion, love—none of it touched me. I barely registered the beautiful Carmen's famous aria, the "Habañera," when the orchestra suddenly broke off on a soaring high note. The singer froze, her mouth open in bewilderment. Silence descended on the hall.

A small, scrawny man picked his way across the stage and stopped at the edge of the orchestra pit. His voice crashed through the silence:

"Comrades! There's an air raid! Please, everyone, proceed down into the bomb shelter in an orderly fashion." This act wasn't in the program.

After I left the air-raid shelter, I walked back to the aeroclub and established myself for the night on one of the office's cold plastic couches. In the morning, I heard a knock at the door, and a broad-shouldered, well-built man in a pilot's uniform appeared at the door. From his stripes I saw that he was a senior lieutenant. It took him a moment to notice me on the couch, barricaded as I was behind the office desks.

"What are you doing here?" he demanded sternly.

"I'm from Moscow. I was assigned to the aeroclub, and I'm waiting here for the personnel chief."

The officer's face brightened. "We're on the same mission. I'm waiting for the chief, too. I need pilots," he sighed, gesturing sadly toward this former palace of aviation, now utterly forsaken, probably for a long time to come.

"What should we do?" I asked him anxiously. And then an idea flashed into my head. "You say you've come looking for pilots," I said. "Take me. Here are my papers. They're in good order."

The senior lieutenant scrutinized my documents from the Central Aeroclub. "You're highly qualified," he said. "I'll take you, Yegorova. We just have to make sure everything is legal. Let's check with the military commissariat."

In a beat-up pickup truck, we threaded our way through a dense pack of mobilized soldiers and presented ourselves before the commissar. As soon as he learned why we had come, he shook his head. "What's she got to do with us?" he roared. "She came from Moscow. Let her go back there!"

"Let's not waste time, Major," the lieutenant challenged. "We desperately need pilots."

"I can't do it. I have no right to bypass the law. We can't have anarchy here!" the commissar persisted.

Arguing did us no good. We had no choice but to retreat. The lieutenant, who introduced himself as Listarevich, did his best to calm me. "To hell with those bureaucrats!" he said. "Let's go to my unit. We'll figure this out for ourselves."

On the way, we stopped in at a hospital to pick up two wounded pilots, a mechanic, and an Osoaviakhim cadet. Listarevich looked happier. He wasn't going back to the unit empty-handed.

We hurried in our mangled pickup to the 130th Air Liaison Squadron for the Southern Front.[1] The lieutenant was a former pilot and was demonstrating his flying skills, driving the pickup like a madman. The truck catapulted alarmingly along the deeply rutted country road at a hundred kilometers per hour. We ricocheted off the sides of the cab and occasionally took flight, slamming back down on the narrow seat after a nauseating moment of weightlessness.

Finally, we reached the aerodrome, or more accurately, a clearing in the tiny settlement of Tikhy near the Chaplino railway station. Dusty and dog-tired from the bumpy ride, we new recruits appeared before the unit chiefs.

"This is it?" said the major, looking us over.

"They evacuated the aeroclub, Comrade Major," explained the senior lieutenant. "But I managed to find a few 'eagles.'"

"'Eagles'?" the major repeated skeptically, and looked askance at me. I noticed an Order of the Red Banner pinned to the officer's chest. *A real soldier,* I thought. *A combat veteran.* I couldn't miss this chance.

"I'm Anna Yegorova, a former flight instructor at the Kalinin aeroclub, at your command," I reported with gusto.

"But we don't draft females for front-line combat."

"Do you really need to be drafted to fight for your country?" I asked.

"That's true," the major acknowledged, looking intently at me. "Do you have your papers with you, Yegorova?"

I felt a glimmer of hope. "Yes, sir!" I quickly spread my logbook, passport, Komsomol card, and orders to the Stalino aeroclub on the table. After studying my documents, the major turned to a captain who had just walked in.

"Grishenko!" he ordered. "Check out Yegorova's flying skills tomorrow."

I caught Lieutenant Listarevich's eye. He winked at me with satisfaction, as if to say, "Everything is OK. Welcome to the 130th."

---

[1] "Front" in this context (and when capitalized) is analogous to the military formation usually called "Army Group" by the German military, and should not be confused with the term "front" as a geographical area during wartime.

20
An Internal Compass

The next day, Captain Grishenko, deputy commander of the squadron, drew up the route for my flight check: from Tikhy to Simferopol.[1] The flight went well, and I was accepted into the unit.

I received my aircraft, the U-2, on my third day at the front. It was certainly no speedy fighter and no dive bomber, just a simple little wood-and-fabric airplane that gave me years of devoted service. It won our front-line troops' admiration and our enemies' hatred. Near the end of the war, it was reborn as the Po-2 or Polikarpov-2, named for its designer.

Old *frontoviki*[2] remember the many nicknames we gave the unpretentious biplane—some ironic, some downright odd, all of them affectionate. The infantry called it "master sergeant of the front." The partisans named it "truck farmer" or *kukuruznik*[3] for its uncanny ability to land in tiny fields or, as they put it, "on a pig's snout." Experienced pilots referred to the nimble plane as "little duck."

Nicknames aside, the hardy little craft was a tireless workhorse: it ferried wounded soldiers, delivered mail, mapped routes, flew reconnaissance missions behind enemy lines, searched for remote units, and even won fame as a night bomber.[4] It carried top-secret orders to army staff officers and transported generals and marshals, war correspondents, and doctors to and from the front. Exceptionally maneuverable, docile, and easy to fly, the U-2 went places that faster and heavier planes couldn't go.

---

[1] The capital of Crimea, a republic in southern Ukraine consisting of a peninsula bounded on the south and west by the Black Sea.

[2] A Russian term for soldiers who served at the front.

[3] Derived from the Russian word *kukuruza*, meaning "corn."

[4] The 588th Night Bomber Regiment (later designated the 46th Guards Night Bomber Regiment) was composed of all-women pilots and crew and served from 1942–45 at Stalingrad, Novorossisk, Kerch, Warsaw, and Berlin (among other battles). The regiment made the U-2 (later called the Po-2) famous with their many surprise night raids on German rear positions—at extremely low altitude and with the engine cut for the bombing run. The Germans nicknamed the 588th pilots *Nachthexen*, or "Night Witches."

It might sound like routine work, but what unexpected dangers it held for us at every turn! In truth, those missions were combat flights, and hardly routine. Our squadron twice received the "Guards"[5] title.

But back to 1941. The front was retreating eastward. With every battle, our troops mounted fiercer resistance, but still they abandoned their positions and fell back. Retreating divisions often lost communication with each other amid the chaos and had no way of receiving their orders. To restore order and command in the field, we took to the air in our U-2s in rain, fog, and snow, to deliver vital information and communicate orders.

On August 21, I was ordered to fly to the headquarters of the 18th Army. I only had a general idea of where the staff was supposed to be quartered, and my mission was to find and map their precise location. All along the route, Hitlerite fighters combed the skies, just as my commander had warned. If you took the time to gawk at them, they would surely cut you down.

It was a gorgeous late summer day. Ordinarily this would have delighted me, but on that day, I was less than pleased. In a crisp, clear sky, the *kukuruznik* would be defenseless against the Fascist hawks. We certainly couldn't outrun them, and plywood "armor" doesn't stop bullets. Our only defense was to dive down toward the ground and spread our wings low over the withered fields, flying so close to the earth you could hear the landing gear cutting the feather grass of the steppe.

At "tree-shaving" altitude, I constantly scanned my compass, clock, and map, all the while monitoring the ground. The earth scrolled by, dangerously close, mere feet below my wings. The first settlement passed below me at exactly the time I'd calculated. The compass was a miraculous instrument, to be sure, but I wasn't on friendly terms with it. I preferred to cross-check my map with checkpoints on the ground. As a flight instructor, I'd seldom had the opportunity to fly long distances or to make "blind" flights in clouds or at night, relying completely on the instruments.

When towns stopped flashing by under the wings and only the bare steppe stretched out before me, I started to worry: was the compass lying to me? Maybe the magnetic deviation wasn't right. I seemed to be flying right of course—or was it left? "Trust the compass," I told myself. "It won't fail you."

Just then, I saw two distant points in the sky, rapidly approaching. Messerschmitts,[6] I guessed. Suddenly, they were upon me, roaring over my head,

---

[5] After 1941, Soviet military formations that distinguished themselves in battle were awarded the honorific title "Guards."

[6] The Messerschmitt Bf 109 was the Luftwaffe's most important fighter after 1935 and saw action in the Spanish Civil War. Small, fast, and maneuverable, the Bf 109 was cheap to produce and was built in great numbers, even during the war years, when the supremely versatile Focke-Wulf Fw 190 fighter bomber came along. Despite the Fw 190's purported superiority, however, it never quite managed to supplant the ubiquitous Bf 109.

brazenly flaunting their spidery swastikas. Machine-gun fire spat at me from above. The "Messers" quickly evaporated, then returned, hating to miss such easy prey. They covered me with their black shadows, but with all their speed, they couldn't manage to shoot down the docile little U-2. They flew off, and I released my breath with relief. Now I could return my attention to the land blinking by beneath me and hopefully get my bearings.

I climbed to around a hundred meters and immediately knew where I was. There in front of me was the headquarters of the 18th Army. I landed on a small field that had three U-2s parked on it. My passenger, a captain of the Dnieper River Fleet, told me to wait and went inside. Pilots from the unit re-fueled my tanks, offered me a slice of watermelon, and filled me in about events at that part of the front.

On the return trip, I let my mind wander a bit, and I was immediately punished for it. I became confused and disoriented. I flew aimlessly this way and that, searching desperately for any recognizable checkpoints. But all I could see was the desolate steppe, soundlessly unfolding below me.

I pulled myself together and turned east, flying exclusively by compass for a while until I saw a railway station. Dipping down as low as I could, I didn't quite manage to read the station name, so I landed to ask someone what station it was. (We often did this.) Pokrovka, they said. What a relief— all along I'd been lost not too far from my base at Tikhy.

When I got back to the aerodrome, Major Bulkin, commander of the squadron, frowned at me. "What took you so long, Yegorova?"

"I was delayed at the 18th Army Headquarters," I fibbed.

It was the liaison officer at the 18th who revealed the truth—about the Messerschmitt encounter and the evasive maneuvers that saved me.

"Take a rest!" said Bulkin. "Tomorrow you're flying there again."

21
Abandoned

The next day, I flew to a different place instead—to Kalarovka, near Melito-pol. I was to deliver a liaison officer carrying operations orders to the staff headquarters of the 9th Army. It was a gorgeous day with unlimited visi-bility. Hoping to avoid running into any more Fascist "hawks," I flew low enough to shave leaves from the treetops. Ahead I could see a small village drowning in a sea of lush green. Climbing slightly to avoid hitting the trees and chimneys, I spotted a sprinkling of white village huts surrounding a broad valley. I turned toward my passenger, a lieutenant colonel, and made a gesture, as if to say, "Here we are, Comrade!"

On my landing approach, a strange movement on the ground caught my eye. Along the road out of Kalarovka, a frantic mass streamed from the vil-lage. A roiling chaos of people and soldiers mingled with cattle, carts laden with household items, and military vehicles. Half-ton trucks sped along the side, and infantry men hurried along in small clusters instead of the usual orderly marching columns.

I landed the airplane on a hill near a windmill, taxied up very close to it, and shut the engine down. "Something is wrong. Stay here until I get back," muttered my passenger. The liaison officer ran down the path to the village.

While I waited, I searched for something to camouflage the plane. Find-ing nothing, I sat down under the wing to wait. An hour passed, then twenty more minutes, then thirty—and still no lieutenant colonel. The crackle of gun-fire rose from the valley, along with the terrified lowing of cattle and the roar of vehicles and fleeing people. Panic seized me. There could be no doubt now. The battle was coming our way. I crawled out from underneath the wing and hurried toward the village to get a better look.

From the hillside, I could see the entire village as if it were drawn on the palm of my hand. The valley cut the village in two. The streets on the eastern side were packed with troops, and the western streets were completely de-serted. But right behind that emptiness, I could see the front line a half-kilometer away, a thunder of war advancing from the west.

In minutes, I suddenly realized, the fighting would tear into the silence of those pensive little houses perched along the valley's edge. And so it did. The first explosion smashed into the quiet streets; then a second rang out, then a third. One of the hut roofs caught fire. A slender poplar bent double under the force of that sinister battle wind. Frightened birds swirled up into the sky. The blunt snouts of tanks scrolled across the landscape as if across a movie screen. They ground along on their caterpillar tracks, spitting flames. Their gun barrels seemed to point right toward my little hill, where the U-2 presented an excellent target.

Indeed, a shell burst right next to the windmill, sending me running toward the airplane. A full two hours had passed, and still no liaison officer. He must have forgotten all about me. *What the devil am I supposed to do?* I thought. The Hitlerites would be upon me any minute. I had to save the aircraft.

The next shell exploded right next to the plane, splintering planks on the fuselage and wings. I shot into the cockpit and tried to start the engine. Nothing. I needed someone to hand-prop the plane. I spotted a military truck tearing at top speed down the road, rattling along with three good tires and a bare rim. I sprinted down the hill, trying to wave him down. The teen-aged driver tried to swerve around me, so without thinking, I whipped out my revolver and furiously riddled the remaining tires with bullets. He stopped, cursing me, and pulled out his rifle.

"Drop it!" I suggested, nodding toward his weapon. "You'd better help me start my plane."

The driver gaped at me. I don't think he was expecting to hear a female voice. I put away my revolver.

"What do you want?" he said frantically. "Can't you see the Fascists are here? They've broken through the front line. I've got to catch up with the others!"

"You'll catch up," I told him. "But I've got to get the plane started, and I need your help."

"To hell with the plane! Get in the truck. Let's get out of here before it's too late."

I glanced desperately at the U-2 as another blast shook her, shredding the little airplane's fabric skin. The plane seemed to shiver with cold.

"They're going to destroy it!" I screamed, and yanked open the truck door. "Get out! I'll only need you for a minute!"

"You're out of your mind!" the boy said, obeying me at last. "Where's the plane?"

I pointed up the hill, toward the windmill. "You've gone mad!" he shouted. "Look, they're shooting the place to pieces! Your bird is about to go up in flames. Just come with me in the truck!"

I refused. He looked all around, then seized my hand and pulled me, sometimes crawling, sometimes running, up the hill. The shells had already made a ruin of the windmill, its broken wings hanging down listlessly. The airplane, too, was riddled with bullet holes.

As I climbed onto the wing, my terror finally caught up with me. Shock waves from the explosions had torn out the front seat and flung it into the instrument panel in the rear cabin. A thought flashed through my mind: what if the plane was too damaged to fly? I jumped into the cockpit and made a cursory inspection. The damage didn't seem too serious.

"Take hold of the prop!" I cried, but the driver had already done it without my invitation. "Pull it through a few rotations. Then pull down on the blade as hard as you can and jump out of the way."

"And a-one!" he cried, yanking hard, and the propeller roared to life. The young driver vanished, as if whisked away on the propeller slipstream. For an instant I saw his truck disappearing behind the hill.

The Germans peppered the U-2 even more feverishly with bullets. I climbed out of the cabin to turn the aircraft so it pointed in the right direction. I don't know where I found the strength to muscle the tail around. Fear probably played a large role, along with the desperate desire to save myself and the airplane.

I took off right under the Fascists' noses and headed eastward. The sun had set, and twilight enveloped the land. I had no working instruments, but the engine was purring contentedly, and I was alive. But how would I land in the dark? I circled the area, searching for the aerodrome. Below me lay wires, railroad tracks, mines, and tall piles of mine waste, but I could see none of it. Finally, I caught sight of a feeble light twinkling in the distance. Could it be a signal?

The squadron had given me up for dead when the hour of my scheduled return passed, especially after some pilots from the retreating 6th Army liaison unit landed and reported to the Major Bulkin that they had last seen me flying over the occupied village. Only my loyal mechanic refused to believe I was gone. He felt strongly that I was alive, and he stubbornly waited at the aerodrome for me. It was he who had built the small fire on the landing strip.

After I landed, I sat in the cockpit for a long while. I couldn't believe I had managed to escape the Fascists' claws. I took off my helmet, wiped the sweat from my forehead with the sleeve of my flight suit, and sat in a stupor. Thus ended another routine day at the front.

When mechanic Dronov finished inspecting the broken aircraft, he said, "You flew back here on confidence alone, Comrade Commander. But don't worry. We can fix her right up."

In the morning, Dronov reported that the U-2 was again airworthy. My *kukuruznik* looked as good as new. "Thank you, Kostya!" I cried. It was the first time I had ever called him by his first name. He blushed, muttered something unintelligible, and started rearranging aircraft covers for no apparent reason.

"You have a gift from God!" the other pilots teased when I appeared before Squadron Commander Bulkin to report on my mission. "It's natural-born instinct. A pilot's intuition. Turn off all the instruments, take away your map, and you'll find your way home all the same. We had already toasted to your memory at dinner!"

"Sure, I'll find my way home," I replied. "Especially when I'm angry."

"What are you angry about?" they said.

"How could I not be angry? The liaison officer ordered me to wait for him. Then he never showed up. He betrayed me!"

"Yegorova!" the squadron commander cut in. "General Korolev, the chief liaison officer of the front, contacted me to find out if you made it back from your mission. The officer who flew with you apologizes for leaving you. He was not able to get word to you."

"But why did he abandon me in Kalarovka?" I shot back angrily.

"He didn't abandon you," said Bulkin. "He needed to deliver the order to retreat to the staff officers, so he hailed a truck out of Kalarovka to try and overtake them."

"What's the point of delivering the order to retreat when the army is already retreating?" I demanded.

"He was just trying to carry out his mission, but he was late. So he had no choice but to go east along with the staff. He begs your forgiveness," Bulkin repeated.

"Before he begs forgiveness, he'd better find out whether I am alive or dead."

I felt hurt and betrayed. *What kind of officer, and what kind of a gentleman*, I thought, *would leave a woman to die like that?*

22
Thief

Occasionally we flew missions to the staff of the Southwestern Front, which at that time was encamped in Kharkov.[1] Utter chaos prevailed at the aerodrome there. Planes were constantly taking off and landing, often simultaneously. There were always "horseless" pilots wandering around in the parking area. Many of them had lost their airplanes in combat. A few had simply crashed right on the landing strip.

Our commander sent me and a navigator named Irkutsky to search for an aircraft that had gone missing at the Kharkov airfield. The pilot had gone inside to deliver a package, and when he returned, his U-2 was gone.

We scouted every aerodrome and landing strip of the Southern and Southwestern Fronts, but to no avail. We landed at an aerodrome in the town of Chuguev, hungry and cross, hoping to find something to eat. The town was evacuating amid constant enemy bombardment. They wouldn't give us even a crust of bread at the aerodrome cafeteria because we didn't have our military ration tickets with us. Irkutsky went to see the commander there to sort out the problem, and I headed out to the airplane.

To my astonishment, I found a major sitting in my seat, shouting "Contact!" to another major, who was reaching for the propeller to start the plane. I sprang onto the wing and thrashed the major with my fists, shouting wildly, "Thief! Thief! You should be ashamed!"

He turned his face to me and pronounced with absolute composure, "Why are you screaming like you're bidding at a bazaar? You could have just told me politely that it's your plane, and we would have gone to find another 'unmanned' one."

With that, the first major lit out of the cockpit and stalked away from the parking lot with a broad stride, the second major mincing along after him. I felt kind of sorry for them.

As our armies retreated, the squadron often changed bases. We'd usually carve out a new landing strip near a small forest or village. Bombs and shells constantly rained down on our airfields and parked aircraft. Despite the hardships and privations, our liaison squadron remained in good spirits.

---

[1] Or in Ukrainian, "Kharkiv." The second-largest city in Ukraine, located in the east of the country. The city changed hands several times and was heavily damaged during WWII.

"Your assignment today is to reconnoiter and find out whose troops are maneuvering in this region," ordered Bulkin one day, placing a mark on the map.

Flying daytime missions in a slow, fabric-and-plywood aircraft was not what I'd call pleasant. Even infantrymen with rifles used us for target practice. But orders are orders.

The soldiers on the march turned out to be ours, retreating from encirclement, I figured. They looked exhausted, carrying their wounded comrades and weapons on their shoulders. When they saw the red star on my wings, they waved their arms, helmets, and caps wildly at me.

Suddenly, four Messerschmitts came screaming out of the air above me and dove toward the retreating soldiers. I saw tracer bullets for the first time, a flaming thread, shattering the column of troops. Some men fell. The rest fled into the forest.

After a few strafing runs on the column, the Fascists turned their wrath on my U-2. I weaved between the trees and followed every curve of the winding creekbed, nearly touching the water with my wheels. It worked. The German pilots dropped off and flew away.

As always, my mechanic Dronov welcomed me ecstatically at the parking area even though I constantly brought him holes to patch or an engine that needed work. Somehow, he always managed to have the plane ready for my next mission.

Many Muscovites served in our squadron, and no wonder, since it was formed not far from Moscow, in Lyuberets. Every morning, our first question to the radio operators was: "Hey, fellows, what's happening in the capital?"

The situation was grave in Moscow. Air raid warnings howled almost every night. The enemy stood at the gates of the city. Ordinary Muscovites faced those terrible days with uncommon courage. Citizens in all kinds of peaceful professions—chefs and scholars, office and steel workers, artists, bakers, and engineers—enlisted in voluntary people's militias and prepared to defend the approaches to their beloved city to the last.

Moscow was ready for the fight.

How many salty tears mothers and widows spilled during that first year of the war! If we could have gathered them into one huge flood of tears, they would have washed the earth clean of Fascists.

But that first winter, we also shed our first tears of happiness. I will never forget the moment when a young radio operator burst into squadron headquarters and shouted from the doorway, "Guys, we've crushed the Fascists near Moscow!"[2]

---

[2] By early December of 1941, the German Army Group Center had advanced so close to Moscow that some Wehrmacht officers claimed they could see the capital's spires through their binoculars. In extreme cold and deep snow, Western Front commander General Georgy Zhukov, newly reinforced with troops from the Far East, launched a

All of us pilots swirled about the room in a wild fantastic dance. We ran riot with joy, laughing, singing, and hugging each other. Our eyes glistened with happy tears. It was the Red Army's first victory over the Fascist invaders, who had swept through all of Europe with impunity and attacked our motherland.

Finally, the Fascists had stumbled. The victory near Moscow had tremendous political significance for all of us, and our spirits began to lift.

---

massive counteroffensive on December 5 against German troops ill prepared for winter. By December 13, the Soviets had pushed the front back twenty to forty miles, and Sovinformbureau famously announced that the Germans had failed to capture Moscow. By January, the Red Army had advanced nearly 200 miles at some sectors of the front. Although the counterattack eventually stalled, the Battle of Moscow was viewed by many as the first major German defeat, which had a huge effect on morale.

23
We'll Meet Again after Victory!

After capturing Mariupol and Taganrog,[1] the Hitlerites began an offensive on the southern front, aiming toward Shakhty, then to Novocherkassk and Rostov-on-Don.[2] We flew many missions a day to various army staff headquarters.

Kharitonov's 9th Army resisted the Fascists at Novocherkassk and held them fast. But the Germans finally occupied Rostov-on-Don in late November, and we moved our airbase to the town of Voroshilovsk[3] that very day.

A week later, our troops counterattacked, recapturing the city and pressing the enemy westward to the Mius River at Taganrog. We moved to the settlement of Filippenko, and the headquarters of the Southern Front moved to Kamensk, in the Northern Donets Basin.

In Filippenko I received my mother's letter, the first from her since the war began. I felt such relief! All these months I had worried about my family, whether they were suffering somewhere under German occupation. Mama wrote that the Fascists had advanced almost to our home Kuvshinovsky district, but the Red Army managed to liberate the nearby town of Kalinin in mid-December. The Germans had not occupied Torzhok, but the Nazi antichrists had destroyed it—all those churches and ancient cathedrals, razed to the ground.

Mama also said that Konev's[4] staff had set up its headquarters not far from our village, and some of the commanders had quartered with her. She thought they were very nice. They brought her sugar, and she boiled herb tea

---

[1] Both are port cities on the Sea of Azov, just north of the Black Sea. Mariupol is in southeastern Ukraine, and Taganrog is across the border in southern Russia.

[2] Located in southern Russia, 760 miles (1223 km) southeast of Moscow, Rostov-on-Don lies on the Don River. Known as the "Gateway to the Caucasus" (and therefore, to the USSR's oil), the city sustained heavy damage in the war.

[3] Now called Stavropol. A city in southern Russia, in the northern Caucasus, 1007 miles (1621 km) southeast of Moscow, the city was named "Voroshilovsk" from 1931–61 (and "Kommunarsk" from 1961–91) after Soviet military and political leader Kliment Yefremovich Voroshilov.

[4] Ivan Stepanovich Konev (1897–1973). Fought with the Red Army in the Civil War. Colonel-General Konev commanded the Kalinin Front during the Battle of Moscow and was promoted to Marshal in 1944 for his role in liberating Ukraine. His forces (with Marshal Zhukov's) captured Berlin in 1945.

for them in the samovar. They told her the latest news of the front as they sat around her table sipping tea. She asked them about me and showed them my letter with its military postmark. "Your daughter's alive, Stepanida Vasilevna, alive and well," they reassured her. "Right now it's quiet on the part of the front where she is."

"Maybe they were lying to me, Little Daughter, but if so they lied very politely and convincingly," Mama wrote.

"As for me, do not worry a bit. I am all right, except that my heart aches for worrying about my children and grandchildren. I've had no news from Yegorushka[5] since the beginning of the war when he sent a note saying he was leaving to whip the Fascists. Kostya's fighting somewhere on the Southern Front. Kolya was terribly wounded and is in the hospital. Zina's trapped in Leningrad, which is still under siege. She's a foreman at a metalworks factory. My poor little grandson Vanyushka was killed in battle. We received his death notice already. Maria looks worse than dead from grief. I've heard nothing from Alexey except the happy news that he had a daughter named Lily right before the war. Vasya's in Norilsk, writing letters requesting to be transferred to the front, but nobody answers them.

And how are you, my dearest daughter? Take care of yourself. Dress warmly. I've knitted you some mittens with only two fingers in them, so they'll be easier to shoot with…

At the end of the letter, Mama prayed for her children's survival and for a stronger Red Army, that we might cleanse the enemy from our pure Russian soil forever.

Letters to the front were generally optimistic. Our families and friends wrote that everything was all right, that they were well fed and provided for, and that they were working with all their might to rid the world of "mankind's bitterest enemy—fascism."

"You'll be home soon," they always said, "after victory is won." Our loved ones wrote us these holy lies to deflect our worry and to help us bear all that was to come. Our letters home were simple and to the point: We are alive, we are healthy, and we're fighting the Fascists.

A letter came from Viktor that autumn. He said he was flying the "little ones" (that's what we called fighters during the war) on the Northwestern Front, that he had shot down nine Fascist aircraft, and that he'd been awarded the Order of the Red Banner and two Red Stars. "When will we meet again, Anya?" Viktor asked me in his letter.

He answered the question himself. "After victory!"

---

[5] Diminutive of "Yegor," the name Anna's mother christened her grandson, and Anna's nephew, Yuri.

24
Greenhorn

The winter campaign of 1942 shattered the myth of the invincible German warrior. We had yet to turn the tide, but our first small successes instilled in our troops a renewed faith in victory, a fighting spirit. Hope characterized that winter for the troops of the Southern Front.

Together with the Southwestern Front, our armies penetrated the enemy's defenses near Balakleya, forming the Barvenkovo Salient, a bulge in the German lines south of Kharkov. Every soldier anxiously awaited the radio dispatches detailing Grechko's and Parkhomenko's daring cavalry raids behind German lines. Day after day brought encouraging reports to our headquarters of how our cavalry's brazen attacks in the bitter cold and black ice of the Russian winter were throwing the Hitlerite camps into panic. Then one day the radio fell silent.

Without the daily dispatches, our commanders were blind and deaf to each other's movements. Amid such fierce fighting, the exhausted cavalrymen desperately needed to return to our rear for food and rest. But how could we bring them home now, with the radio mute? How would we find them?

"Let's send the U-2," offered General Korolev, liaison commander of the Southern Front.

"The U-2?" echoed the army commander doubtfully, glancing reflexively out the window. Snow swirled madly behind the fogged panes. "Who could possibly fly a mission in this weather?"

"The pilots of the Liaison Squadron," answered Korolev.

On one of those February days, when a blizzard had formed huge snowdrifts along the streets of Filippenko, I was called to the squadron headquarters. They explained the situation at the front and ordered me to fly to Barvenkovo, find Parkhomenko's and Grechko's cavalry corps, and deliver a package marked "Top Secret" to them. General Korolev would accompany me there, and I would return on my own.

A brutal wind tossed the airplane violently. The engine shuddered as if with fever, as a howling snowstorm drowned out its steady hum. Everything was going to be all right, I told myself. Still, how could I find anything in this endless, solid curtain of snow? It swallowed the little biplane, gripping it fast in its sticky embrace. Icy flakes pelted my face like tiny needles and frosted over my goggles. Visibility was practically zero. My only hope was my intuition and flying experience.

Even those reliable counselors are of little use to pilots in a complete whiteout like that one. Still, I somehow made it to Barvenkovo and landed near the railway station. The general climbed out of the cockpit, leaned toward me, gazed at me with sadness in his eyes, and gave me a tiny kiss on my helmet before I flew on.

The storm grew more furious, the swirling snow denser. The U-2 rocked and jerked like a child's swing. Orientation was almost impossible in these conditions. What should I do? Return to base? No: I had no right to do so. I had been ordered to find the missing cavalrymen by hook or by crook. Finding them meant saving thousands of lives.

Whenever I spied the faintest sign of habitation, I landed the plane to find out whether our troops or the enemy's were in the area. Each landing in these extreme meteorological conditions was a leap of faith. Anyone who pilots planes knows what I mean. Three times I landed and took off again, despite a torrent of snow and blasting wind.

Still, I searched, flying as low as I could, examining every dale and ravine. In one small village I spotted tanks, but they opened fire before I could determine whose they were. The blizzard saved me, concealing me from their guns. God knows how my flight might have ended if I hadn't noticed some horses in a narrow ravine. "These are ours," my intuition told me, and I began my descent.

No sooner had I touched down, when two soldiers in cavalry uniforms rushed toward me. I had guessed correctly. "Which cavalry corps are you from?" I asked.

"The 1st Parkhomenko's" they answered.

"I'm from Front headquarters. Are there any commanders here?"

"There's an intelligence commander."

A man in a camouflage uniform approached. He introduced himself as the intelligence commander of the 1st Cavalry Corps under General Parkhomenko. He described the situation and location of their 1st and 5th Corps detachments, and I hurriedly marked my pilot's map. "Good for you, Pilot. Found us on such a nasty day! Here, I'll take the packet to the corps commander."

"No," I replied. "I must deliver it personally."

"What do you mean, 'I must'?"[1] After a slight pause, the officer burst out into a rumbling laugh. "I took you for a man! May I escort you?"

"No. I'll go alone."

"OK, but be careful," he warned. "You'll have to crawl about a hundred meters. See that hut in the distance? That's where you're going. Keep away from that ravine. You'll run into some Germans there."

---

[1] She has used the feminine version of the Russian predicate adjective, "must," which confuses the officer.

I finally managed to place the package in the general's hands. He looked mortally exhausted. He glanced at the order and swore loudly, never suspecting that the pilot's overalls, fur boots, and helmet that stood before him contained a young woman.

A shell exploded somewhere nearby, then another, shaking the earth and flinging up pillars of snowy dust. As shrapnel whistled over our heads, the general stood lost in deep deliberation. Finally, he turned to me and declared decisively, "Here's what we'll do. Fly to Grechko, the 5th Corps, and give him this letter from me. Then fly back to the Front headquarters and get us a radio. We'll keep fighting here for a bit longer."

"I won't be able to make it before dark, Comrade General, and the airplane is not equipped for night flight."

A string of curses followed, directed at the rear support staff who were lagging behind the cavalry corps: the men and horses were starving; the two-way radio didn't work; he had sent a cart the day before to Barvenkovo, but it had disappeared. The general flung up his hands in despair and demanded, "What's the matter with your voice anyway? Do you have a cold?"

"No," I answered, taking the envelope from him. "What message should I give to the Front headquarters?"

"What *messsss*-age?" hissed the general derisively, through clinched teeth. "Are you mocking me, you greenhorn? Do you see the fire your *kukuruznik* has brought on our heads? That's it. You're staying here with us!"

"But you ordered me to deliver a letter to the 5th. Let me fulfill the assignment."

"Go on! Fly out of here!"

Locating Grechko's 5th Cavalry Corps wasn't difficult, since the intelligence commander of the 1st had already mapped their coordinates for me. I landed the plane right in the middle of the village, handed over the envelope, and took off again. I would have to return to the aerodrome at night.

I circled the aerodrome. I knew it was just below me, but I was wary of landing in the impenetrable blackness, for fear of wrecking the airplane. If only someone would at least strike a match or light a cigarette. Finally, I spotted a tiny light and began my descent. I landed without incident, and my mechanic raced up just in time to guide me to parking. As always, Dronov was waiting for me at the aerodrome. When he heard the faint roar of my engine, he rushed to the field and illuminated a blowtorch for me, which I'd seen from the air.

Frozen to the bone and terribly exhausted, I reported to the checkpoint like an apparition. The squadron commander listened quietly to my messages from the cavalry corps, went to the telephone, and asked to be connected with the Front staff. "Do I have permission to sleep?" I asked.

"Of course!" Bulkin said, waving me away carelessly. Feeling slightly hurt, I headed toward the house where I was quartered. Despite the late hour, the owner of the house was still awake. When she saw the state I was in, she started bustling about, exclaiming, "Where have you been to wear yourself out so, sweetie? Here, have a little baked milk. It'll warm you up, dearie."

She helped me pull off my soaked fur boots and overalls and gave me some warm *valenki*[2] to put on. "Would you like to sleep on the stove?[3] It's quite warm," she said.

"Yes, on the stove," I agreed feebly.

My hostess reminded me so much of my own mom. I suppose all mothers are alike in a way. Every time I returned to her hut for the night after a flight, she sat me down at the table and served me Ukrainian borscht and the most delicious pickled tomatoes. Then she would sit down across from me and tell me about her three sons, fighting somewhere in the North. She told me how hard it had been, raising her sons after her husband died. She grieved that she had no grandchildren to look after. When the war broke out, her sons were all drafted, and none of them had had the chance to marry. At this she sighed bitterly, tears streaming down her cheeks. She wiped them away with the hem of her apron and implored, "Eat, little daughter, eat! Maybe somebody's mother is feeding my poor sons somewhere tonight. Who knows? It could even be your mother!"

After downing the heated milk, I crawled up onto the stove to warm myself and quickly dozed off. At midnight there came a knock at the door. My hostess, grumbling, unlatched the door, and a man in an army sheepskin coat walked in. "Where's Yegorova?" he demanded.

I recognized Listarevich's voice and answered, "I am here, Comrade Senior Lieutenant, on the stove."

"I'm sorry, but you'll have to say goodbye to the warmth for now. You're needed at headquarters immediately."

"Noooo! I won't allow it!" wailed my hostess. "Did you ever see such a thing, tormenting a girl like that! She hasn't even dried off and warmed up yet! Don't you have any boys you can send?"

I jumped down from the stove, dressed quickly, grabbed my revolver, and stuck a map into my fur boots. The lieutenant and I stepped outside and into a waiting truck.

---

[2] Singular, *valenok*. Traditional Russian felt boots made from wool, worn in winter by many Red Army soldiers.

[3] A large indoor oven of brick, mud, or stone, typically found in peasant huts and used for both cooking and heating. The top of the stove provided the warmest spot in the hut for sitting and sleeping in winter months and thus was considered a place of honor.

25
Devil's Fellow

The squadron's chief of staff, Senior Lieutenant Listarevich, opened the door of the pickup and said regretfully, "I'm sorry we didn't give you time to rest, Annushka. You've been urgently summoned to staff headquarters to report on the location of the cavalry corps."

Lieutenant Konstantin Semyonovich Listarevich was a good-natured man—lively, cheerful, and quick with a joke and a laugh, but he hadn't been himself lately. He had recently learned of the atrocities the Fascists had committed in his native Belorussia.[1] Worry about his childhood home near Gomel and about his elderly mother, a teacher, and father, a telegraph operator, weighed heavily on his heart. He concealed his emotions and only seemed to become more energetic, working ten times as hard. He had been a fighter pilot in the I-16 until his eyesight failed him at the dawn of the war. Now he took on the responsibilities of chief of staff and squadron commander simultaneously, managing the engineering service, aircraft repair shop, and food service. He'd much rather have been flying missions with us, if he could. But even as busy as he was, he always found time for a chat or an encouraging word to share with pilots before missions.

Although our squadron was intended for liaison purposes, we flew other kinds of missions as well: reconnoitering enemy positions near the front lines, searching for lost units, and establishing communications with them.

That night Listarevich and I flew to Kamensk-Shakhtinsky[2], where the Southern Front Staff was headquartered. We arrived just before midnight and were immediately led to a brightly-lit room. Gathered around a huge table, a

---

[1] Belorussia (the present-day territory of Belarus) suffered mightily during Germany's three-year occupation. The Nazis adopted a savage scorched-earth policy there as they swept through in 1941, partially in retaliation for widespread Belorussian partisan resistance, but also in an effort to exterminate the Jewish and Slavic population, whom the Nazis viewed as *Untermenschen*—"sub-humans" of inferior races. Germany executed hundreds of thousands of civilians, deported hundreds of thousands for forced labor, razed thousands of villages, and murdered an estimated ninety percent of the Jewish population that had not already fled. True figures are difficult to gauge, but Belorussia lost approximately a quarter of its pre-war population—by proportion the highest death rate in Europe.

[2] A town just east of Lugansk in southern Russia, on the Northern Donets River.

group of generals stood studying a map. I froze in bewilderment, unsure to whom I should report.

"You're the pilot who found the cavalry corps, aren't you?" someone finally asked.

"Yes," I said.

"Show me on the map where Parkhomenko and Grechko corps are located."

Two generals politely made way for me as I approached the table. To my chagrin, I could not recall the names of the settlements where I had found the cavalrymen. I grew increasingly distressed, running my finger for a long while along the colorfully marked operations map, but to no avail.

"May I show you on my map?" I asked timidly, knowing the areas were clearly marked there. From my fur boots I produced my worn, large-scale aviation map, marked up with course lines, and far easier for me to read than the operations map. The generals burst into friendly laughter, and my tense nervousness drained away. "Here," I began, pointing to the map.

The generals bombarded me with questions. I gave clear and precise answers, directing them not to the questioner but to one particular general whose kind, round face and sumptuous fluffy moustache put me at ease. He smiled and pointed furtively to another general who was the senior officer there, signaling me to report to him. But I still felt drawn to the mustached officer with the gentle eyes and continued to address him. When I finished, they thanked me and dismissed me. On the way out, I ran into the commander of the Front Liaison Service. "How was it in there?" Korolev asked.

"I told them everything in detail, Comrade General."

"Good," he said, pausing for a moment. I took advantage of the lull. "Comrade General, the man with the whiskers, is he the Army Commander-in Chief?"

"No, that's General Korniyets, a member of the Military Soviet. You liked him, didn't you?"

"Yes, very much."

Listarevich and I flew back from Kamensk at dawn. I had hardly had a chance to warm up and get to sleep before I was awakened again. "Yegorova, you've got to fly to the front line again. The 1st Cavalry Corps needs a radio. You know the way now, so you'll be able to find them," said Bulkin.

Knowing the route didn't make the assignment much easier—same blizzard, same blind flying. It helped that I already knew where the cavalry corps was encamped, except that when I got there, they had disappeared. I searched for quite a while, to no avail, and finally landed near a tiny settlement to ask someone where the cavalrymen had gone. I left the engine running and ran through the snowdrifts toward the nearest hut. I rapped on the window with my frozen fingers, producing a resounding crack that sounded like icicles shattering. An ancient but sturdy-looking man in undershirt, trousers, and *valenki* answered the door. "Grandfather, have our troops been through here?" I asked him.

The old man interrupted me hastily. "Run away from here, Sonny, the Germans are here! They got here late last night," he said, gesturing toward something with his arm.

I turned around and saw Fascists standing around the next hut. *Run!* my instincts told me, but my legs wouldn't obey. I stood there, momentarily paralyzed, as if my feet were nailed to the ground.

The old man came to my rescue, shoving me in the back and bringing me to my senses. I rushed toward my U-2 *kukuruznik*. My beloved corn plane. Machine gun fire crackled from behind me. I looked back and saw that the old man in the white undershirt had collapsed into the snow.

The ghostly image of that stalwart old man who had rescued me, as if straight out of a fairy tale, loomed before me as I fled to my airplane. But this was no fairy tale. A fresh burst of machine-gun fire reminded me of that.

I nimbly leapt into the airplane and hit the throttle. The U-2 lurched forward and skied along the snowy field, faster and faster, lifting off amid a hail of bullets. One of them shattered the mirror on the dashboard. A strip of fabric dangled from the right wing. I felt hot and flushed, yet my teeth were chattering. I finally found the cavalrymen as the sun dropped low to the horizon.

In a school building which the staff was using as its headquarters, I ran into a familiar colonel—the reconnaissance chief. "Congratulations on your safe arrival," he greeted me, then took me straight to Parkhomenko.

"Comrade General, the messenger from the front headquarters is here," reported the colonel, as he handed Parkhomenko the package.

"Tell him to come in," said the general, his eyes still glued to the map. When he lifted his head, I saw exhaustion and many sleepless nights written on his face. Still, he radiated a real cavalryman's proud bearing. He was impeccably shaved, his hair neatly combed. Unconsciously, I stood at attention. It didn't escape the general's eye.

"At ease, at ease," he commanded jovially. "You've brought us good news, then, Eagle. And what about a radio?"

"There it is, sir."

Just then, we heard the rumble of explosions growing nearer. The Fascists seemed to have increased fire. The general pricked up his ears.

"You're the devil's fellow!" he said. "Look at all this trouble you've brought on our heads! You've revealed our location. Do you see what the Hitlerites are doing?"

The general still had no idea that the soldier standing before him was not a boy at all, but a young woman. However, this didn't seem an appropriate time to correct him. The building shuddered with the force of shells exploding ever closer. From somewhere came the tinkle of shattering glass. Fragments drummed on the roof. But Parkhomenko remained unperturbed. He sat calmly at a table, his broad chest thrust forward defiantly, bristling with medals.

I didn't share his calm. I was terribly worried about the fate of my U-2. My assignment was completed. I needed to hurry back to base. Darkness was fast approaching.

"Comrade General, do you have any messages for the Front staff?" I finally ventured to ask.

"Messages?" came Parkhomenko's booming voice. "Are you joking? You see what fire your *kukuruznik* has brought us? It's too late to fly away, lad. Stay here with us. Burn down your bird. Send it to the devil's mother. We'll find you a good horse and teach you to fight with a saber."

I had no intention of burning down my "bird." I was ordered to return to base, and an order's an order. I ran out of the general's office and scurried along a line of huts and fences toward the plane. The way turned out to be very long. At times, the fire pressed me to the ground. Running from one shell crater to another, I recalled the old law of front combat: shells, they say, never fall twice on the same spot. Or so says the theory of probability! Thanks to that excellent maxim, I made it to the airplane safe and sound.

When I tried to start the engine, I realized that it had sustained damage, probably hit by a fragment. More trouble. I headed back to the school building the same way I had come. Cavalrymen bustled about the street, loading equipment into rustic carts, preparing to evacuate.

"So you've decided to stay with us, lad?" Parkhomenko greeted me.

"No, Comrade General, I came to ask for your help."

"What kind of help?"

"I need a horse to tow the plane," I answered.

"I don't have horses to spare right now. You can see the mess we are in."

I somehow persuaded the commander to lend me a good horse. I found a rope and tied it to an axle on the undercarriage, then looped a collar around the horse's neck. As I began leading the horse, a hefty fellow of Kuban Cossack[3] stock appeared.

---

[3] In Russian, *kazak*, from the Turkic word for "free man" or "adventurer." In the 15th century, many Eastern European serfs fled their owners and settled in the Don and Dnieper regions (present-day southern Russia and Ukraine), establishing self-governing communities (called *stanitsas*) of free men known for their military prowess. Groups, or "hosts," of Cossacks were named for the region in which they settled (often named for a river, e.g., "Don," "Kuban," or "Zaporozhian," the latter meaning "below the rapids" of the Dnieper River.) From the 16th century onward, both Poland and, later, Russia employed Cossacks to defend their nations' frontiers and allowed the hosts a degree of sovereignty in return. By the 19th century, the Cossacks had lost much of their autonomy, and their traditional villages no longer functioned in the traditional, communal way. After the Russian Civil War, in which many Cossacks fought with the White Army, a directive from the central government called for (as quoted in Richard Pipes' *A Concise History of the Russian Revolution*) "the complete, rapid, deci-

"Why do you want to save this lousy pile of plywood?" he grumbled, taking hold of the bridle. "Another minute of messing around, and Fritz will bomb us."

"Then let's hurry up so they don't get us," I encouraged him.

"'Hurry up, hurry up," he mocked. "Horses like things done properly. Every rope has to fit just right. What's the use of rubbing sores all over her withers? She'll just die on you."

Finally, the Cossack took the horse by the bridle and shouted sharply, "Come on, girl, off you go!"

I gripped the wing firmly to keep it steady along the rutted road. We joined the line of departing carts and made our way through the thickly falling snow, which concealed us from the enemy shells as nightfall enveloped us.

It was the first and only time I "flew" with a horse as a crewman. Underfed and exhausted from the long raid, the horse plodded at an unhurried pace, without seeing the road. The U-2 sighed miserably over each bump and pothole. With every lurch, alarming cracking sounds issued from inside the aircraft. I followed the plane's every movement as the wings bowed clumsily down to the very snowdrifts, then sprang back up again. The vibrations made my heart ache. I was afraid the wings would buckle and fall off.

Thanks to the horse and the gloomy Cossack, I managed to save the U-2. We stayed the night in a small village. Early in the morning, I inspected the engine. I asked the woman whose hut we'd stayed in to boil a kettle of water. I drained the oil into a cast-iron pot and heated it on the stove. Some of the cavalrymen helped me rinse the carburetor with hot water, pour the heated oil back in, and crank the engine. To our joy, the engine sneezed a time or two, then started with a happy roar.

That February day I felt a flush of gratitude for my aeroclub instructors. All those times they had made us take apart and reassemble the aircraft engine and stay late after flights working with the mechanics had not been in vain. If you want to fly well, you must know your airplane well. That was always the rule. How it helped me that day!

"Will you permit me to fly, Comrade General?" I asked Parkhomenko.

"Fly away!" he said. "Take this package and one of our wounded. Don't be cross with an old man like me. I took you for a male, but of course, you're—

"Well! In war, anything is possible." The general's brown eyes lightened with kindness. He smiled shyly and bade me goodbye with an awkward wave.

---

sive annihilation of Cossackdom as a separate economic group, the destruction of its economic foundations, the physical extermination of its officials and officers, and altogether the Cossack elite."

26
A Pilot for the General

For the first time since the beginning of the Barvenkovo operation, I finally had a good, long sleep. Pleasant dreams swept away my fatigue. The harrowing experiences of those two difficult flights folded themselves away, into the vault of memory. New trials awaited me.

Feeling buoyant and full of energy, I stopped by the squadron staff headquarters. The first thing I noticed was a large sheet of drawing paper tacked to the hallway wall. I would have walked on by it, but one of the pilots appeared in the corridor and said with a sly grin, "Don't be snooty, Yegorova, read it. It concerns you, after all."

"Me?" I said with surprise, and went up to the paper. Some self-styled artist had drawn a caricature of me as a kind of fairy-pilot, winging my way through a snowstorm. Below the friendly lampoon, someone had written, "Women are flying missions while the men are on vacation!"

"How do you like our little joke on the men?" asked Lieutenant Listarevich, who suddenly appeared in the hallway. I blushed and mumbled something incoherent.

"Why so bashful? You taught the men a very good lesson," he said, extending his hand to me. "And congratulations. The commanders have submitted your name for an award for your successful search missions in support of the Cavalry Corps. "

Just then someone poked his head out of an office. "Yegorova, you are summoned to the commander!" he said.

"Fly to the 6th Army. Pick up General Zhuk, the Front Artillery Commander," ordered the squadron commander.

"Yes, sir!" I replied, and began plotting the course on my aviation map.

Evening was coming. In every direction the snowy earth shone pure white, the sky crisp and clear. The world seemed as fresh and tidy as a window scrubbed clean before the holidays. As if there were no war.

As they say, God protects those who protect themselves. And so I flew low, nearly shaving the leaves from the trees, hiding in ravines and behind copses, as if I were part of the landscape.

As soon as I landed, an Emka[1] pulled up to the plane. A general stepped out of it. I reported to him according to the strictest protocol. "They couldn't

---

[1] The nickname for the GAZ M1 (rather like a Ford V8), a Soviet staff car of the late thirties and war years.

have found a male pilot for the Front Artillery Commander?" the general snapped irritably.

I answered his question with a question: "Could you please tell me where we are flying?"

The colonel who accompanied the general told me our destination—a small village. I pulled out my map and spread it across the wing, tracing our route for them with my freezing hands. I climbed into the front cockpit, and the general, in a tall, ostentatious fur hat and a scarf wrapped nearly up to his eyes, arranged himself behind me. We took off.

In my rear-view mirror, I watched my passenger's tired face. When our eyes met, I gestured toward the ground, so festively dressed in its silvery winter raiments, and to the setting sun. But the general still frowned.

Suddenly, a shadow fell over the airplane. I turned to look, and an icy chill ran down my spine. Two Messerschmitts were diving straight for us.

My gear and wingtips nearly scraped the ground as I yanked the plane to the right and back to the left, trying to avoid the machine-gun fire. But the Germans dove at us again and again.

The engine coughed once, twice, three times. The airplane seemed to be desperately gasping for air, as if it were slowly suffocating. Something was terribly wrong, I realized. Below us, the snowy steppe stretched as far as the eye could see, without a dwelling or a puff of friendly smoke in sight. A "wolves' expanse," as we say.

Suddenly, the engine quit altogether. Of all the terrible luck! I turned to my passenger and signaled to him that we were landing. He nodded his head with obvious displeasure. *There's a "Lord of the Manor" for you,* I fumed. *This puffed-up fellow has no idea how much trouble we're in. He's acting like I'm landing just because I feel like it. This would have to happen when I'm carrying the "god of war" himself.*

Our troubles continued to mount. I made a power-off landing, as fierce gusts buffeted the tail and wings, trying to turn us over. The little plywood and fabric plane was no match for the stubborn steppe wind. But I gripped the control stick just as stubbornly.

All the while, the two "Messers" showered us with bullets. I leapt out of the plane to help the general, who was bundled up so thickly he could barely move. Glowing rays of fire pierced the snow all around us as we ran into the woods. We stumbled in the snowdrifts, fell, and got up to run some more. My general was breathing hard. His age and his sumptuous clothing weren't cut out for a lot of running. Suddenly, the sky went quiet. I asked the general to wait for me under the trees.

"Do you really expect me to wait here until the cows come home?" the artillerist interrupted angrily, catching up to me. "I have no intention of standing around waiting in this weather. We need to leave the plane and look for some sign of habitation before we freeze to death."

I glanced at my plane with alarm. Every gust of wind shook it convulsively. *If this wind gets any stronger, it will break the plane in two,* I thought, ignoring my passenger's suggestions. *I need to anchor it somehow.*

I climbed into the cockpit. "What the devil are you doing?" the general demanded.

"I'm getting a rope. We're going to tie down the plane," I said.

"Excuse me? We'll be here until nightfall! Once it gets dark, we're done for."

"Darkness or no darkness, it doesn't matter," I said. "I have no right to abandon the plane in this condition."

"Look here—" he started, but seeing my face, my passenger realized that I would not change my mind. He took the rope from me.

With great difficulty we towed the plane tail-first to the trees, where I examined it carefully. The "Fritzes" had smashed the U-2 quite thoroughly. It was full of hundreds of holes, one propeller blade was wrecked, a cylinder was missing, and the oil and gas tanks looked like sieves. It was a wonder the plane hadn't caught fire.

Working together, we quickly tied the plane to the tree trunks and camouflaged it with branches. We took out the documents we needed, figured out which direction to go on the aviation map, and set off into the steppe.

We sank into the snow up to our knees, breaking through every few steps and falling deeper into the drifts. The darkness made the going even harder. We walked for an hour, then two, then three...

Cottony snow poured from the sky endlessly as if from a torn sack. At times it seemed that someone had decided to bury every inch of the earth in snow, once and for all. Walking became more and more difficult. But the worst of it was that my exhaustion was quickly giving way to indifference. I dropped my head low, hiding my face from the stinging snowflakes. That sensation at least occasionally brought me back to reality.

Or maybe it was a dream. After all, I could hear the steady clatter of jackhammers, the muffled cries of passing workers in the tunnel, my brigade friends' jokes. Tosya Ostrovskaya whispered something in my ear, but I couldn't make it out. Then Tosya started shaking me by the shoulders. I couldn't understand what she wanted. Why was there snow in the tunnel? It tickled my cheek so gently, wrapped my hands with such warmth—like a wool mitten—that I wanted to stay forever in its cozy embrace.

Tosya was shaking my shoulder again. Wait, this wasn't my girlfriend Tosya. This crude, booming male voice couldn't be hers. With extraordinary effort, I barely opened one eyelid.

"What's your name?"

"Anna."

"You've got to stand up, Comrade Anna. Get up and start walking right now!" This time I made out the words quite clearly. "You'll freeze to death before long."

I didn't have the strength to take a single step. I sat back down heavily in the snowdrift. "I can't go any further. Go ahead without me."

"Get up, Anna. Get up!" said the general, tugging at me. "If you fall asleep here you'll freeze to death!"

"Yes, yes, yes, get up," I echoed mechanically. Finally, I understood where I was. "Of course, I will get up and walk."

My mind knew what to do, but my feet refused to obey. If only I could find the strength to stand, to take one more step into that desolate, frozen steppe.

The general pulled me by the hand, and I started walking. I leaned on the artillerist for the first few steps, then gradually began to overcome my mortal fatigue. With every step I felt stronger, leaving the moment of death farther behind me. The wind's wailing no longer seemed so ominous, and the bottomless darkness didn't frighten me any more.

By morning, we came upon some of our soldiers—the very artillery unit General Zhuk and I had been flying to meet. Our hands and faces were frostbitten. The men led us into a hut where an iron stove was lit. Sleeping soldiers covered the floor. I sat down on the floor in the doorway and immediately fell asleep. The radio operators transmitted my whereabouts to the squadron and told them that the U-2 needed major repairs.

Pilot Spirin soon arrived with my mechanic Dronov, then flew back to the squadron to bring back the necessary parts. It took us the entire day to find that unknown stretch of forest where we'd concealed the airplane—fortunately we spotted a dark blemish on the snow where the oil had leaked out—and to tow the U-2 to a village.

Konstantin Alexandrovich Dronov swore mightily when he started examining the damaged aircraft. He threatened to mail a thousand devils to the addresses of certain German pilots, even to Hitler himself, and promised to hammer a wooden stake into the Fuhrer's grave one day. Despite all the curses, he did his work well. He set up a tent over the engine to protect himself from the wind and took off his gloves. I stayed nearby to help him.

"Comrade Commander, you shouldn't be hanging around the airplane engine. If it sees your face, it might get scared and not start," my mechanic joked.

It was true—my face was quite frightening. Frostbite had turned it completely black. I smeared fat on my skin and put on a moleskin mask—fur-lined, with slits for the eyes and mouth. I looked like a carnival sideshow. The air force issued these masks to all pilots, but we seldom wore them when we flew.

Dronov invented various pretexts to send me back into the hut to get warm. Eventually, he gave in, and we worked together.

I could never be an aircraft mechanic. What extraordinary people they are, what masters of their trade! "Golden Hands," as we call them. They work and work, going without sleep or food, until a plane is ready to fly again.

They send their pilots into the sky, and then they wait patiently for them to fly home again.

It's the waiting I couldn't stand, especially in wartime, on those awful days when a pilot is overdue, and the mechanic can only hope for a miracle. He waits at the airport, tidying up, perhaps lighting a cigarette to pass the time. When he recognizes the distinct hum of his very own plane, he rushes to meet it, overjoyed when his pilot steps out safe and sound. But when a pilot fails to return, his mechanic's grief knows no bounds. And still, he continues to hope, staring unendingly into the empty sky, waiting.

This time, Dronov didn't have to wait for me. We returned to the squadron together. He showed our comrades all the holes he had patched in the frost. "Eighty-seven holes I counted in the plane, and Annushka and the general—not a scratch! It's the tail number, the 'devil's dozen,' that did it!" Dronov joked. But I knew it wasn't the "lucky" number thirteen on my tail that protected me on my flights. It was the capable hands of my mechanic.

Our terrible night in the steppe must have made quite an impression on the general. He told General Korolev, the liaison chief, that he was transferring me to an artillery-spotting squadron. "I need strong-willed pilots," he said.

The other pilots told me I was out of my mind. "You're a pilot, not a barrage balloon," they argued heatedly.

"Don't worry, lads. I agree with you," I told them. "I'm not interested in hanging like a target over the front line. But to tell you the truth, I'm sick and tired of being an air taxi driver. Anyway, our U-2s themselves are little more than targets for these Messerschmitts. I want to fight for real."

"If I could do anything at all, I'd be an attack pilot," I said.

27
The Party

In April of 1942, when we were based at Voyevodovka, near Lysychansk, Ukraine, I was nominated for party membership by our Battalion Commissar, Alexey Vasilyevich Ryabov, and our party organizer, Ivan Yosefovich Irkutsky.

I liked Ryabov and Irkutsky. Whevener I was upset, I would go looking for them. To be frank, Major Bulkin was rather rude and arrogant, and we didn't much like him. But Commissar Ryabov was different. He often flew missions, like any ordinary pilot, and he was someone you could talk to openly and honestly. He never scolded us without reason, and when he did, we didn't feel offended.

Irkutsky was just like the commissar—sympathetic, kind, attentive, and an excellent navigator. "Yegorova, we're compatriots!" he told me one day. "I was born near Torzhok village, too! Have you gotten any letters from your mother?"

"No, I haven't heard from her in a long time," I said. "I'm afraid the Fascists may already be there, committing their atrocities. I'm so worried about Mama."

"No news from my mother, either," he said quietly, then bent his head down closer to me and added, "Our Komsomol organizer told me that Komsomol is recommending you to become a party member. I'll vouch for you. I've been a party member since 1939 and a Komsomol since 1928. You see how old I am already!"

"Oh, come on! You're only thirty-one," I told him. "What did you do before the war?"

He told me his life story. His father died in the Imperialist War when Ivan was six. Ivan worked on the farm in the village until he was fourteen, then went to an institute in Moscow. "In 1939 I finished the School of Airborne Navigators in my hometown of Torzhok, etcetera, etcetera." He finished his story, laughing at his "etceteras" so youthfully and naturally that I ventured: "Are you married, Ivan Yosefovich?"

"No, Yegorova, I haven't had the chance. I had a girlfriend once, but when I went into the army, she didn't wait for me. She got married."

That's how the party organizer and I always used to talk to each other—heart-to-heart.

"Commissar Ryabov will give you a second recommendation," he added. "He told me so."

"Thank you!" I said. "I'll try not to let you down!" I said gratefully and ran to my plane.

Commissar Ryabov presided over party meetings in the squadron. They were usually quite brief. We mainly discussed candidates for party membership.

Ryabov was neither an orator nor a theoretician. He was just a good man. He spoke sincerely and passionately about how we must each fulfill our individual assignments to the best of our ability and follow the orders of the Southern Front command if we were to achieve victory. The true mission of all Soviet people, he said, was to crush the enemy.

Then came the party nominations. When my turn came, the party delegate handed me my candidate's card, then asked out of the blue, "By the way, Comrade Yegorova, you're not by any chance the sister of Vasily Alexandrovich Yegorov, are you?"

"No," I answered quickly.

For many years I agonized over my treachery. How could I so thoughtlessly disavow my brother? He'd been the father I never had. Even now my soul burns with bitterness and shame when I recall that episode. Why had I answered that way?

Many years later, when Vasily had been rehabilitated and had come to Moscow, I confessed to him what I had done. He thought about it for a moment, then smiled. "You were probably afraid they wouldn't let you fight in the war," he said.

"I was scared to death," I admitted.

"My little coward," he said and kissed me, as if to say, *I forgive you for what they made you do.*

28
Order of the Red Banner

We flew mission after mission. They never seemed to end.

"Yegorova, your mission is to search for 'Katyushas'!"

"Yes, sir!" I repeated.

Katyushas had just appeared at our sector of the front. The commanders had described the exact location of the heavy trucks loaded with the sheathed rockets I was to find. I was also to deliver a classified packet to a General Pushkin.

Spring had come, and with it the mud and foul weather. Heavy rains poured unceasingly. Visibility at the aerodrome was abysmal, around a hundred meters. When I took off, dense fog closed in, and the rain turned to sleet.

I climbed to nine hundred meters, where the fog was a bit thinner. Suddenly, the aircraft began shuddering violently. Glancing outside, I noticed that the wings, fuselage, and even the propeller were covered with an even crust of ice.

The engine was still turning, and the control surfaces still worked, but the plane didn't respond to my inputs. I was losing altitude. I pushed the stick forward to descend more quickly, but something told me the ground was quite close already. Houses flashed by, then a forest, a river, a ravine. I shut down the engine, pulled back on the stick, and *Bam!* The airplane slammed down, heavy with ice. I did everything I could to slow the airplane down, although the U-2 didn't have any brakes.

Finally, the U-2 rolled to a halt. Silence. I couldn't see two steps in front of me through the thick fog. I was afraid I would lose the plane if I walked away from it. I would have to wait until the fog cleared. I cleaned the ice off the plane and calculated my approximate location based on my speed and the duration of the flight.

When the fog finally dispersed a bit, I noticed a haystack right in front of the aircraft's nose. How had I missed it?

I never did find General Pushkin and his "katyushas" that day. On the way home, I flew into another snowstorm. I somehow managed to land in utter darkness, but I couldn't even see to taxi. I only found the parking ramp because my mechanic heard the "voice" of his plane and ran to meet me.

The squadron commander gave me a lengthy scolding. "Tired of living, are you?" he raged. The other pilots regarded me with gloomy silence. They had apparently turned back because of the weather. But the liaison commander of the Southern Front, General Korolev, congratulated me, and an official from the political unit handed me a package.

It was one of those parcels randomly sent to front-line soldiers from kind souls back home. The box was full of wonderful things! Neat little packs of tobacco, a bottle of vodka, knitted wool socks, beautifully embroidered towels, a bag of dried fruit, and, most interesting of all, a hand-stitched tobacco pouch with an embroidered inscription on it: "To a dear soldier, from Marusya Kudryavtseva—a keepsake." Inside the pouch was a photograph of a good-looking young woman and a letter asking the "dear soldier" to whip the Fascists quickly and return home after a quick victory. At the bottom of the box lay a notebook with ten envelopes, all addressed to Marusya, the city of Mary, Turkmen Republic.

I gave the tobacco and vodka to my mechanic and the towels to the hostess with whom I was staying, and I kept the dried fruit and socks for myself. I passed on Marusya's hopeful photograph, letter, and envelopes to Viktor Kravtsov, a handsome twenty-two-year-old Kuban Cossack. No matter where we based, the village girls couldn't take their eyes off him. He pretended not to notice them.

"Viktor, have a look at this photo." I teased "Isn't she a lovely girl? You should write to her. I'll bet she'd rather get a letter from you than from me. It would make her so happy to know that her package made it into the hands of a handsome young soldier, a pilot even!"

"Ridiculous!" he muttered, but he did accept the notebook and envelopes.

On Red Army Day, our squadron gathered to celebrate. Chief of Staff Listarevich solemnly read a decree from the Presidium of the Supreme Soviet: Lieutenant Spirin was awarded the Red Star, and Junior Lieutenant Yegorova, the Order of the Red Banner.

I had just returned from a mission and had slid into the back row a bit late. The roar of the engine still rang in my ears, and I didn't hear the names called. Suddenly, everyone surrounded me, congratulating me for the award.

For what? I wondered. I had made it to the front by chance. I carried out my orders as best I could, like any soldier would. I confess, it was quite difficult at times, but I just kept trying. My mind floated back to previous missions. It did seem ludicrous at times to fly missions in broad daylight armed only with a revolver! Those Messerschmitt aces had little trouble shooting down our defenseless U-2s.

The familiar voice of my mechanic Dronov interrupted my ruminations. "Comrade Commander, what's wrong? You look pale," he said.

"I'm fine. Why?"

"You are called to the Presidium!" he whispered.

Leonid Romanovich Korinyets, member of the Front Military Soviet and the very same general whose friendly face had put me at ease when I had reported to the commanders about the cavalry corps, handed me the award.

29
A Hooligan on the Road

In May of 1942, the armies of the Southwestern Front launched a major offensive toward Kharkov. Our Southern Front joined the operation to liberate the city and destroy its occupiers.[1] Before flights, our liaison squadron was briefed about the latest combat operations at the front. We would then fly to one or another army, division, or corps to verify those reports.

On the morning of May 20, I was to fly to the 9th Army with a top secret package. Although a navigator or liaison officer usually accompanied me, for some reason I flew alone on this mission.

At the approaches to the town of Izyum,[2] I could see our troops' frantic movements along the fields and roads. In Svyatogorsk and Izyum—in fact, throughout the Northern Donets valley—scores of fires raged.

Since childhood, I've always hated fires. In the village, we used to say, "A thief at least leaves the walls standing; a fire, nothing!"

I still remember the night the wheat burned in our village. We used to dry the bundles of harvested wheat in the threshing barn by heating it from below with a big brick furnace. One night our threshing barn caught fire. A spine-chilling scream rang out into the quiet night. "Fire! *Fi-re!* We're burning!" We

---

[1] Now known as the Second Battle of Kharkov. On May 12, 1942, the Soviet Southwestern Front (supported by the Southern Front) launched simultaneous attacks from the northeast and southwest of Kharkov, in a planned pincer movement to surround the city. Most historians contend that the Soviet effort was ill-advised in conception and botched in execution—the Red Army had underestimated German strength in the area and was walking into a trap. Stalin would not listen to his commanders' warnings. (According to historian Alexander Werth, Khrushchev made this claim in his "Secret Report" of 1956 to the XXth Congress; of course, Khrushchev had his own motives for doing so.) German forces counterattacked, resulting in the encirclement of Group Bobkin and the 6th, 9th, and 57th Armies. By the end of May, more than 200,000 (and possibly many more) Red Army troops had been captured or killed, and the way was cleared for Paulus's victorious 6th Army to advance to Stalingrad. The extent of the catastrophe was kept from Soviet citizens and soldiers at the time—an announcement at the end of May put Soviet losses at "5,000 killed and 70,000 missing."

[2] The Red Army had seized a bridgehead over the Northern Donets River at Izyum which formed a westward salient into German lines south of Kharkov and, in effect, laid a trap for the Soviets. As Soviet troops (including the 9th Army) pushed west via Barvenkovo, a German counteroffensive on May 18 pressed north toward Izyum, pinching off the bulge and encircling four armies and many senior officers by May 23.

jumped down from our beds and rushed madly around in the darkness of our *izba*. The boys ran out of the hut half-dressed, but Mama was so frightened that she couldn't find the door. She grabbed the samovar instead of the door-knob. She might still be standing there if my younger brother Kostya hadn't run back to the hut. "Mama, calm down! The fire's out, the wheat is safe," he cried. "Kolya sent me to tell you everything's all right!"

Even in wartime, with whole cities burning, I still couldn't get used to the sight of those ravenous flames. My heart pounded with anxiety, just like when I was little, as I looked down upon the blazing Donets River valley. It seemed that all Russia was ablaze.

Above, a dogfight raged between a pair of our I-16s[3] and six Me-109s — an unequal battle. But our "Ishachki" masterfully evaded the Messerschmitts' fire and made a frontal attack, seizing the advantage.

I must confess, I was so entranced by the dogfight that I failed to notice the German fighter swooping down on me from above like a hawk. A burst of machine gun fire flashed. If only there were some little ravine or hollow to drop down into! Instead, an unbroken field undulating with last summer's corn stretched out before me as far as the horizon. A solid wall of forest rose to my right, and to the left I could see a town.

The plane caught fire. Suddenly, the cockpit became so hot and smoky I could scarcely breathe. I landed quickly and leapt from the plane, tearing the smoldering tatters of my flight overalls from my body as I fled into the woods.

This seemed to drive the German pilot into a blind rage. He dove low, strafing me as I ran. In 1941 and even 1942, the Hitlerites could still enjoy the luxury of falling upon a lone, fleeing Russian soldier and emptying their guns at him.

I ran and ran. Occasionally I would throw myself to the ground, pretending to be hit, hiding my head under a cornstalk. When the "Messer" passed

---

[3] The Polikarpov I-16 was a small, highly maneuverable monoplane fighter ("I" indicates *Istrebityel*, or "Fighter") developed by engineer Nikolai Polikarpov. Entering service in the mid-1930s, the I-16 proved itself in the Spanish Civil War — Republican troops called the little airplane *Mosca* ("Fly"), and the Nationalist side dubbed it *Rata* ("Rat"). Soviet pilots who found the aircraft unwieldy to handle nicknamed it *Ishak* ("Donkey") or the more affectionate diminutive, *Ishachku* ("Little Donkey"). The first low-winged monoplane with retractable gear to fly in any air force, the I-16 was a leader in fighter design but was considered rather obsolete by mid WWII (and gradually replaced), outmatched by the faster and more powerful Messerschmitt Bf 109. Pilots at Soviet Air Force training schools joked, "If you can fly the I-16, you can fly anything."

The I-16 became associated with fierce Soviet resistance. It was the first Soviet aircraft to employ the legendary Red Air Force *taran* technique — ramming an enemy aircraft when all other combat measures had failed. One hour after the Germans invaded, an *Ishak* pilot rammed a Heinkel 111 bomber, destroying both aircraft.

by to make a turn, I leapt from the ground, pressed the top-secret packet to my chest, and ran some more.

When the Fascist ran out of ammunition, he flew away.

All quiet in the forest. Not a soul anywhere near. And suddenly, I was swept with a longing to lie down in some little clearing, close my eyes, and doze off, just like I used to do when I was little. Young foliage had already begun pushing its way out of the skeletal winter branches. Spring was coming into its own. I had never feared death, but suddenly a fierce desire to live seized me. It would be terrible to die in the spring. Life tasted a millionfold sweeter in springtime.

But my plane had burnt to ashes, and along with it the mail sack and my leather flight jacket. What was I to do? I had to somehow find the 9th Army staff headquarters.

I searched and searched. Finally, I noticed a telephone wire hanging from some tree limbs. I followed it, hoping it would lead to some kind of command point. After about thirty paces, I ran into a couple of soldiers winding the wire around a spool.

"Where's the checkpoint?" I asked them.

"What checkpoint?" they shouted, continuing to work. "This place is occupied."

I made my way out of the forest and hurried across some fields to a desolate road. A few straggling soldiers and small cavalry detachments marched haphazardly, avoiding the road.

Suddenly, a truck raced toward me along the road. I stood in its path, waving my arm for it to stop. It drove around me. An Emka appeared. I tried to flag it down, but it, too, sped right past me. Without hesitating, I pulled my revolver out of its holster and fired into the air. The driver put the car into reverse and braked near me. The front door opened, and a dashing captain sprang out. He deftly snatched my weapon, twisted my arm around behind my back, and felt in the left pocket of my soldier's blouse for my documents.

I wasn't going to stand for such treatment. I quickly whipped my head around and sank my teeth into the captain's arm until I drew blood. The car then emitted a stout general, demanding to know who I was and why on earth I was going on like some kind of hooligan in the middle of the road.

"Who do you think you are?" I shot back, presenting the general with my papers. Actually, my papers were quite impressive. They ordered all military units and civil organizations to provide me, the bearer, with whatever aid I required to fulfill my assignment.

"Where are you headed?" the general asked, suddenly very courteous.

"To the Staff Headquarters of the 9th Army."

"Get in," the general offered graciously, then added with concern, "How did you get so badly burned?"

I told him the whole story and suddenly found myself in tears. I don't know if it was from the pain or the insult, but my burned arms did hurt very badly. And when the captain had twisted my arms, he had scraped off the skin, and now they were bloody and raw.

"Don't cry, dear," the general said soothingly, "Or those salty tears will sting your face. You're here now, and we'll get you to the 9th Army in no time."

Unfortunately, in wartime such notions as "now" and "in no time" tend to become somewhat elastic. It wasn't until three hours later that we found the 9th Army, where I delivered the package to the operations chief.

The medics applied an ointment to my face and bandaged my hands. I ate voraciously at the field mess, and that night a military truck delivered me to the aerodrome.

The squadron welcomed me home like a long-lost brother. Narodetsky, the provisions chief, brought me sweets instead of the hundred grams of vodka that pilots usually received after flights. He knew that I never drank my ration and would give it away to the mechanic or the other pilots, so he often spoiled me with something tasty instead.

I once learned the hard way that receiving special treatment from the provisions chief had consequences. When we were stationed in the forests near Voroshilovgrad,[4] the front was quiet for a time. We pitched our tents among the trees and made very few flights. One day Narodetsky invited me on an excursion to Voroshilovgrad. At the town supermarket, a wide-brimmed straw hat with a sumptuous bouquet of artificial flowers on it caught my eye. I stood by the counter for a long while admiring the hat. Narodetsky noticed me eyeing the exquisite creation and, after whispering briefly with the saleswoman, presented the hat to me.

The hat hung proudly from a nail in my tent. Once, as I was returning from a mission, I caught sight of the beloved squadron dog Druzhka,[5] who had been with us ever since we were based at Tikhy, wearing the hat. My pilot-comrades had cut holes in it for Druzhka's ears and tied it fast to his head. The dog dashed around, barking joyfully in his extravagant finery. The pilots hid from me in their tents, snickering. Viktor Kravtsov scolded me: "That's what you get for accepting gifts from the provisions chief!"

This time, when I returned to the squadron safely, my face and hands and even my boots badly burned, no one seemed to mind about the candies from Narodetsky.

"Don't fret over the airplane, Yegorova. You can always get another one," Engineer Malikov told me. "The main thing is that you're alive, and the package is delivered. An airplane isn't a living thing."

---

[4] Called Lugansk (or "Luhansk" in Ukrainian) before 1935, from 1958–70, and again after 1990. An industrial city in the Donets Basin of eastern Ukraine.

[5] "Buddy" or "Little Friend."

Volodovo village—My childhood home, 15 October 1988.
"With tears in my eyes / and tenderest sorrow, / I wandered my home village, /
A place so dear to my heart." *Note: Yegorova may have adapted this poem
from a similar 1966 verse by "village poet" Nikolai Rubtsov.*

Above: Vasily
Alexandrovich
Yegorov, 1934
(my brother).

Left: My family. *Back Row:*
Aunt Anisya with her
husband, and Mama. *First
row:* Grandfather, Grand-
mother's brother the priest,
and Grandmother.

ПЛАНЕРИСТЫ ... УБА МЕТРОСТРОЯ 23-IV-1936

Above: Printed on front: Metrostroy Aeroclub Glider Pilots, 4/25/1936. *Written on back:* Metrostroy aeroclub pupils at the Maliye Vyazmy aerodrome, with instructor Miroyevsky. In the war, Miroyevsky dies flying Il-2s. *(Yegorova is seated, far left.)*

Left: Anna — Metro engineer

Timofeyeva (Yegorova) Anna Alexandrovna. Kuban, 1943.
Flew 277 missions in Po-2s and Il-2s.

1943. By the Shturmovik, after a mission.

On the right, Konstantin Listarevich, who brought me to the front.
On the left, Squadron Commander Pyotr Grishenko.

Dronov. 1975. Po-2 mechanic of the
130th squadron.

Mikhail Nikolayevich Kozin.
Commander, 805th Attack Aviation
Regiment of Berlin, Order of Suvorov.
Died near Chelm in 1944.

Pilots Zubov and Rzhevsky.

Misha Berdashkevich's squadron "Storm the Fascists." Berdashkevich sits
2nd from the left, to the right, Vanya Sukhorukov. Standing left to right:
Misha Zubov, Zhenya Ageyev, and Ivan Pokashevsky

At Ivan Pokashevsky's grave. On the right, Ivan's brother, Vladimir.
On the left is Regiment Commander Pyotr Karev.

Captain Tit Kirilovich Pokrovsky. Ace
pilot with a difficult fate. He died before
my eyes—blown up in the air by a
Fascist rocket—and fell like a
burning torch into the Sea of Azov

My tail gunner Dusya Nazarkina. 1943,
Timashevskaya. Died August 20, 1944 at
the Magnuszew Bridgehead, Warsaw.

Pilots of the squadron after a mission.

Women armorers.

On the left, our regiment commander
Mikhail Nikolayevich Kozin. On the right,
MiG-3 fighter regiment commander,
who covered us Il-2s on the field of battle.
230th Div., 4th Air Force, 1943.

My family: Anna, Vyacheslav, sons Pyotr and Igor, 1952.

Kim Green, Anna Yegorova, and Margarita Ponomaryova in Moscow in 2005.

(Anna Yegorova with her husband and sons.) In my garden in 1955.

Anna with medals.

Anna by an Il-2 at the Monino (*Air Force*) Museum.

The Timofeyevs: Vyacheslav Arsenyevich and Anna Alexandrovna.

The inmates at the Küstrin camp weaved this purse for me from straw. Georgi Fyodorovich brought it to me under his medical gown. You can see the Air Force emblem and my initials on it. I keep it as a symbol of friendship and devotion to the motherland.

Photo origin unknown.

Pavle Trpinac, *(his wife)* Milena Trpinac, Anna Timofeyeva-Yegorova,
Vyacheslav Arsenyevich Timofeyev (*Anna's husband*), and *(son)* Dushan Trpinac.
Yugoslav Professor Pavle Trpinac, awarded the Order of the Patriotic War
for saving Soviet soldiers in the German 3-C Küstrin camp.

Yulia Fyodorovna with daughter Lyuba and son Kolya.

May 24, 1987. My regimental comrades, 4th Air Force—805th Attack Aviation Regiment, 40 years after the Great Patriotic War, at a reunion at VDNKh.

On Victory Day in Red Square, 1994.
The surviving veterans of the 805th Shturmovik Regiment.

Anna mural portrait.

38
Wing to Wing

We finally received our new silver airplanes, equipped with a separate cabin and high-caliber machine gun turret for the tail-gunner. We were delighted with this innovation, which would protect our tails from enemy fighters.

We were desperate to get to the front, but bad weather delayed us. Well into March, the winter still seethed, with no sign of abating. When the last frosts yielded and the sun broke through, we ascended into the sky and steered a course to Saratov.[1] The sky shone clear and blue, a good omen, we felt, as we combat friends flew wing to wing in a mood of celebration.

We caught sight of Saratov in the distance. After such a long flight, we were dangerously low on fuel. Each of us landed in turn, clearing the runway quickly to make way for the next plane. One airplane lingered too long on the runway, and the next pilot, Junior Lieutenant Pivovarov, had to go around. His engine quit, and the airplane abruptly banked and plummeted to the earth, killing Pivovarov. In shock, we all landed our planes anywhere we could find a spot.

I had seen much death in this war, but to lose a comrade here, deep in the rear where we least expected it, was unbearable. I had just shared a table with him at breakfast that morning. As he raked a cascade of fair hair back from his high forehead, he cut his eyes toward me slyly and said to Pilot Sokolov, "Volodya, do you have any idea who Yegorova plans to give her hundred-gram vodka ration to after our combat flight?"

"I'll put it on the landing 'T' so you and the other drunks can find the aerodrome by the scent of alcohol instead of wandering around lost and landing wherever you deem fit," I retorted.

Why had I spoken so rudely to him? I berated myself. Always, this alter-ego of mine was lying in wait inside me, ready to burst out at the worst moments. Maybe I did have a "partisan character" like my brother Vasya said. I tried to keep it in check, but today I had failed disastrously. I couldn't forgive myself.

The second leg of our journey, from Saratov to Borisoglebsk,[2] took less time than the first. As I approached the field, I noticed that my left main gear would not extend. Long after the rest of the regiment had landed, I circled the

---

[1] An industrial and transportation center in southern Russia on the Volga River, 532 miles (856 km) southeast of Moscow.

[2] A town in Voronezh Oblast in southern Russia, around 200 miles east-southeast of Voronezh.

airport, flying different abrupt maneuvers to try to snap the undercarriage down. Nothing worked, and my fuel was getting low. On the radio, I received the order to make a belly landing.

I hated the idea of purposely wrecking the new airplane, so I decided to land with the right main wheel extended. I carefully put the plane into a right-banked slip. The right wheel softly kissed the runway, and I tried with all my strength to hold the bank as long as possible. As the airplane slowed, the left wing dropped, and the airplane ground to a halt, tracing a half-circle around the left wing. It had run out of fuel.

A crowd surrounded the airplane, as I sat under the canopy in a stupor, drenched in sweat. Captain Karev climbed onto the wing. "Come on out of there! I would welcome you with flowers, but unfortunately Borisoglebsk doesn't have a florist's shop. I owe you a bouquet!"

Before the day was done, the mechanics had hammered out the propeller, straightened and painted the left wing, and returned my plane to the flight line with the others.

In the morning we took off for the front. We refueled at Tikhoretskaya and set a course for Timashevskaya,[3] in the Kuban, where we would merge with the 230th Air Attack Division of the Fourth Air Force.

In Timashevskaya we met a woman who had sent all nine of her sons to the front—Alexander, Nikolai, Vasily, Filip, Fyodor, Ivan, Ilya, Pavel, and the youngest, Sasha, who died in 1943 at age 20, posthumously awarded Hero of the Soviet Union. Not one of her sons returned home from the war.

The staff had already moved to the new base and had arranged our accommodations in a nearby school. A few of the other pilots and I stayed in the house of a young woman whose husband was at the front.

Doctor Kozlovsky, as always, arranged a bath house for us. This time, instead of some ruined hut, he set it up in a big van by the river. A long line of eager people formed behind it.

---

[3] A town in the northern Caucasus just inland from the Taman Peninsula and around 45 miles (72 km) north of Krasnodar.

39
The Taman Peninsula

The regiment's new chief of staff, Captain Yashkin, called all flying personnel to the staff dugout to report on the situation at our sector of the front. When he introduced himself, he told us his background. He had come straight to the regiment from the military academy, where he hadn't even had the chance to graduate. He was from a worker's family in Leningrad—his father had worked all his life at the "Red Nailmaker" factory and had died of starvation during the siege.[1] Yashkin ran his fingers nervously through his unruly hair and wiped the tears that streamed from his clear, blue eyes. Fate, I thought, was just like nature—a brilliant, sunny day could suddenly bring storm clouds when you least expected it.

The captain then stood up from the desk, straightened his soldier's blouse and holster as if shaking off painful memories, stood to attention, and began his report.

The first spring thaws of 1943 brought a breath of victory to the Kuban region, he told us. A red banner once again fluttered over the city of Krasnodar.[2] The Red Army had advanced hundreds of kilometers deep into occupied territory, liberating parts of the northern Caucasus, the Rostov region, and a sliver of Ukraine and had gained the approaches to the Sea of Azov. The Hitlerite high command responded by pulling about a thousand aircraft from the 4th Air Force and two hundred bombers out of the Donbass and concentrating them at airfields in the Crimea and Taman to provide air support for their troops. Our commanders responded by transferring three more air corps to the Kuban to join the 4th and 5th Air Forces, the Black Sea Fleet Aviation,[3] and two divisions of long-range aviation already deployed there. An unprecedented concentration of air power was gathered along a relatively

---

[1] On September 8, 1941, German (and Finnish) forces surrounded Leningrad and blockaded the city for 872 days (also called the "900-day siege"), until January 27, 1944. With heating fuel and food supply routes cut off, three million Leningraders had to live on tiny rations. In *The 900 Days: The Siege of Leningrad,* Harrison E. Salisbury cites estimates of Leningrader deaths during the siege ranging from 600,000 to 2 million as a result of exposure, starvation, disease, and enemy shelling.

[2] A city on the Kuban River and the capital of the Krasnodar region, in the Kuban, 956 miles (1,538 km) south-southeast of Moscow.

[3] A naval airborne unit, or naval air force, attached to the Black Sea Fleet

small sector of the front. One of the greatest air battles of the Second World War was about to begin.[4]

"The Germans are still wearing black to mourn their fallen soldiers at Stalingrad," Captain Yashkin went on. "But our army, inspired by the victory at Stalingrad, is pursuing the Fascist hordes all along the front, from Leningrad to the Caucasus. The Hitlerite plot to capture the oil fields of the Caucasus and control the Black Sea coast has failed. The enemy has fled to Rostov-on-Don and Taman. To prevent our troops from breaking through, the enemy has constructed a solid line of defense from Novorossisk to Temruk, with concrete pillboxes, anti-tank and anti-infantry fortifications, dense minefields, and all manner of artillery. They're calling it the 'Blue Line.'"[5]

Taman... I found myself daydreaming, recalling what I'd learned at the Metrostroy school about the Taman Peninsula. Greeks had lived there 1,500 years ago. Since then, Khazars, Genovese, Mongol-Tatars, Turks... I thought of Lermontov's "Taman."[6] I have always loved Lermontov. Before the war, Viktor Kutov gave me a tiny volume of Lermontov's poems. Now, I carried it with me in my journeys at the front.

"In order to threaten their flanks," the captain's voice broke my reverie, "and to keep the German Fleet away from Tsemess Bay,[7] a naval infantry

---

[4] In April–May of 1943, a furious struggle for air superiority raged over the "Kuban bridgehead" in the northern Caucasus which, according to historian Von Hardesty in *Red Phoenix: The Rise of Soviet Air Power*, marked a pivotal moment for Soviet aviation—in which the Soviet Air Force's role shifted from primarily defensive to offensive. The Kuban bridgehead fortifications stretched from the Kuban River delta, southwards across the Taman Peninsula, to Novorossisk on the Black Sea coast. The Germans hoped to defend the approaches to Crimea from the east, while the Soviets sought to oust Germany from the northern Caucasus and, thus, from a rich source of oil. Both sides deployed heavy concentrations of aircraft to the region, and for the first time (according to Hardesty's *Red Phoenix*), Soviet aircraft factories relocated to safety beyond the Ural Mountains began supplying up-to-date aircraft (such as the LaGG-3 and Il-2) in large numbers.

On April 17, 1943, the Germans launched a massive offensive against the beachhead at Myskhako, flying more than 1,000 attack sorties on the first day alone (according to Hardesty).

[5] The line of defense fortified the center of the "Kuban bridgehead," stretching across the Taman Peninsula from Novorossisk, a Black Sea port city in the south of the peninsula to Temruk, a city at the mouth of the Kuban River (which empties into the Sea of Azov) in the north. The Germans nicknamed their position the "Blue Line" because of the abundance of water barriers.

[6] "Taman" is the fourth short story of Mikhail Lermontov's classic 1840 novel *A Hero of Our Time*. It begins, "Taman is the worst little town of all the seacoast towns in Russia."

[7] The bay in the Black Sea on which Novorossisk is situated, more commonly called the Bay of Novorossisk.

landing detachment has landed at the outskirts of Novorossisk, near the fishing village of Stanichka, and occupied the bridgehead, called Malaya Zemlya.[8]

"The Hitlerites attacked the bridgehead with infantry, tank, and artillery forces. Day and night, the shelling never ceased. Not an inch of land was safe from bombs and shelling.

"Our regiment is going to help those naval infantrymen destroy the Fascist scum on the Taman Peninsula…"

---

[8] The name means "Small Land."

40
First Battle

After the briefing, we pilots stepped outside the cramped dugout to await our orders. *Who would fly the first combat mission?* we all wondered. *Maybe it'll be me,* I thought nervously.

All of us were terribly agitated, even the veterans, but we laughed and joked to hide our emotions. Rzhevsky told a joke about a little girl who asked her father to tell her all about locomotives, back when they were still brand new. He talked for a long while, even showing her a drawing, and then asked her, "Well, do you understand it all now?"

"Sure, Papa!" his daughter answered. "Just one thing: where do you harness the horses?"

The pilots all laughed. A short, robust little fellow named Volodya Sokolov skipped up to me and with great effort adopted an expression of utmost seriousness. "Annyuta, let's exchange statures!" he said.

"Yes, let's, Volodya!" I replied. "I love high-heeled shoes, but I'm embarrassed to wear them because of my height. How are we going to do it? And what's in it for me? After all, I'm 170 centimeters, and you're only 160. I stand to lose ten centimeters!"

Suddenly, the chief of staff broke in: "Sokolov, Yegorova, Vakhramov, Tasyets, Rzhevsky, report to the commander!" Our laughter and anecdotes evaporated. We rushed into the dugout.

The commander described the route to us, a rather zigzag, indirect course. "All the better to skirt the enemy's anti-aircraft guns," he explained.

"You must stay close in flight formation and do everything exactly as I do," added Navigator Pyotr Karev, our flight leader. He showed us our route on the chart. I was to be Karev's right wingman.

I can scarcely describe my feelings on the eve of my first combat flight in the Shturmovik. I felt no fear. Instead, a feeling of satisfaction flooded over me. I had no reason to hang my head now. I had been included in the first combat sortie! The only woman among so many men, and *such* men—attack pilots!

Five regiments comprised our 230th Attack Air Division—four attack and one fighter regiment, most separated by many miles. Four LaGG-3s[1] from the

---

[1] The Lavochkin-Gorbunov-Goudkov-3 fighter, named for its designers, was introduced in 1941. Pilots were not impressed with the airplane's lethargic acceleration, erratic handling, and poor maneuverability, and it quickly gained a reputation for

fighters' regiment that shared our aerodrome would escort us on the mission. The more daring fighter pilots didn't relish such assignments. Among themselves they referred to these escort sorties as "nursing" jobs. They would rather be hunting for enemy planes, shooting them down, and going home having "won" a few kills. But whatever their attitude, they saved my life that day.

We sat on alert in our cockpits, awaiting the signal, a green flare. I scanned the instruments and ran my fingers over all the switches and levers, making sure they were in their proper positions. Sergeant Rimsky, my mechanic, bustled about the airplane, polishing and re-polishing the sparkling-clean canopy glass, adjusting a parachute strap on my shoulder, and asking repeatedly, "How else can I help you?"

"Thanks, my friend. I just need to be alone for a few minutes to collect my thoughts," I told him gratefully, glancing ahead and to my left at Karev's airplane. The flight leader seemed quite calm. He rested his hands outside, on the edge of the cockpit, and sang to himself. *Isn't he the least bit worried about this mission?* I wondered. But the hissing of the green flare cut short my ruminations. It arced over the field, its glow gradually dying out as it fell. It was time! We took off and turned toward Malaya Zemlya.

Terrified of lagging behind the formation, I did my best to stick tightly to Karev. When he rocked the plane back and forth, I imitated his maneuvers. When he dove toward the ground, I followed. When he fired, I fired. I dropped my bombs the moment I saw his bombs falling. Still, I lost the formation after the fourth target run—not just lagged behind them, but lost them altogether. What the devil was I to do? I was flying alone among an unbroken curtain of exploding missiles. I searched desperately for the formation. I made a U-turn toward our territory over the settlement of Myskhako.[2]

Dozens of aircraft, ours and the enemy's, dotted the sky over Tsemess Bay. Airplanes plummeted into the sea. Pilots bailed out and drifted helplessly down toward the water while enemy launches sped from the opposite shore toward them. I was seeing my first real battle.

To a combat rookie, it was impossible to make sense of the chaos over the Taman Peninsula. Two fighters dove like hawks toward me. At first, I

---

dangerously lousy performance. Heavy losses, in addition to the highly-polished plastic-impregnated-wood surface—evocative of a shiny casket—prompted pilots to nickname the airplane "*Lakirovanny Garantirovanny Grob*" (based on its abbreviation), meaning "Guaranteed Lacquered Coffin." The underpowered LaGG-3 was a poor match for the Messerschmidt Bf 109, but its airframe could take a pounding, so it was refitted with a new radial engine and upgraded to the more successful Lavochkin La-5.

[2] In February 1943, a Soviet seaborne team landed at Myskhako and occupied a small beachhead there, southwest of the German-held Black Sea port of Novorossisk, to threaten the right flank of the Kuban bridgehead (as described in the previous chapter). The Soviets called the nineteen-square-mile bridgehead "Malaya Zemlya."

thought they were our *Yaks*, until I saw the tracer rounds flashing to my right. When the airplanes rounded back toward me for another attack, I noticed the white crosses on their fuselages. They attacked brazenly from all sides, as if I were no threat whatsoever, but to no avail.

The Shturmovik was slower than the Messerschmitts, and at one point, the enemy fighters raced ahead of me, practically right into my sights. I pressed all the triggers simultaneously, but nothing happened. I had emptied all my ammunition over the target.

Our fighters rescued me just in time. They drove the Fascist vultures away and even shot one of them down. I made it back to the aerodrome in one piece.

Captain Karev reproached me harshly for lagging behind the formation. I couldn't have agreed more, and I humbly acknowledged his criticisms.

On that flight pilots Vakhramov and Sokolov were shot down by anti-aircraft guns near the target. After a few days, they made their way back to us. One of our launches retrieved Vakhramov and his tail-gunner from the sea. Sokolov had managed to steer his machine toward our territory and land it on the bank of the Kuban River.

41
Tit Kirilovich

I learned to follow the flight leader as he maneuvered, skirting the treetops or ramming the throttle in to accelerate and climb with him. I learned to strafe tanks, a risky endeavor indeed. Tank cannons fired very accurately, and impulsive pilots paid for their miscalculations with their lives.

So many combat missions... I recall the gray strip of the Kuban River flashing beneath us, a tumult of mountains peeking through a patchy low overcast. I remember stalking our target, unseen, from the sea, the blue expanse of water shining through the dispersing fog. I can still see the anti-aircraft gunfire flickering far below, the tiny clouds of explosions leaping in a wild dance around the plane as we crossed the front line.

I will never forget the feeling a pilot has seconds before the attack begins, one of utmost tension and concentration. In that moment nothing exists for him except the flight leader and the target.

Everyone was exhausted from constant combat flights without respite. Our ranks were thinning. The weather often turned wretched, pinning us close to the ground so that everything that could fire took shots at us. The machines came back literally riddled. The mechanics could barely patch them up.

We flew missions over the Chushka Spit and the Blue Line. We attacked enemy ships in the Black Sea and raided their aerodromes, railroad junctions, and rear echelons of troops and equipment. We prepared diligently for every mission.

One day, while we were waiting for the order to take off, we lay "sunwise" in a circle, head to head, telling funny stories in turn. Anyone who told a joke that didn't make us laugh would get a thump on the forehead. The game eased our frayed nerves a bit, but it didn't still our hunger pangs. Dinner was late, and everyone kept casting greedy glances at the road to the Cossack village. The women who prepared food for us would be bringing food from that direction any minute.

"It's coming, it's coming!" Vasya Kosterov, a Muscovite with a strapping *bogatyr*'s physique, shouted joyfully. But just at that moment, the staff messenger ran toward us and cried, "Combat crews, to the regimental commander!" We put dinner out of our minds and rushed to the dugout.

A hatless and medal-studded Lieutenant Colonel Kozin stood by his desk, unhurriedly expounding upon the details of our mission. Not one of his wavy, fair hairs strayed out of place, as if he were fresh from the barber shop.

A light breeze from the window wafted across him, carrying a strong aroma of cologne. His pipe rested in an ashtray made from a flattened shell-case.

"A dense concentration of enemy echelons, comprised of personnel and equipment, has convened at the Salyn railway station on the Kerch Peninsula," he pronounced. "Your assignment is to bomb and strafe these echelons so that the enemy cannot ferry them across the Kerch Strait to Taman. Pilot Usov will be the flight leader. Let us think through this and choose our route together. I think it might be best to fly across the Sea of Azov just above the water, then unexpectedly pop up over the station for the initial strike..."

The flare soared over the airfield. We taxied to the start point and took off in turn. Six LaGG-3 fighters took off right after us. We began letting down at the approaches to the Sea of Azov, but the Germans' coastal defenses opened intense anti-aircraft artillery against us. In horror, I watched Captain Pokrovsky's airplane burst into flames and plummet into the sea like a blazing torch.

Our formation seemed to lose momentum for a fraction of a second. Then the remaining airplanes quietly drew up behind the flight leader, filling the empty space, and we pressed on toward the target.

Oh, God! Why did you take him? The old prayer from my childhood suddenly came flooding back to me.

Tit Kirilovich Pokrovsky... When he came to our regiment, he was already a veteran combat pilot with three Orders of the Red Banner—one from Lake Khasan,[1] one from the Finnish War, and one from the early days of the Great Patriotic War. "Such a great pilot, and only a flight group commander?" some of the pilots grumbled.

Born in 1910, Kirilich (as we called him) was older than all of us, and his funny stories about his flying adventures always had us laughing. We worshipped him. But he was a reserved fellow and often kept to himself. Once, after dinner, we organized a dance at the aerodrome. Pokrovsky sat by himself, looking sad and lonely, so I invited him to waltz with me.

"Thanks, Yegorova, but let's go for a walk instead," he said. It was a lovely, warm evening, and the moon shone brightly. We strolled through the village, and he told me about what had happened to him at the beginning of the war.

By the end of 1941, he had been shot down for the ninth time. His regiment had no airplanes left, and only five or six pilots had survived. They were transferred to a training regiment, which also had no airplanes.

Tit Kirilovich tried everything to get back to the front. He stated his case to the regimental commissar, heatedly describing his and other pilots' grow-

---

[1] A lake in the Russian Far East, near the border with China and North Korea. She is referring to a twelve-day border conflict (called the "Changkufeng incident" in Chinese, after a disputed hill occupied by the Soviets) in July–August 1938 between the Soviet Union and Japanese troops occupying Manchuria.

ing desperation. But as Pokrovsky grew increasingly indignant, the commissar called in the "Special Section" to settle the issue.

The "Osobist"[2] conducted the discussion that followed as if it were some kind of NKVD interrogation, complete with the requisite rudeness and arrogance, all the while making deliberate, detailed notes. Pokrovsky lost his temper, calling the Osobist a good-for-nothing idler, always sniffing around the aerodrome for some "easy bait" to inform on. "You earn your bread cowering far away from the front, accusing honest people of crimes!" the pilot fumed. The Osobist placed the interrogation report into his folder without asking for Pokrovsky's signature, buckled the folder closed, and left.

Soon Pokrovsky was arrested and sent before a military tribunal on the most malicious trumped-up charges. For "evading the front" and "anti-Soviet propaganda," he was sentenced to execution by firing squad.

The pilots in his regiment were outraged. They convinced a young telegraph operator to send an urgent cable to Mikhail Ivanovich Kalinin himself. Apparently the telegram made it because Pokrovsky was rehabilitated, his rank, Party membership, and awards restored. With that horror behind him, Pokrovsky was assigned to our 805th Attack Aviation Regiment. And now, in a momentary burst of flames, we had lost a fearless pilot and a brave and honest man forever.

After Pokrovsky went down, we lost our fighter cover somewhere in the dogfight that was unfolding above us. After a while we crossed the coastline, emerging over the enemy airfield Bagerovo instead of the Salyn railway station. Around thirty twin-engine bombers painted with white crosses were lining up on the ramp for refueling. Several Messerschmitts were already making their takeoff run. Without hesitating, our flight leader Pavel Usov opened fire on them. "Attack those rats!" Pasha shouted to us across the airwaves.

We fell on the Fritzes with all our Shturmoviks' firepower. Usov set two Messers on fire before they could take off, and we blazed away at the line of bombers on the ramp. After thoroughly combing the aerodrome, we climbed out and headed toward Salyn Station. We emptied our bomb payloads on the echelons and turned back across the Kerch Strait toward home. It was a successful mission, but it had cost us five flight crews.

The mechanics silently gathered the covers to the airplanes that hadn't returned, rolling them up like shrouds. My eyes still burned with images of my combat friends plummeting toward the sea and earth. I crawled out of the cockpit and, without taking off my parachute and helmet-headset, jumped

---

[2] The NKVD's "Special Section" or *Osoby otdel* was formed as an arm of the Cheka shortly after the Revolution to supervise the military. During WWII, the OO's task was to root out spies, collaborators, and deserters. The term *Osobist* stems from **Osoby** and basically means "special agent."

down and ran from the parking area. Unable to restrain myself any longer, I collapsed onto the ground and sobbed violently.

"Yegorova, you must be exhausted," came the regimental commander's voice from above me. "Rest a little, pull yourself together. I won't assign you to the next combat mission."

"No, no! I'll fly!" I protested. "Please don't ever make exceptions for me. It's insulting!"

Already, my airplane was being refueled, the bombs hung, the machine guns, rockets, and cannons loaded. I saw the green flare launch into the air, and I once again hurried to the cockpit, drying my tear-stained face as I ran.

42
Pyotr Karev

Pyotr Timofeyevich Karev, a Muscovite, was the best flight leader in the regiment. The young pilots idolized him. I always felt safe when he led a mission. He had an uncanny ability to cheat death, despite his recklessness. Right before an attack, he'd tell a joke or make a funny comment, and I would almost forget that we were in the middle of our third or fourth bombing run over the target.

He was resourceful as well as audacious. On one occasion, a bomb fell off one of our aircraft on the takeoff run. The pilot and tail-gunner just managed to escape and flatten themselves to the ground before the bomb exploded. But the plane still carried five 100-kilogram bombs. Our takeoff clearance was cancelled.

Still, we had a mission to fly. So Karev gave the order to turn the start position around by thirty degrees. The planes began taking off, one by one, passing quite close to the burning airplane loaded with bombs, shells, and missiles. We tensed for the explosion as we passed, but it didn't happen until the last plane, piloted by Karev, was in the air.

One night Commander Karev drank 300 grams of vodka before dinner. Each pilot was rationed a hundred grams of vodka per combat flight. So Karev figured, since he had just flown three missions in a row that day, he'd enjoy his three vodka rations in a row as well. Afterward, he made a beeline to the dugout of the anti-aircraft gunners who protected the airfield. He seemed determined to straighten them out.

"What's wrong with you guys?" he slurred. "You're flinging too many shells into space without hitting anything during these 'Lapot' raids![1] I'll prove it. I'm going to take off in the 'Il,' and you shoot at me. I'll shoot back at you, and we'll see who wins."

---

[1] Soviet soldiers called the Luftwaffe's Junkers 87 *"Lapot"* (or "Bast shoe," a roughly-woven sandal made of tree bark and worn by Russian peasants) because of its fixed gear. The Ju-87, or *"Stuka,"* was a *"Sturzkampfflugzeug,"* or dive bomber, with a notorious wailing siren (affixed to some planes). It made its service debut in the Condor Legion during the Spanish Civil War and terrorized ground armor extremely effectively in Poland, Western Europe, Greece, and the Soviet Union. But the Battle of Britain revealed its vulnerability, as RAF fighters found the sluggish airplane easy to shoot down. As a result, the Focke-Wulf FW 190 fighter began to replace the Ju 87 as a primary ground support fighter bomber in late 1943.

Although Karev didn't get to implement his experiment, not one witness to that dispute doubted that he would have emerged victoriously. We considered him infallible.

We loved him. He was both straightforward and affable, and he wasn't afraid to get his hands dirty. He wouldn't think twice about heaving a heavy bomb onto his shoulder and hauling it to the aircraft. The girls who armed the airplanes doted on their volunteer helper and vied with one another to wash his collar liner or his handkerchief. Pyotr always declined, thanking them and smiling as he sang, "So many lovely girls, so many tender names..."

Quick with a funny anecdote, Captain Karev was also fearless in battle and was frequently selected for the most dangerous missions. As regimental navigator, he taught us tactics: how to attack a railroad echelon or a tank column, how to bomb bridges and ferries, and how to zigzag along the course. We discussed how to correct for surface winds when bombing or strafing.

The regiment adopted his innovative method of maneuvering inside the flight group. Previously, we'd been ordered to remain rigidly in formation, regardless of circumstances. But Karev insisted that we maneuver inside the formation within certain limits—we could fly higher or lower than the flight leader and even change the distance between planes if need be. This tactic sharpened our awareness and made it more difficult for enemy fighters and anti-aircraft guns to take aim at us.

On one mission, only two crews out of six made it back home, Captain Karev's and mine. I was his wingman. When we finished our attack and climbed out over the water, we spotted what looked like gigantic white mushrooms floating on the sea—the parachutes of our downed pilots. I had two bombs left, but a couple of Messers still hung in the sky behind us, ready to finish us off. Just then I noticed a loaded barge, and the temptation proved too great. I doubled back right in front of the Messers and pulled the emergency bomb release lever. The aircraft jerked and rocked uncontrollably, as I fixed my eyes on the barge.

How are you feeling now? I thought gleefully. *Ha! Take that!* The barge listed steeply and slid into the deep. Suddenly, a horrible doubt stabbed me like a needle prick to the heart. Whose barge was it? I hadn't thought to look at its identification markings. Granted, it had sailed from the enemy-occupied Kerch shore, but such "evidence" is the devil's favorite kind of joke...

When I reported on my mission to the commander, I didn't mention a word about the barge. But the mystery was solved when my flight leader and the fighters radioed that an enemy transport had been destroyed. Our division commander, General Semyon Getman, pinned a silver medal that said "For Bravery" on my soldier's blouse, next to my Order of the Red Banner.

43
The Blue Line

One day near the end of May 1943, Regimental Commander Kozin gathered all the flying personnel at the airfield. "Comrade Pilots!" he said excitedly. "All those who are prepared to fulfill a special mission for the Northern Caucasus Front Command, step forward!"

Everyone took a step in unison.

"No, that won't work!" he smiled. "It looks like I'll have to choose. Major Kerov, take three steps forward."

Pavel Kerov was commander of the First Squadron and a veteran attack pilot. We younger pilots admired his enviable calm. He looked more like a schoolteacher than a fearless *shturmovik*.[1] He never raised his voice at us if we did something wrong. He would just look sadly at us with his languid, gray eyes, shake his head, and walk away, swaying like a sailor, leaving his subordinate to contemplate the ill-conceived deed.

Once, when our regiment had only six functioning planes, Kerov led an impossible attack on a heavily-defended Don River ferry, surprising the enemy from their rear. He brought back the whole group safely, actually supporting one riddled aircraft's wing with his own wing, like a wounded friend's arm draped across his shoulder.

Pavel Kerov stepped forward.

"Sukhorukov, Pashkov, Frolov...," the commander called, glancing down the row. "Yegorova," I heard my name. "Strakhov, Tishenko, Grudnyak, Sokolov, Zinoviev, Podynenogin..."

All of us took three steps forward.

The regimental commander selected nineteen pilots, including three squadron commanders, all of the flight group commanders, and any senior pilots with combat experience. General I. E. Petrov, commander of the North Caucasus Front, and General K. A. Vershinin, 4th Air Force commander, addressed us soon thereafter.

"Your task, Comrades, may seem simple, but it will actually be quite difficult to implement," General Petrov pronounced, adjusting his pince-nez and stammering slightly. "Our troops are poised to break through the Fascist defenses along the Blue Line. But before they do, we need to camouflage the advancing forces with a smoke screen. That is where you come in."

---

[1] The term refers both to the Il-2 attack plane and its pilot.

Just then, the general looked right at me. I felt my shoulders clench, as if to buffer the question I knew was coming: "What is a woman doing here?" But General Petrov said nothing, and his gaze slid to some other pilots who were standing near the mock-up of the Blue Line. I sighed with relief.

The general explained that we had to create the smoke screen at a very precise moment so that it would blind the enemy just as our infantry was seizing the trenches along the main line of the Fascist defense.

General Vershinin then told us how we were to carry out the plan. We would fly without bombs, missiles, or machine gun ammunition. There would be no turret guns or tail-gunners in the rear cabin. We were to fly right above ground level, the lower the better. Instead of bombs, balloons full of smoke-producing gas would hang from our bomb racks. Once the gas mixed with air, the smoke screens would form.

"The most difficult aspect of this flight is that you must not under any circumstances maneuver," said General Vershinin, bending over the map. "That's seven kilometers of straight flight at extremely low altitude. Is it clear why you mustn't maneuver?"

"Because the smoke screen will be broken otherwise," one of the pilots offered.

"And a broken smoke screen means that the attack will stall," remarked Petrov, stroking his red mustache. "That's why the screen has to be solid, unbroken, and straight as a ruler, so that not a single searchlight beam can penetrate it."

"This is how you will do it," Vershinin continued. "As soon as you see smoke appear from the plane in front of you, count three seconds and pull the triggers. Do not maneuver. You will be flying under fire, over fire, and through fire. I wish you all a good day's work and a safe return home."

As General Vershinin bade us farewell, he added, "If anyone has changed his mind, don't be afraid to speak up. It's your right to refuse this mission. We need for the pilots flying this assignment to have every confidence that they will succeed and return to the aerodrome."

No one said a word.

On the morning of May 26, the eastern horizon barely blushed with traces of pink when we loaded onto a military truck for the airfield. The always happy and sociable Lieutenant Colonel Mikhail Nikolayevich Kozin was gloomier than a thunderhead, perhaps because he hadn't been included in the mission or maybe because he was worried we might not survive.

And the pilots? What was their mood before such an important mission?

By then I had gotten to know them all quite well. I watched my combat friends, sitting in front of me with their spines pressed against the bench seat. They were recklessly bold and gallant in battle, and so ordinary, even a little ridiculous with their feet on the earth. They all somehow reminded me of my brothers.

Grisha Rzhevsky. He was playing with a kitten, his new "talisman", which was wriggling wildly inside his new fur-lined leather jacket. My brother Yegor also loved animals. Mama would always find newborn kittens and puppies hidden under Yegor's bed or the kitchen table along with plates of milk. Whenever they started mewing or yapping, Mama would get angry and threaten to punish Yegor, but she could never bring herself to follow through. Yegor grew up, joined the army, and went to war. He did not return.

Kolya Pakhomov. He sang his favorite song quietly to himself:

Come to the fence, young Cossack girl,
Get me ready for the march before sunrise…

Tolya Bugrov. He was excitedly telling Valentin Vakhramov something, and both of them were hanging onto each other and giggling like little boys, as if both of them weren't going to be cast headlong into a firestorm in a few minutes.

Misha Berdashkevich's blue eyes were twinkling as if he were amused about something. His handsome face was disfigured by so many burn scars. Could he be reminiscing about the time he escaped from the hospital and returned to the regiment wearing only a hospital gown?

Tasyets, a Greek by nationality, sat lost in thought. He was probably figuring out how to make a better target approach or how to draw Fascist fighters off the attack. He was an excellent theoretician.

Semyon Andryanov, commander of our Third Squadron. He had his arm around his colleague, Boris Strakhov, commander of the Second Squadron. They stared silently into the expanse of the Kuban steppe, just awakening after a long winter. Both of the twenty-year-old commanders were trying their best to look mature, assuming an air of utter sternness. Andryanov had even gotten himself a pipe, and he kept it between his lips all the time. It wiggled up and down at the corner of his lips when he talked. His eyes shone with such youthful ardor that it almost seemed a shower of sparks might burst out of them.

Filip Pashkov, Andryanov's deputy. He was such a gentleman. Even now, he was holding onto me to cushion me from the truck's jolting as we rattled over potholes on the way to the airplanes. He was telling me about his hometown of Penza, about his mother and sisters, and about his father, who was injured in the Imperialist War and died when Filip was three years old.

"When the war is over, let's go to Penza!" he said. "I'll show you everything, *stanishnitsa*.[2] The writers Radishchev and Belinsky have house-museums there, and of course Lermontov's Tarkhany estate. You know Alexander Ivanovich Kuprin. He's one of ours, too—from the village of Narovchat, near Penza."

---

[2] The nickname basically means "female dweller of a *stanitsa*," or Cossack village

For some reason, Pashkov never called me by my first or last name, my rank, or even my title. It was always "*Stanishnitsa*, how are you?…"

"And what *forrrrr*-ests we have! So many *muuuush*-rooms! *Berrrrrr*-ies!" he cried in a singsong voice, rocking back and forth. He was obviously embellishing a bit, as inveterate mushroom hunters are wont to do. "There are such marvelous meadows in our forests. You can practically mow down the mushrooms with a scythe! And Mama is such an excellent cook! You'll come, won't you?"

One day Pashkov failed to return from a combat mission. We thought he had been killed. Ahh, the war… amid so much grief, there were also miracles. After five days, our Filip made it back to the regiment with his tail-gunner, both unshaven, dirty, with their clothing in tatters, but happy.

"I heard that you cried bitterly over me, Anna!" Filip said later, calling me for the first time by my given name. "Thank you! But it would be better if you believed I was alive. You should always believe I will come home."

In the end, Pashkov didn't come home. He died somewhere north of Novorossisk. I waited and waited for him, trying to believe he would survive, as I promised I would do. But the sky over the aerodrome remained empty and silent. After he died, I wrote to his mother and sister in Penza, where he'd so often invited me to visit him after the war.

On this day, however, we were all still alive and clattering toward the aerodrome. Suddenly, a loud banging interrupted my reverie. Some of the pilots were pounding on the truck's cabin, yelling at the driver, "Stop! Stop! Where are you going?"

The driver braked, and the pilots shouted, "Turn around, quick!"

Apparently, a cat had crossed the road on the way to the airfield—a bad omen.

Another time, the men made the driver stop when they spotted a woman carrying a yoke laden with empty buckets.[3] I wouldn't say we pilots were superstitious exactly, but it never hurt to take precautions, we figured.

Amid all this, Doctor Kozlovsky was trying to persuade one of the pilots to let him measure his blood pressure before the flight. "Doctor, take my kitten's blood pressure instead! He's very restless and naughty today," said Rzhevsky, reining in the doctor, to laughter all around.

"Perhaps you've forgotten, Grisha, that last night you fed him five pork chops?" Doctor Kozlovsky retorted.

The jokes flew back and forth. We needed them, needed the laughter. To an outsider, we might well have seemed like a truckload of drunken idiots, but we were quite sober.

At last, we reached the aerodrome. As always, the mechanics, armament specialists, and instrument technicians bustled about the planes, preparing

---

[3] An old superstition in Russia has it that seeing a woman with an empty bucket is bad luck.

them for combat. They never failed us, there under the open sky, in any weather.

Tyutyunnik, the mechanic of my Il-2, rushed to report to me that the aircraft was ready. Wiping off his work-hardened hands, he helped me into my parachute and adjusted something in the cockpit. Once we got the engine turning, he thrust a pickled apple into my palm. How he got it, I'll never know. He shouted into my ear, "If your mouth gets dry, bite into this!" and rolled off the wing like a marble, blown off by the propeller slipstream.

I turned on the radio. I heard our flight leader, Major Kerov's, voice in my earphones giving me a clearance to taxi. In front of me, Lieutenant Pavel Usov's Shturmovik taxied practically wing-to-wing with Ivan Stepochkin's.

The two were inseparable, even though they were nothing alike. Usov was a short and stocky Russian, with plump cheeks that seemed puffed up from so much laughing and teasing. He even walked with a jaunty, dancing gait. Stepochkin was tall and handsome, with black eyes and curly hair, like a gypsy. He was quiet and pensive.

One day, the two friends were strolling together in Timashevskaya and decided to peer into the village church. The priest was delivering a sermon about the benefits of fasting. A skeptical Usov began vigorously debating the priest, and Stepochkin, try as he might, could not extract his friend. Apparently, the priest's argument convinced Usov in the end. When they left the church, he declared decisively, "I am going to fast!"

"In that case, I will raise the issue of Communist Usov's expulsion from the All-Union Communist Party of Bolsheviks, on the grounds of religious belief," Stepochkin replied and crossed to the other side of the street.

At dinner that night, Pavel Usov, in his usual humorous way, expounded upon the benefits of fasting. It was better not to overeat after the Easter fast, as believers used to do, he was saying. "Better to eat leaner fast day foods to give the stomach a break," he asserted enthusiastically.

"Then why did you order that second helping of steak, Pasha?" someone asked. A fighter pilot named Volodya Istrashkin stuck a half-liter jar of homemade grape wine on the table and said, "Here you are, my friend, to help you digest your food better. I believe I heard the priest say he was permitting wine and ale today!"

Vanya Sukhorukov, from the town of Ivanovo. On the ground, he was as quiet as a blushing girl, but in the air, he was unrecognizable! He was awarded the Hero of the Soviet Union for leading a successful attack in the Caucasus in November of 1942. I was to fly a two-plane formation with him on that mission.

And suddenly, we were at the airfield, climbing into our planes. Major Kerov was the first to take off. We quickly caught up to him and settled into formation. I glanced back toward the east, where a glorious rising sun unfolded its vivid rays across the sky. To the west, along our route, the sky was dark, and smoke and fog blanketed the earth like a shroud.

The Blue Line greeted us with four layers of long-range artillery fire. Exploding shells blocked our way like a wall. Our group broke through this cover fire at minimal altitude and pressed on to the village of Kievskaya. Tracers cut through the sky. Oerlikon[4] shells painted the morning with their red globules. Metal splinters pelted the airplane's defensive armor. Enemy mortars and high-caliber machine guns pounded us.

We were flying through utter hell. But we had to fly perfectly straight and level. The sea was raging with fire, and I found myself unconsciously pressing my back against the seat. The seconds dragged on endlessly. All I wanted was to close my eyes and shut out the inferno all around me.

Suddenly, I saw smoke erupting out of the plane in front of me. "Twenty-one, twenty-two, twenty-three," I counted three seconds — three long, slow seconds! Finally, I pulled the triggers. What would be, would be. The pilot in front of me did the same — as instructed, we flew arrow-straight, not diverting a centimeter from our course or altitude. I desperately wanted to see if our plan had worked, but I could not so much as bank to get a look.

Finally, Kerov and all our Shturmoviks turned right and climbed out, back toward the east. We returned to the airfield escorted by our fighters. Over the radio we heard Kerov's voice, deep and calm, like his character. "Thank you, Little Brothers! You've done a great job!" he told the fighter pilots.

I felt a surge of joy and relief. All nineteen of us had made it home. We heard Kerov again in our earphones. "Attention, Humpbacks!"

"Humpbacks" meant us. Our Shturmoviks got that nickname because of how the cabin perched, like a hump, atop the fuselage. I listened intently.

"For successful completion of the mission and for the courage displayed in laying the smoke screen, all of you will receive an Order of the Red Banner," came Kerov's voice through the ether.

Silence. The engine of my "Ilyushin" steadily rotated, carrying me to the airfield. Among us we had an agreement that the most severely damaged aircraft landed first. But I took my turn, unaware the plane had been hit.

I taxied to the ramp and shut down, only then letting myself succumb to mortal exhaustion. Mechanics, technicians, armorers, and pilots who had stayed behind swarmed around the cockpit like bees. "Are you wounded, Comrade Lieutenant?" a young woman armorer named Dusya Nazarkina shouted. "You've got blood on your face!"

"No," I said. "My lips are cracked and bleeding, that's all."

A mechanic pointed to the yawning hole in my left wing. "It's a good thing that shell didn't explode. You'd be scattered all over the place," he said.

---

[4] Oerlikon is a suburb of Zurich, Switzerland known for producing anti-aircraft guns. Since 1936, the Zurich-based company now called Oerlikon Contraves (derived from the latin *contra aves*, or "against birds"), under various names and ownership, has been a leading developer of anti-aircraft weaponry.

"Look, your elevator trim tab's hit, too." I had flown all the way back without noticing my "Ilyusha" was wounded.

The regiment assembled at the aerodrome under our regimental combat banner. We who had flown the mission stood a little apart from the rest. General Vershinin, the 4th Air Force Commander, thanked us and pinned an Order of the Red Banner on each of our soldier's blouses.

That night we learned that our troops had broken through the cursed Blue Line! When we deployed the mixture, a white wall of smoke had instantly grown and swelled all along the enemy's defensive line. It had done its job, enveloping the enemy's pockets of resistance, and blinding their infantry. Unable to see what was happening in front of them, the Hitlerites deserted their forward positions in panic. Our troops broke into the first trench and managed to advance two kilometers beyond.

Learning of their success felt as good as any award.

44
A "Dame" on a Ship

Bitter fighting raged on in the Taman Peninsula. The regiment settled into a routine, usually flying several combat sorties a day.

Most of our missions took us over the roiling waters of the Sea of Azov and the Black Sea. I've been afraid of water since childhood—I never learned to swim well. Flying over open water, I would listen with heightened awareness to the engine. It never sounded quite right over the sea. I hoped my seat belt would save me in the event of a water landing, but the other pilots didn't have much faith in it. What if it didn't release quickly enough? My friends always laughed at me when I buckled myself in, but the harness gave me some peace of mind.

The sea swallowed Boris Strakhov, a fair-haired fellow from Gorky, the regimental favorite. He went down over the Chushka Spit, as flight leader on a mission to bomb a railroad ferry. The pilots watched as four Focke-Wulfs[1] fell upon his wounded plane like jackals. It banked steeply and plunged into the deep.

The next day, sailors brought us his body, which had washed up on the shore near Anapa.

In wartime, we rarely buried our pilots because they usually perished and disappeared in combat zones. But we lay Strakhov to rest with full military honors. The regiment was inconsolable.

I cried bitterly over Borya's casket. I could not believe that he was gone. I kept imagining that he would sit up, look at me with his gray-green eyes, twirl an imaginary mustache, and ask me, "Why are they drafting girls into the war?" With these words, he would offer me a wildflower he'd picked by the revetments,[2] just like he always did.

His best friend Ivan Sukhorov could scarcely overcome his sorrow. Vanya grew thin and gaunt, his cheeks hollow. He spent all his spare time sitting by Boris's grave.

---

[1] The Focke-Wulf Fw 190 fighter-bomber entered the war in September 1941, engaging the RAF in the skies over France and the English Channel and outperforming the British Spitfire Mk V. By autumn 1943, it had supplanted the Junkers Ju 87 as the main attack aircraft on the Eastern Front. Fast and light, the versatile aircraft also rivaled the Bf 109 as a fighter, but came along too late to replace it.

[2] A type of fortification built on a slope, (or along cliffs or trenches) to protect a shoreline from erosion or to absorb the energy of incoming artillery or stored explosives.

I thought of Ivan and Boris in happier times. Ivan had once borrowed my new English wool greatcoat for a trip to visit his girlfriend to ask her to marry him. But when he returned to the regiment, he avoided me. I cornered Boris to ask what was wrong with his friend.

"You see, the question is very delicate," he said. "You won't tell anyone, will you?"

Ivan had arrived home to find that his girl had run off to the front. There was no wedding. So his hometown friends had given him a bottle of home-made whiskey to share with his combat-pilot comrades. He wrapped it in my tailored greatcoat and cradled it like a baby all the way back to the regiment. On the last leg of the journey, in a truck from Krasnodar to the aerodrome, the driver hit a bump that tossed everyone out of the truck. They all survived, but the bottle shattered. When Ivan got home, he washed the coat and hung it on one of the village fences to dry, hoping the alcoholic odor would evaporate. "As soon as it dries, he will return it to you," Boris confided seriously.

I burst out laughing. I pictured Ivan flying out of the truck, embracing the swaddled bottle as if it were his new bride. "I'll ask the commander for a new greatcoat. From now on, this one belongs to Ivan," I told Boris. "Let it remind him of his hometown friends' gift."

That's how life was at the front. Rare moments of youthful élan alternated with grief and loss, combat flights and attacks.

I was summoned to Regimental Headquarters and ordered to lead a formation of four Shturmoviks, again to the Chushka Spit. We were to attack the enemy's infantry and equipment reinforcements that had just ferried across the Kerch Strait. I demurred, meekly asking Kozin, the regimental commander, to let me fly as regular flight crew instead.

"And who exactly is going to lead the formation, in your opinion?" Mikhail Nikolayevich demanded, staring at me point blank. "All we have left are a bunch of young greenhorns. Usov, Stepochkin, Zinoviev, Tasyets, Pashkov, Balyabin, Mkrtumov—they're all dead. Bugrov is burned all over. Tryokin is terribly wounded. So who do *you* think should lead flight missions?"

He turned away from me, wiping his eyes with his gloves. I briskly repeated the order and hurried out of the dugout.

"Only the condemned are sent to fly to a target like that in such horrible weather," Pilot Zubov grumbled when he heard about the mission. My nerves betrayed me. Instead of explaining the mission to the crew to calm them down a bit, I shouted orders in a harsh, irritable tone. "Everyone to the planes! Go!" I barked.

After takeoff, my wingmen took their positions in the formation. The four LaGG-3 fighters joined us from their base closer to the front.

It was impossible to fly straight through the labyrinth of anti-aircraft batteries to the Chushka Spit. I decided to make a deep attack run from over the Sea of Azov. The low overcast worked in our favor.

The minutes over open water and wetlands ticked by impossibly slowly. I knew well that any engine or airframe malfunction meant aircraft and crew would vanish without a trace. I glimpsed the sandy banks of the Chushka Spit through occasional windows in the overcast.

Death swirled all around us—in the form of a Focke-Wulf, diving out of the clouds, or from the earth, as anti-aircraft shells or stray bullets.

On the approach to the target, we fell under fierce anti-aircraft fire. I glanced back and saw that my wingmen remained in their positions. I remembered what Squadron Commander Andryanov always said: "You have to outsmart the anti-aircraft guns."

I prepared to attack, veering the plane back and forth, changing altitude and speed. My wingmen did the same. We raced through the first belt of enemy defenses, then the second. There was the target! The Chushka Spit stretched for eighteen kilometers, like an unfinished bridge across the Kerch Strait. The long, narrow strip, washed by two seas, swarmed with Fascist rats. So many men, tanks, weapons, and trucks littered the land that we could hardly see the sand beneath.

We dove, dropped bombs, fired guns and cannons. We soared out over the Hitlerites' heads, climbed out, and dove to strafe them again. I could make out burning trucks, an explosion, fleeing infantry, and tanks crawling every which way, crushing their own soldiers. *Take that, you swine, for all our grief!*

I was running out of ammunition. I turned the plane toward home, looking around to see that everyone was with me. A chill ran down my spine. My face flushed hot, and my mouth went dry. Where was Zubov's plane? How could I have lost him? Was he shot down?

Only three crews remained, plus the four umbrella fighters in a nearby dogfight. I flew home, watching the ground intently. I hoped I might catch sight of Misha Zubov's plane. How on earth had it happened? Why had I yelled at him before the mission?

We had just crossed the front line when I spotted a Shturmovik lying on a low knoll near the wetlands. The tail number said "23." It was Zubov! He and his tail-gunner had climbed out of the cabin and were waving at us and shooting flares from atop the wings. I made a steep bank over them and waggled the wings as if to say, "I see you. Wait here for me," and flew away.

At the regiment, I reported to the commander on the mission and immediately took off in a Po-2 to collect Zubov and his tail-gunner.

Later, after Misha and I had flown many missions together, he confessed to me: "You know, Anna Alexandrovna, I wasn't afraid of the bad weather and the Chushka Spit that day. I was afraid of you. I told myself, 'Mikhail, no good luck can come of a dame on a ship.' But when you made that turn over us and then came back to get us in the Po-2, I forgot my doubts about you and 'dames' in general. Please forgive me."

45
My Tail-Gunner

Division Command decided to send me to Stavropol to be trained as a navigator. Attack and fighter aircraft didn't have navigators. Every pilot did his own navigation. But each attack and fighter regiment had a staff navigator, who effectively served as Deputy Regimental Commander. Squadron navigators did double duty as Deputy Squadron Commanders.

I had no interest in climbing the ladder of promotions. I just wanted to fly. I categorically refused to be sent to take navigation courses, so our Division Commander, General Getman, ordered Major Karev to escort me there under guard. I had no choice but to submit.

After two months, I boarded a train back to the 4th Air Force's base in Krasnodar. From there, I happily flew back to my regiment as if I were coming home. But my joy faded when I learned that twenty-three-year-old Squadron Commander Semyon Andryanov and his tail-gunner Potseluiko had been killed. My words stuck in my throat. Only my thoughts and memories functioned. All I could think of was the marvelous album full of drawings Andryanov had once shown me. "You have a real talent, Comrade Commander," I told him.

"You're wrong, Yegorova," he said. "It's only because I had a great drawing teacher in school, in Nizhny Tagil. I went to his drawing club whenever I could. As long as I can remember, I've always loved to draw."

"You should go to art school after the war, Semyon Vasilyevich," I told him, addressing him for the first time by first name and patronymic. "I'm no art expert, but I think your drawings are quite good."

"I love flying, Annushka," he said, unexpectedly affectionate, calling me by my nickname. "But after the war is over and we defeat the last Fascist, I'm going to study art seriously."

Semyon Andryanov didn't live to see victory or to draw any more pictures. He died leading a dangerous, low-altitude tank-bombing mission eight kilometers west of Krymskaya.

I flew the old one-seater Shturmovik longer than anyone in our regiment. I considered it lighter and more maneuverable than the two-seater. But when I returned from my navigation courses, I had to start flying the two-cockpit Il-2.

On one recent mission, I had caught hell from some "Messers." We were flying to Temruk, a city on the eastern bank of the Kuban River and just south of the Sea of Azov. Our orders were to knock out a bridge across the river, one that Karev's group had already destroyed once before. How many times were these cursed Fritzes going to keep rebuilding it?

The main route from the Chushka Spit mooring to the Blue Line crossed that bridge, so it was heavily defended by anti-aircraft batteries, not to mention the nearby defenses of the Blue Line itself. Three crews had already perished near Temruk and the bridge: Podynenogin's, Mkrtumov's, and Tasyets's.

Captain Yakimov led the mission to the bridge. Slightly older than the rest of us, he had a graceful, athletic build and a rather haughty, condescending way about him, as if he looked down on us. He went over the flight with us and, for some reason, assigned me and my one-seater, the only airplane with no tail-gunner, to fly in the back of the six-plane formation!

After we dropped our bombs and climbed out over the Sea of Azov, some Messerschmitts intercepted us. Our four "Laggs" were engaged in a dogfight nearby, so it fell to our tail-gunners to beat off the pursuing "Messers." I felt quite vulnerable in the rear of the formation with no tail-gunner.

The "Messers" repeatedly tried and failed to split the formation. We knitted together in a tight group, wing-to-wing. My aircraft's aft hemisphere lay unprotected, so of course, I took a hit—to my right side. I yanked the plane left, but too late—a second round hit my "Ilyusha." Then the "Messers" scattered, turned back toward me, and attacked my rear from all sides.

After another hit from close-range, I engaged *forsazh* mode,[1] shoved the control stick forward to gather some speed, shot past the group, and squeezed into position between the leader and his right wingman, Volodya Sokolov. That's what saved me.

At the flight analysis, Captain Yakimov reprimanded me. "You. Broke. The. Flight. Formation," he articulated distinctly, pronouncing every syllable. "Pilot Sokolov might have taken you for an enemy aircraft and unloaded his machine guns and cannons on you!"

"And why," I asked him impudently, "when the Fascists started shooting at me, didn't you regroup the formation into a defensive circle and draw off the fighters to your side?"

Silence reigned. Yakimov turned red. Finally, Volodya Sokolov broke the deathly silence: "Comrade Captain! How could I possibly take Yegorova's Shturmovik for an enemy plane with that blue scarf of hers sticking out from under her headset?" The pilots burst out laughing, dissolving the tension.

---

[1] Literally "boost," or "power augmentation." Similar to "War Emergency Power" in U.S. military aircraft of that era, "forsazh" is an emergency power setting to increase the engine power setting beyond safe limits, used only for a few minutes at a time because of the additional stress placed on the engine.

We pilots were always quick with a joke after moments of mortal danger. As the palpable chill of fear melted away, the joy of seeing, breathing, living another day would burst out of us in the form of hearty laughter and teasing.

After the mission to Temruk, I got an Il-2 with a second cockpit for a tail-gunner. Before I took the navigation courses, I had flown the plane a few times with different gunners, just for practice. I even took my mechanic Tyutyunnik once.

Usually, gunners were selected from the ranks of mechanics, observer-pilots of obsolete planes, and ground-forces gunners—really, anyone who was willing to fly and could shoot—and trained in short-term courses. These aspiring tail-gunners usually had no flight training and knew little about how to aim at in-flight targets. They had only their great desire to beat the Fascists. A silly popular song about tail-gunners circulated throughout the division:

Over the hills, the "Il" reels and turns,
In the front cabin the pilot-hero reels and turns,
Another lad sits in the rear seat,
He's an air gunner, that's his beat...

There were girls, too, among the "lads," and also "lads" the age of our fathers. Squadron Adjutant Boiko suggested that I take my pick.

"What do you mean, 'take my pick'?" I asked in surprise. "If there's a spare tail-gunner somewhere, give him to me. I can't very well steal a tail-gunner from a crew that's already flying together. That won't do."

"We do have one without a crew, but he's a bit peculiar. We're planning to send him to the ground forces. You're the Deputy Squadron Commander now. You have the right to choose a good tail-gunner."

"What's the name of the tail-gunner you're planning to send away?"

"Makosov."

"Give him to me."

"I strongly advise against this, Comrade Lieutenant," said the adjutant.

"Send him to my plane anyway," I said.

Shortly after that, while I was chatting with the squadron engineer and a lieutenant-technician, I heard a chuckle from behind me: "Here I am."

I turned to find a round-faced fellow of about eighteen, with a broad smile spreading across his face and dimples crinkling his plump rosy cheeks. His cap sat pushed to the back of his head, and a lock of fair hair peeped out, combed painstakingly to one side.

"Who are you?" I asked.

"Sergeant Makosov. Captain Boiko sent me to you."

"Well then, Sergeant Makosov, report to me properly."

"How odd! I've never seen a female pilot before," he said and started giggling again, shifting from one foot to another, apparently unaware of how to stand at attention.

"What's your position in our regiment?" I asked him.

"Tail-gunner."

"Have you ever flown before?"

"Only in the tail-gunners' course. I just finished."

"Do you want to be a tail-gunner?"

"Very much. But they haven't assigned me to a pilot yet."

"How well do you know the equipment in the rear cabin, firing aspects, and enemy aircraft silhouettes?"

"Well enough."

"OK. Tomorrow you will be tested."

The next morning, Makosov climbed into the rear cabin of my Shturmovik. He answered all my questions without hesitation, smiling all the while. That's how I got my new tail-gunner.

Personally, I wouldn't take that job for anything. It's terrifying. You sit in an open cockpit with your back to the pilot, with a high-caliber machine gun mounted on a pivoting half-turret in front of you. Fascist fighter planes fire point blank at you from the rear, where there are no trenches or hills to hide from the bullets. All you have to protect you is a machine gun that sometimes jams, and you have to fire it while being flung back and forth by the pilot. How could anyone stand it?

Makosov played a very active role from our first combat flight together. When he spied an enemy aircraft, he would fire a signal flare toward it to warn everyone. When I would climb out after the target approach, he would continue firing at ground targets. He protected our tail very well. Best of all, he would report to me over the intercom everything he saw in the air and on the ground.

"Comrade Lieutenant," I would hear now and then, "there's an anti-aircraft gun firing from the woods on our right!"

"Comrade Lieutenant, six tanks are on the move from Novorossisk toward Malaya Zemlya, and they are shooting."

And again: "Comrade Lieutenant, Shturmovik number 'Six' has been hit and is going down over the sea..."

Nothing seemed to escape his notice. I was happy for his success, and I encouraged him whenever I could. Our commanders awarded him a "Distinguished Combat Service" medal for completing ten successful missions and for shooting down a "Messer."

Makosov always kept his machine gun in excellent condition, constantly cleaning and lubricating it in his spare time. He would sit for hours in the rear cockpit practicing his aim at our planes as they passed.

I trusted my tail-gunner completely. I knew he wouldn't let me down. He never panicked when a fighter attacked him. He simply opened fire, in a calm and businesslike fashion, and hit the target. He received another medal, "For Courage," for helping to shoot down a Me-109. At the flight analyses, he was often set forth as an example to other gunners.

As always, he blushed, flashing his broad smile and his dimples. The women-armorers started to look with interest at Tail-gunner Makosov.

46
Herotown

In between combat flights or in bad weather, we attended squadron and regimental Komsomol meetings, often late at night. I recall some of the topics on the agenda: "All As One to Destroy the Fascist Beast," or "Helping Each Other in Combat—Rules for Komsomols."

We also occasionally found time to relax amid the rigors of wartime work. Tail-gunner Zhenya Berdnikov tirelessly organized the regiment's amateur performances. He was a jolly fellow, often telling jokes and tall tales for hours on end. You couldn't help but laugh when he would start dancing like Charlie Chaplin, staring goggle-eyed and singing tunes from his films.

Once when we were based in Timashevskaya, Berdnikov suggested we act out Leonid Lench's sketch "Dreams That Come True." Everybody gladly took all the roles except one—no one wanted to be the deranged Führer. So our Komsomol leader Rimsky had to play the role himself. The performance went splendidly, and we decided to perform it for the local villagers.

A mechanic named Vanya danced the "Yablochko" and then the "Russian Pereplyas" with some woman-armorers named Nina Piyuk and Dusya Nazarkina. Masha and Vasya told funny stories. Berdnikov and Yulia Panina sang "Ogonyok." Everyone loved how Vadim Morozov recited the poem "Wait for Me."[1] Then came the "Dreams That Come True" sketch.

All went well until the conversation between Napoleon and Hitler. From the deathly silent hall came a sudden loud swear, and an object came hurtling onto the stage toward Hitler. Everyone laughed except the actor, who was hit in the head with a rubber galosh, which knocked the Hitler wig right off his head. We never performed that sketch again because nobody was willing to risk playing that particular despicable personage.

After the performance, an old man came up to Rimsky and apologized. "Forgive me, Sonny! I didn't mean to hurt you. It's just that… if I could, I'd strangle Hitler with my own two hands! The Fascists shot my two brothers and burned down my house…"

How could anyone fail to understand the man's grief?

---

[1] A famous 1941 love poem by Konstantin Simonov which was such a favorite among soldiers that many carried it with them at the front. The poem begins, "Wait for me, and I'll come back…"

☆ ☆ ☆

On September 16, 1943, our troops liberated Novorossisk.

Troops landed just north of Kerch, on the Yenikal Peninsula and cleansed the Chushka Spit of Fascists on October 9. They landed in Eltigen, south of Kerch, on November 1.

You won't find Eltigen on maps anymore. It's now "Geroyskoye," or "Herotown." The seaborne assault force made landfall in Eltigen at night in storms and high seas that lashed the rocky shores. They crossed the Kerch Strait from Taman in rickety boats, over thirty-odd miles of furious seas, under ceaseless artillery fire and unblinking search lights.

Grounded by terrible weather and muddy airfields, we pilots knew nothing about the landing until days later. That week, a few airplanes attempted the takeoff run, but each time the landing gear sank into the mud up to mid-wheel. It wasn't until November 7 that we could join the fight.

Major Karev, the regimental navigator, led the group. He instructed us not to use the brakes on the takeoff run because the undercarriage could get stuck in the muck and cause the six-ton plane to overturn. Also, he warned us that if mud clogged the gear mechanism, the undercarriage might not retract, and if it did, the suction of the mud might prevent us from extending it again before landing. In that case, we had to crank it down, thirty-two turns of the emergency winch with the right hand, as we flew with the left. He advised us to keep the oil cooler flap closed on the runway so it didn't get clogged with mud and overheat the engine.

On the takeoff run, mud totally engulfed the airplanes. Not all of us managed to escape its gummy embrace. Two out of nine airplanes nosed over on the runway.

We set a course for Eltigen, a fishing village between Churbashkoye and Tobechikskoye Lakes, on a low, sandy beach where the coastal hills and cliffs angle down toward the sea. A little north of Eltigen lay the port of Kamysh-Burun, where the Fascists' naval craft were based.

This time, containers of ammunition, food, and medical supplies replaced our usual cargo load of bombs. Stormy weather had already kept our troops at Eltigen waiting for provisions long enough. We had to drop this load right "on the nose" for them. We had to consider wind direction and speed and our groundspeed, meanwhile evading all manner of Fascist fire from the ground.

We managed to deliver the cargo to our boys near Eltigen, just in the nick of time, according to journalist S. A. Borzenko, Hero of the Soviet Union, who participated in the battle there. He wrote, "The situation was catastrophic. It seemed that all was lost. Somebody suggested that we send our final radio message: we are dying, but we won't surrender… Nobody counted on a miracle… Suddenly, artillery from the Taman roared into life. But it was only the beginning of our retribution. The Shturmoviks added their fire from treetop level, then set up a smoke screen, enveloping the shore like fog… From above, we had a perfect view…"

47
Thank You, My Friend "Ilyusha"

When the Hitlerites fled the Taman Peninsula, we crossed the strait to the Kerch Peninsula.

I was ordered to lead a six-plane group to the Baksa region, north of Mitridat Mountain. We didn't have a specific target. We were to fly along the front line and find a target for ourselves.

Over and over I told my wingmen on the radio, "Maneuver, maneuver, maneuver!" I didn't relax either, thrusting my Shturmovik this way and that, accelerating and decelerating. As flight leader, I knew I would catch the brunt of the anti-aircraft fire.

Suddenly, it came. I peered into the greenery below me and caught sight of tanks camouflaged amid the foliage! I dove and fired my anti-tank missiles at them. "Maneuver and attack!" I shouted into the radio.

I spotted a cargo truck in my optical sights and let fly a storm of fire from the autocannon. The ground rushed at me with such force that it appeared to be falling on me. My fingers squeezed a trigger again. In a flash, a lethal rocket swooped toward the ground. I pulled back on the stick, and the Shturmovik obediently pulled out of the dive. I had already dropped a load of bombs, so the plane climbed easily. My air-gunner, Makosov, unloaded his machine gun at the fleeing Fascists below. And *that's* what a ground attack in the Shturmovik is like!

Just as we finished the attack and turned home, the "Messers" found us. One of the groups engaged our cover fighters in a dogfight, and the other attacked our "Ils." It was an unequal fight, the six of us against ten Fascist planes. We formed up in a defensive circle. I could see two fighters plunging into the sea a ways off, one with a red star on the fuselage, the other bearing a black-and-white cross. An Il-2 was sinking to the bottom right before my eyes.

We had to make it at all cost, I told myself. We aimed at anyone who faltered or who raced forward and exposed his belly to our cannons. One "Fritz" spat smoke and lagged behind. We hit another one, and it dropped to the earth like a stone. The "heroes" started scattering then. They seemed less inclined to fight when the odds shifted in our favor.

The "Messers" disappeared just as the anti-aircraft guns came to life again. A red-hot anti-aircraft shell fragment punctured the plexiglass section of the canopy and flew right by my face. I noticed blood on the armored glass that separated my cabin from the tail-gunner's. Was Makosov wounded? That same instant, I felt the plane pulling to the right—the control rods were severed. Better yet, my wingmen were heading off to the east, and my aircraft wasn't responding to my control inputs. It had turned west, toward the enemy.

I was alone. Treacherous chills ran up and down my body. I summoned all my strength and skill. The "Thin Ones"[1] smelled easy prey and pressed in on me from all directions, directing their glowing tracers again and again at my injured machine.

I somehow turned the Shturmovik toward home. The engine coughed and sputtered, but it was at least still turning a bit. The machine was holding on, and so would I.

I clenched my teeth and fought to control the unresponsive airplane. I was flying at the lowest possible airspeed and still losing altitude. The earth drew closer and closer, and I still had to cross the Kerch Strait!

Suddenly, I saw some object flying up out of the infantry trenches. *Grenades?* I thought. No. It was our soldiers, ecstatically greeting the passing "red-starred" airplane by tossing their helmets into the air. They were just so happy to see me and their beloved "Flying Infantryman."[2]

I had made it. I had made it to our lines.

As I crossed the strait, our fighters drove away my pursuers. At last, I saw the airfield. I flew straight in to land, ignoring all proper approach procedures. Rules were the least of my worries. I couldn't get her down fast enough, as far as I was concerned.

Stillness. How amazingly quiet it was back on the earth! But what was that? Why were my hands covered with blood? My shirt was bloody as well. I hadn't felt the shell fragment hit me. But what about Makosov? I launched out of the cockpit straight to his. He was alive! The weight lifted a bit from my heart.

Pilots were sprinting across the airfield toward my airplane. An ambulance painted with a red cross raced our way at top speed, followed by a tractor that would quickly tow the crippled aircraft from the runway. Swallowing tears, I clung to the wing and whispered, "Thank you, my friend 'Ilyusha.'"

Makosov was loaded onto a stretcher. He was trying to stand up and kept repeating, "Comrade Lieutenant! Don't send me to the hospital! Let our doctor fix me. I'll get better and fly again soon. Don't choose a new tail-gunner!"

"OK, OK, Makosov," I said soothingly. "I'll ask them to treat you at the battalion clinic. Get well soon. I'll be waiting for you!"

---

[1] The Russians nicknamed the Messerschmitt-109, or Me-109, "Thin One" because of its narrow silhouette.

[2] Another nickname for the Il-2 among Soviet soldiers.

48
The Weightlifter

Things had changed in the regiment since the appearance of the fair sex. Our pretty female armorers had quite a positive effect on the male personnel. Some of the pilots believed that beards protected them from bullets, so many of the men had started growing them. But when the armorers arrived, out went the beards. The pilots started shaving and changing their collars more frequently. The mechanics' usually greasy overalls suddenly became snow white from regular washing in buckets of gasoline.

They were even wrinkle-free, pressed under mattresses while the men dreamed.

Soon the girls set about altering the military-issued men's shirts and underwear, which were much too large for them. One of the armorers, a Cossack girl from the Kuban named Nina, was a particularly good seamstress. When the men started seeing evidence of her talent, they approached her, blushing awkwardly, to ask her to tailor their shirts to fit their figures better.

The girls were issued thick-soled boots from England, which they called "Churchills," to be worn with foot wrappings.[1] They learned to sew stockings from these leg-wrappings, which we called "zebras" for their uneven striped coloring. Everyone was always trying to lay hands on a bit of ink or some acrichinum[2] from the apothecary to dissolve in water and dye the homemade stockings. In summer, the armorers wore lightweight slippers fashioned from airplane-cover material instead of the heavy "Churchills." But no matter what they wore, they were lovely young women.

It was only a matter of time before love bloomed.

On my way to visit the injured Makosov, I heard sniffling from behind the last revetment. I walked toward the sound and found Armorer Dusya Nazarkina sitting on a shell box, sobbing bitterly, hiding her face in her lap.

Someone has hurt her, I thought, but I immediately rejected the idea. She was cheerful and hardworking, and everyone at the regiment loved her. It was a pleasure to watch her attaching bombs and missiles or loading cannons and machine guns. In her soldier's blouse and riding breeches, sun-faded but

---

[1] Under their boots, Red Army soldiers wore bandages around their feet, which was thought to prevent frostbite better than socks.

[2] A common drug then used to treat malaria, giardia, and other parasite infections; also known by a number of synonymns, such as "quinacrine," "mepacrine hydrochloride," or "Atabrine"; could also be used as a dye.

always clean and pressed, she bustled around the Shturmovik with extraordinary speed and dexterity. I always wondered how she managed to hang hundred-kilogram bombs under the fuselage. "Before the war I worked in Moscow at the 'Red Bogatyr' factory, and in my spare time I went to a weight lifting club!" she jokingly explained.

And here the "weight lifter" was, sobbing disconsolately. I shook her by the shoulder, but she didn't respond. So I sat down next to her on the box, took her head in my hands, and put it into my lap. Her garrison cap, which she was clutching for dear life, was wet and crumpled. I quietly stroked Dusya's head.

After ten minutes of weeping, Dusya began to tell me through her tears about her great love for Seryozha Bondarev. He was an aircraft mechanic, but he had substituted for another tail-gunner on a mission with Pilot Khmara. The two had not returned.

"I don't want to live without him!" she wailed. "Just yesterday we confessed our love for each other, kissed for the first time, and vowed to get married after the war. Now he's gone. Seryozha's dead!"

She fell to the ground moaning, crying softly with her face in her hands. I ran to the staff dugout to fetch some water and took some ammonia from the clinic. Dusya gradually quieted down, then asked suddenly, "Comrade Lieutenant! Anna Alexandrovna! I ask you, I beg you, let me be your tail-gunner. I know all the enemy plane silhouettes. I know how to shoot well. Take me! I want revenge for Seryozha."

"I already have a tail-gunner. Makosov," I said, bewildered by Dusya's unexpected appeal.

"But he's wounded. Will he be able to shoot after such a serious injury? His right hand is severely damaged."

I tried to talk Nazarkina out of it. I told her how terrifying it was to fly as a tail-gunner in a ground attack plane, how few of them survived. "We pilots are at least protected by armor," I persisted. "The gunner is totally exposed to Fascist fighters in that open cockpit. Your Seryozha may be alive yet. We know so many pilots and gunners who have come back from 'the dead.'"

Dusya didn't listen to a word I said. "Take me. I'm filling out my application to the commanders now. Please support me in this."

I couldn't convince her otherwise. After about two weeks, Colonel Tupanov, chief of the political department, dropped by the regiment and resolved the issue. Nazarkina became my tail-gunner. To my knowledge, we were one of only two all-female crews in ground attack aviation.

I hated to part with an experienced tail-gunner like Makosov, especially since he had asked me not to choose another crewman, but orders are orders.

I started flying with Dusya Nazarkina in 1943. To my amazement, she handled her responsibilities no worse than Makosov on our first combat flight. She became my second pair of eyes, her voice on the intercom describing what she saw. Sometimes I would catch a glimpse of her through the armored glass that separated us, back to back. She would be furiously working her machine gun, its barrel rising and falling as it spat fire. Her small figure literally whirled around the compartment. How lucky I was in my choice of tail-gunners!

49
"This Is 'Birch Tree'... How Do You Read?"

We received our third reinforcement of aircraft and flying personnel since we'd begun fighting in Taman. The regiment joined the 1st Belorussian Front at our new base in Karlovka, near Poltava, where Tsar Peter the Great defeated the Swedes.[1]

Recently our troops had destroyed a large enemy contingent nearby. All sorts of abandoned German equipment lay strewn about the field, near the former Russian redoubts. Headquarters deemed this an ideal firing range and built an observation tower and an imitation front line, complete with trenches populated with wooden "soldiers," ersatz wooden "cannons," tanks with white crosses, and trucks.

Our young reinforcements from the Far East were experienced pilots but had yet to see combat. We had to teach them what previous veterans had taught us, how to bomb, shoot, and navigate to the target. I admit, we "old timers" didn't relish training the young pilots. As we left the front, we were counting on a brief rest in the rear. We just couldn't summon much enthusiasm for dropping cement bombs on a firing-range stage set. The trainees were sick of practicing as well and eager to test their mettle at the front.

Our Regimental Navigator, Major Pyotr Timofeyevich Karev, was named Deputy Commander of the 805th, and I was appointed Regimental Navigator. I was very nervous about my new position, and I rushed to see Kozin, the Regimental Commander, to "clarify our relationship."

Everyone loved our commander. A brave pilot, he was strict, but fair to his subordinates. He sang songs with us, danced, and shared our sorrows. Our friendly collective called him "Dad."

Kozin had recently visited his family somewhere in the deep rear. When he returned, he showed me a tiny photo of his daughter. A girl gazed out of the photo with eyes wide and trusting, looking so like her father's. Two braids emerged from beneath a scarf tied under her chin. "An heiress!" said Mikhail Nikolayevich, laughing.

---

[1] Poltava is an industrial city in the black-earth region of eastern Ukraine and also the name of the surrounding province. In 1709, Peter the Great of Russia defeated Charles XII of Sweden at the Battle of Poltava (fought just northwest of Poltava). A turning point in the Great Northern War (1700–21), the battle effectively launched Russia as a great European power and signaled the end of Sweden's military supremacy.

"You know, Lieutenant," he added, "When my wife heard there was a female pilot in the regiment, she got jealous."

"Let her get jealous," grinned Shvidky, the regimental *zampolit*.[2] "That can sometimes be useful..."

Amid these recollections, I climbed down into the commander's dugout and reported to him with a formal salute. "Comrade Commander, allow me to address you!"

"Go ahead," Kozin nodded with a reproachful look.

"Why have they appointed me the Regimental Navigator? I don't think I can handle it. Everyone will laugh! What about Berdashkevich, commander of the Second Squadron, or Sukhorukov, or Vakhramov? It makes more sense for one of them to be navigator of a men's regiment!"

"Are you finished?" the lieutenant colonel asked sharply. "Then about face! Forward march! On the double! Get on with your duties as Regimental Navigator, and don't ever bother me with this matter again."

I came to enjoy my new duties, which included teaching classes to the flying personnel and guiding "combat missions" on the radio from the observation tower. After all, I had studied navigation at Kherson, taken navigator courses at Stavropol, and taught classes on navigation when I was an instructor at the Kalinin Aeroclub. So I suppose it made sense that the commanders had chosen me as Regimental Navigator.

I recall standing atop the observation tower, looking out over a stupendous panorama. Planes taxied on the airfield, a lush carpet of green. American "Flying Fortresses"[3] took off to fight the Germans somewhere near Poltava. A small river flowed by Karlovka's gardens and the nearby redoubts of Peter the Great that stopped Charles XII in his tracks. All around, the larks sang their hearts out.

The telephone rang. I picked up the receiver and heard the flight leader's voice: "Get ready! We're taking off."

Somewhere beneath me, the tower's radio station whirred into action. I picked up the microphone, blew into it, and said, "Hello! Hello! Hello! This is 'Birch Tree.' How do you read?"

"This is "Mignonette-2![4] This is Mignonette-2! I hear you loud and clear. Do you approve 200?"

"Two hundred approved."

---

[2] A deputy political commander, or political commissar, who conducted indoctrination lectures and supervised party organizations in military units. He was also responsible for maintaining troop morale and resolving disputes and disciplinary problems.

[3] For a short period beginning in June 1944, a few American shuttle-bombing bases existed in Ukraine. The bases were removed after a devastating German night bombing raid at Poltava destroyed most of the bombers on the ground.

[4] *Reseda odorata* (common name "mignonette") is a fragrant flower native to the Mediterranean and southwest Asia.

"Mignonette-2" was Major Karev, and "200," a code for a bombing and attack clearance. I still don't know why the communications chief gave all the men feminine call signs like "Mignonette," "Violet," "Lilac," and "Volga." He even gave me a masculine call sign once—"Hawk."

A Shturmovik formation circled over the firing range, diving steeply at the target. The pilots worked diligently to maneuver the target into their sights and fire at the dummies in short salvos, then release their bombs and make a climbing U-turn. Karev, "Mignonette-2," carefully watched the pilots' work and patiently corrected them:

"Khukhlin! Reduce your dive angle!"

"Ageyev! Don't slow down!"

"Tsvetkov, decrease your speed, or you'll wind up ahead of the group."

"Good man, Kirillov, you hit the target," the voice of Mignonette-2 echoed over the firing range. From our many missions together in Taman, I already admired his daring, but my respect for him deepened as I watched how meticulously he guided the young pilots.

Karev's group headed off toward the airfield. I heard another voice on the radio. "Birch Tree, this is Mignonette-17. This is Mignonette-17. Do you approve 200?"

"Two-hundred approved,"

"Do you have a toothache, little Birch Tree?" the voice said. Indeed, my teeth did hurt. Could he see that my cheek was bandaged? I curtly cut off the too-familiar voice from the ether.

"Mignonette-17, mind your own business! Reduce your dive angle!"

The pilot ignored me and dropped his bombs in a steep dive. "Mignonette-17, quit improvising, or I'll close the test range!"

"Roger," he answered merrily and swooped in for another attack, a very accurate one, I had to admit. The pilot—Ivan Pokashevsky—departed the range in a descent, shaving the treetops, leaving a song behind on the airwaves.

50
A Father's Gift

Lieutenant Pokashevsky stood out among the new arrivals, with his broad face, mop of dark hair, and mischievous gray eyes. Instead of a proper uniform, he wore a quilted jacket over an old-fashioned soldier's blouse and civilian trousers. His worn boots looked like they had seen quite a lot. He wore his *shapka-ushanka* slid so far on the back of his head it seemed on the verge of falling off.

Ivan told us he'd been shot down and taken prisoner by the Germans. During transport to Germany, he and two other captured pilots cut a hole in the train floor and jumped off the train one night. They fled into the forests and joined some partisans. Pokachevsky fought with them for seven months and won an Order of the Red Star. Then the pilots were sent to Moscow, and Ivan found himself in our regiment.

As soon as his father learned Ivan was alive, he sold his apiary to buy an airplane. He wanted his son to fly his very own airplane. He thought Ivan would be safer that way.

Finally, Pokashevsky received his uniform and his assignment to the Second Squadron. One day his father, Ivan Potapovich Pokashevsky, came to Karlovka and brought his elder son, Vladimir, the director of a collective farm.

"Let my lads serve with you," Ivan Potapovich told the Regimental Commander confidentially. "Volodka's sat around on the *bronya*[1] long enough, like he's really so indispensable! It's time he knew honor! But as for our arrangement, don't make any special allowances for them. Make 'em follow army regulations just like everybody else."

A clear blue sky and bright sunshine—so warm it almost seemed like summer— greeted the crowd at the aerodrome. Citizens of Karlovka and nearby towns waved banners and portraits of party leaders. Standing apart from the other airplanes was a new Shturmovik with an inscription on the fuselage: "From Father—to the brothers Pokashevsky."

Ivan Potapovich's sons helped him onto the wing and stood on either side of him. The division political department chief, Lieutenant Colonel Dyachenko, climbed onto the wing as well and opened the meeting. He praised

---

[1] A wartime document permitting men eligible for army service to stay in reserve if their work was deemed vital to the war effort—for example, defense industry workers and scientists.

the collective farmer's patriotic deed and spoke passionately about the coming combat missions and certain victory.

Then it was Ivan Potapovich's turn. The old man gave a start and was about to step forward, but his sons grabbed him to keep him from falling off the wing. He only managed two words, "Brothers and Sisters!" before his voice broke. His sons leaned toward him, whispering something to him, trying to encourage him.

After a moment, he went on. I will never forget his short speech, in the eloquent language of a simple peasant: "I have two sons. I give them both to our homeland. I'd go myself to fight the invaders if I weren't so old."

The old man wanted to say something more, but his emotions overwhelmed him. He waved his hand, bowed to all four sides, and kissed his sons three times. Everyone erupted into applause, and the orchestra burst into a flourish of trumpets. Dozens of hands reached up toward Ivan Potapovich and began tossing him into the air.

Henceforth, the brothers crewed their father's airplane: Ivan as pilot, and his brother Vladimir, as tail-gunner.

From the tower, I watched the Pokashevsky brothers' work through my field-glasses. Excellent! They had hit all their targets. Suddenly, a plane headed toward the test range without my clearance. "This is 'Birchtree.' This is 'Birchtree.'" I rattled out quickly. "Report who is flying over the range."

No answer. The plane made a U-turn and dove toward the tower. *He's crazy!* I thought. He must have confused the signal "T" on the tower for the cross on the firing range.

"Everybody into the trench!" I shouted as the radio operator and a technician threw themselves in. A bomb exploded. The blast blew away the tent and shook the tower, showering bomb fragments everywhere. For some reason, instead of holding on to the handrail, I grabbed the microphone and telephone and rolled down with them, shouting: "Signalman! Fire a red signal flare! Drive him away from the firing range!"

Red flares sailed into the air. The pilot understood his error and flew off. His aim wasn't half bad. I wish it had been the right target, but oh, well, training is training.

The next group arrived, led by Squadron Commander Misha Berdashkevich, a kind-hearted Belorussian who bore a terrible sorrow. His father died fighting with the partisans, and his mother was shot by a Nazi firing squad for being a "partisan sympathizer."[2]

---

[2] Guerrilla or resistance fighters harassing an occupying force behind enemy lines.

According to Alexander Werth's *Russia at War*, Stalin broadcast an appeal on July 3, 1941 for a sustained partisan uprising in German-occupied territories. Local civilians, Jewish refugees, and soldiers trapped behind enemy lines in eastern Poland, Ukraine,

"Artillery fire from the right!" he told the group to introduce the training scenario, and the pilots performed anti-aircraft altitude and course maneuvers.

"Four 'Fockes,' to the right of the sun!" came the flight leader's voice again, and the group set up a defensive circle.

A defensive circle, or "life buoy," as we called it, was a combat formation to protect a formation from "Messers." Let's say an enemy fighter attacks our Shturmovik. The planes following ours in the circle can then cut off the attack with head-on fire. We also often attacked the target in the circle formation.[3]

The twelve ground attack planes dove, their guided missiles flying toward the ground. *Boom!* came a powerful salvo blast. After that, cannon and machine-gun cut the target to pieces, and the planes released their bombs just as they recovered from the dive. When the dust settled, I couldn't find any trace of the target in my binoculars.

May passed uneventfully. The young pilots learned to shoot and bomb accurately and to maintain the flight formation even while maneuvering. Once they learned to attack the target in squadron-sized groups, the regiment was ready to depart for the front.

Finally, we got the OK. Our 805th Ground Attack Aviation Regiment, incorporated into the newly-formed 197th Attack Air Division, joined General Polynin's 6th Air Force, part of the 1st Belorussian Front.

Many pilots remembered the Division Commander, Colonel V.A. Timofeyev, from when he directed the Poltava and Orenburg flight schools. When he was introduced to the flight personnel, he looked to me like a tsarist army

---

and Belorussia began an organized resistance movement which gained momentum in 1942, as the Nazis' intent to exterminate much of the population became clear. (Werth quotes a German officer who testified at Nuremburg, "among the purposes of the Russian campaign was the reduction of the Slav population by thirty millions.")

Werth notes that Belorussia's partisan movement was the largest in Eastern Europe, with an estimated 360,000 fighters by the end of 1943. Belorussian villages in partisan areas often suffered the brunt of the Nazis' brutal reprisals. Hundreds of villages were burned to the ground, their inhabitants executed or deported. Werth quotes an order from Hitler of December 16, 1942, demanding brutal repression of partisan bands: "The troops ... have the right to use any means, even against women and children, provided they are conducive to success. Scruples of any sort are a crime against the German people...."

[3] A description of the circle formation, from Von Hardesty's *Red Phoenix: The Rise of Soviet Air Power 1941–1945*: "An interval of 1,300–1,600 feet separated the (column of) attacking Shturmoviks.... The Il-2s approached the target in line astern, diving sequentially with the first plane forming a loop. The circle would then be maintained until the objective was destroyed or the ammunition ran out.... As a closed loop, the circle provided effective defensive fire against enemy fighters."

officer straight out of the movies. His tunic and breeches fit him like a glove. His high-heeled boots with knee-pads gleamed as if lacquered. His elegant crowned service cap sat a bit higher on his head than was strictly necessary, and he wore fine leather gloves on his hands.

"*He's* definitely from the rear," grumbled my airplane's mechanic, Gorobyets.

"No, he's not," objected pilot Zubov. "He was in the Civil War. Can't you see the medals on his chest?" said Zubov. "He also fought on the Kursk Salient."

"And by the way, Timofeyev was arrested in '38 as an enemy of the people and spent two years in a Chita prison. But the charges were unfounded. His teacher interceded on his behalf, and Timofeyev was rehabilitated," Zubov informed us.

"How do you know all that?"

I was a cadet at the Orenburg Flight Academy. Vyacheslav Arsenyevich told us all about the Civil War. He used to give the best lectures, like nothing I'd ever heard—how to use a fork and knife properly, how to smoke gracefully without staining your fingers, how to dance and invite a lady to dance."

"What?! Two years into the war, and you're learning how to dance?" snapped Pilot Tolya Bugrov, whose face was mottled with burn scars.

"Did he teach you how to select a good wife as well?" snickered Zhenya Berdnikov.

"S-T-O-P chattering!" shouted Major Kuznetsov, the regimental staff chief.

And that's how my "relationship" with Vyacheslav Arsenyevich Timofeyev began…

The 197th redeployed to the devastated land of Belorussia. Day after day, thick morning fog cloaked the aerodromes and delayed our missions. We'd taxi to the start positions and cut our engines to wait. When wind finally tore away the misty shroud, group after group bombed the front lines, suppressed enemy artillery fire, attacked columns of German troops, and burned trucks and tanks—our usual work.

51
Death of the Commander

On July 7, 1944, our troops liberated the town of Kovel[1] from the Hitlerite invaders. We transferred to an aerodrome in that region, where I was ordered to fly a reconnaissance mission. I was to fly along the roads with a film camera and record the enemy's concentration there.

On the way, I made a detour to a neighboring airfield to pick up my fighter escort. A pair of fighters awaited me there with their propellers already turning. They took off while I circled the field.

I immediately contacted their leader on the radio. "I'm going to be conducting visual reconnaissance and taking some pictures. Please stay close by and cover me, OK? Acknowledge."

Instead of replying "Roger" or repeating back my directive, the leader paused, then said in a hoarse, sarcastic tenor: "Hey, you 'humpback!' Why are you tweeting like some common dame?"

After another pause, the leader added, swearing irritably, "To think you're in a Shturmovik! It's disgusting to listen to you!"

The insulting "common dame" comment got my goat at first, and I had to restrain myself from firing back an angry retort. They had no idea they were taking orders from a woman, I realized. I began to see the humor in the situation.

On the way home after the mission, I contacted the vectoring station and reported on the situation in the area I had reconnoitered. A familiar officer from our division replied, "Thank you, Annushka!'

The fighters went mad. They started performing all sorts of aerobatics around my plane! One of them would barrel roll, the other would do a wingover. When they finally calmed down, they flew alongside my "Ilyushina," saluted me from their cockpits, and waved.

As we flew by their airfield, I bade the fighters farewell: "Thanks, Brothers! Go ahead and land. I can take it from here."

But my bodyguards escorted me all the way to my aerodrome. They circled the field as I landed, and only then waggled their wings goodbye and disappeared over the horizon.

As I reported on the mission to the regimental commander, I noticed everyone was grinning. All of a sudden, they burst into hearty laughter.

---

[1] A city in northwestern Ukraine, not far from the Polish border. Kovel has belonged to Lithuania, Poland, Russia, and Ukraine at various points in its history.

"Lieutenant Yegorova's started bringing her fiancés right here to the air base," commented Karev warm-heartedly. The pilots laughed, and so did I. After all, I'd made it home without a scratch, mission accomplished.

Our army passed through Polesye,[2] on our way to liberate the longsuffering Polish people. Narrow fields of unharvested rye flashed by beneath my wings. Roads snaked from hut to hut like ribbons. I came upon tiny hamlets with Catholic churches, houses with shingle-covered roofs, and wooden crosses at every crossroads.

On the way to attack the enemy's reserves near the city of Chelm, I heard the regimental commander's voice on the radio: "Yegorova! Look right of course—there's artillery hidden in the undergrowth. Unload all your guns on those rats!"

I banked steeply to the right, pushed over into a dive, and, spying the artillery, opened fire. Anti-aircraft guns roared to life. "Vakhramov," ordered the commander, ignoring the code, "Hit the battery with your guided missiles!"

Closer to Chelm, a motorized column of tanks, trucks, armored transports, and tanks of fuel crept along the road. "Maneuver, fellows, maneuver!" the flight leader reminded us, with a turn leading us toward the attack. "Aim. Fire!"

Smoke curled toward our planes from the ground, as small-caliber fire and four-barrel Oerlikons started their rat-a-tat chatter. I so wanted to turn back and open fire on them, but they had already slid by, and an armored vehicle was looming temptingly in my sights.

We climbed higher for bombing, the sky densely pockmarked with black explosions. We ignored them and dropped our bombs. It was time to pull out of the dive, but the flight leader continued his headlong plunge toward the earth. Amid a sudden salvo of artillery fire, Kozin's plane seemed to linger for a moment, and then flash bright with flames. His Shturmovik tumbled into the swarm of military vehicles and sent up a massive pillar of fire.

It's impossible to find words for the feeling that enveloped us at that moment. In a rage, we flung attack after attack toward the enemy column. It seemed that no force on earth could stop us. We didn't withdraw from the battlefield until we ran out of ammunition. Nobody on the ground shot at us after that.

---

[2] A former province of eastern Poland located in the watery lowlands known by the same name (also Rus. *Polesye,* Ukr. *Polissya,* Pol. *Polesye*) and also called the Pripet Marshes. This large, wooded, boggy region (of about 104,000 square miles), intersected by numerous rivers, covers northern Ukraine and southern Belarus and constitutes the largest swampland in Europe.

We flew home separately, each tortured by the same bitter, guilty thought: we hadn't been able to protect "Dad." We had also lost our tailman, Viktor Andreyev, a reserved but kind pilot from Saratov and one of the best "hunters" of us all.

A despondent mood greeted us at the aerodrome. The fighters had already radioed ahead with the awful news. Usually, the mechanics met their airplanes enthusiastically, but that day their eyes were full of tears.

The commander's mechanic was overcome with grief. He retreated to the revetment, violently hurling tools, chocks, and whatever else found itself in his way.

Everyone spontaneously drifted toward the regimental command post. The chief of staff emerged from the dugout, climbed onto a shell-box, and said, "Regimental Comrades! The commander would be disappointed in us. Where is our fighting spirit? Where is our combat readiness? There's a ruthless war on! We can't forget that for a minute! I want everybody to return to his post. Pilots of the Third Squadron, remain here for a combat assignment. We shall avenge our lost comrades. Mikhail Nikolayevich Kozin, Viktor Andreyev, and the others have all given their native land the most precious gift they had—their lives."

52
On to Poland

The Polish 1st Army fought heroically, side-by-side with us on our sector of the front. Together, the Soviet Army and the Polish troops advanced swiftly into Poland.

Many Poles had fled to the Soviet Union when the Nazis occupied their motherland. A group of them formed the "Union of Polish Patriots" in April of 1943, and that union eventually grew into the new Polish Army.[1]

In May, the USSR State Defense Committee founded the 1st Polish Division, named after Tadeusz Kosciuszko.[2] Our nation paid all expenses. The Polish patriots were stationed in small villages not far from the old Russian city of Ryazan. There on the sloping banks of the Oka River, they plotted the liberation of Poland. (If you take a train today between Moscow and Ryazan,

---

[1] This is the official Soviet line that Yegorova would have learned from *Sovinform-bureau*. The reality is far more complicated. First, although many Poles were indeed refugees, hundreds of thousands more languished in Soviet Gulags, having been captured and deported from Poland when the USSR and Germany partitioned Poland as per the 1939 Nazi-Soviet Pact. (The Soviet Union occupied eastern Poland to the Bug River on September 17, 1939, prompting Stalin's foreign minister, Molotov, to declare that Poland had "ceased to exist.") Numerous officers, soldiers, and "politically suspect" citizens became Soviet POWs, and many of these simply disappeared.

Second, Polish communists and Stalin created the Union of Polish Patriots in 1943 for their own (unstated) political purposes—to counter the Polish government-in-exile in London (which harbored few illusions about Soviet designs on Poland and was closely aligned with Britain) and to orchestrate Soviet-Polish relations, planting the ideological seed for a Soviet-controlled puppet government. The Union's propaganda machine became even more crucial after the government-in-exile broke off relations with Stalin in April of 1943, following the German "discovery" of mass graves of Polish soldiers at Katyn. (The graves were actually unearthed long before, but Goebbels saved his bombshell for later, as the Wehrmacht began to falter, in a carefully orchestrated stroke of propaganda genius. The Soviets parried this by accusing the Germans of perpetrating the massacre at Katyn, but the USSR officially admitted to the killings in 1990.)

[2] Tadeusz Kosciuszko (1746–1817). A Polish officer who led a 1794 uprising against occupying Russian and Prussian forces and served time in the Peter and Paul Fortress in St. Petersburg as a result. He also fought with the colonies in the American Revolutionary War and was made a brigadier general in the US Army at the end of the war.

The Kosciuszko Division later expanded into the 1st Polish Army.

you'll notice a monument to Soviet-Polish brotherhood-in-arms high on a hill, bronze "Katyusha" rockets rising nearly thirty meters high.) Finally, in March 1944, the 1st Polish Army was formed.[3]

When the Polish soldiers and officers stepped onto their native land, they knelt and kissed the ground and then embraced each other. We understood how they felt. The Polish people greeted their liberators—both Polish and Soviet soldiers—with jubilation, smiles, and tears, carrying food and flowers out to the soldiers in the street. What suffering, what humiliations these innocent Poles had endured during those black years of Fascist occupation! We knew all too well.

Polish pilots in the "Krakow" and "Warsaw" Regiments fought shoulder-to-shoulder with us Russian pilots and even rivaled us in skill and courage. Many times the "Warsaw" Fighter Regiment flew cover sorties with Shturmoviks.

From Chelm, our air division pressed on rapidly, liberating Lublin and Demblin, which earned our 6th Attack Aviation Corps the name "Lublinsky" and our 197th division, "Demblinsky." In Lublin, we found the notorious Hitlerite death camp Maidanek, where one and a half million women, children, old people, and prisoners-of-war were executed.

Representatives of the 805th visited Maidanek along with delegations from many military units. We saw that hell with our own eyes—ovens and gas chambers where the Hitlerite butchers exterminated countless human beings.

---

[3] The 1st Polish Army (basically the military wing of the Union of Polish Patriots) indeed fought with distinction as part of Marshal Rokossovsky's 1st Belorussian Front. According to Norman Davies' *Rising '44: the Battle for Warsaw*, more than 100,000 men fought with the 1st Polish Army, around 43,000 of them drafted directly from Soviet Gulags, and tightly controlled by Soviet-trained officers and commissars. Its strength grew as it swept towards Polish territory, and the symbolism of Poles marching into Poland with the USSR as their patron was lost on no one.

But Ms. Yegorova's endorsement of the armies' happy alliance seems to reflect more the official view than the actual attitude of many Russians and Poles, for whom mutual distrust would not evaporate so quickly. An earlier attempt at a Polish Army on Soviet soil had failed earlier in the war. When the USSR and the Polish government-in-exile re-established diplomatic relations in 1941 (after Germany invaded the USSR), the Soviets granted "amnesty" to many captured Poles and attempted to form a Polish Army on Soviet territory under General Wladyslaw Anders. Recriminations quickly ensued. The Soviets alleged that the "Anders Poles" were avoiding the fight, while the Poles complained of meager rations, supplies, and arms from the Soviets. Furthermore, they were understandably resentful about their capture and imprisonment and had no wish to be controlled by Moscow (whose promise to "liberate" Poland elicited much skepticism). So Stalin and Churchill agreed to let the Anders Army evacuate via Iran in 1942 and fight with the Allies under British command, leaving bitterness on both sides.

I recall entering a long barracks and seeing the huge piles of children's shoes in all different sizes, their murdered mothers' purses... I couldn't help weeping, and I wasn't the only one.

When we returned to the regiment, we organized a meeting. We commemorated the dead with a minute of silence. Afterward, various people from our regiment made brief speeches, full of hatred for the Fascist vandals and steadfast determination to avenge their unspeakable atrocities. Everyone vowed to continue the merciless fight, all the way to Berlin.

Our regiment re-deployed to the Polish town of Parczew.[4] The hostess of the apartment where Dusya and I stayed always met us with a jar of milk after our flights. She would pour it into a glass, right on the porch, and urge us to drink it. The host, a tall, proud Pole in home-stitched clothing, often emerged, insisting that we enjoy "Pani Yuzefa's" hospitality. We couldn't resist, of course, especially when the hostess offered us homemade curds as well.

One day I returned from the aerodrome alone. The hostess met me with a look of horror. "Matka Boska! Virgin Mary! Where on earth is Panenka Dusya?" she exclaimed with alarm.

Dusya's at the aerodrome," I lied, not meeting the Polish woman's eye. "She's on duty at headquarters today."

Pani Yuzefa blew her nose into her apron, hastily wiped her eyes, and crossed herself. I hurried out of the house, a weight pressing on my heart. That day Dusya flew a combat mission, and she hadn't returned.

Our commissar, whom we called "Zampolit Shvidky" in the old-fashioned way, had flown a sortie in my airplane. He took my tail-gunner with him. Flight leader Berdashkevich reported that he had never made it to the target. He had turned back somewhere on our side of the line and had not been seen since.

A search plane departed and returned without finding them. The next evening, the two appeared, exhausted but unhurt. Apparently, the engine had started coughing as they approached the target. Shvidky managed to turn the plane and glide to our territory. He put it down in a marsh near a lake. They barely made it out of the aircraft.

The flight had left Dusya quite upset. "Anna Alexandrovna! I want to fly only with you. Don't send me with anybody else!" she pled with me.

"OK, Dusya, OK," I said soothingly. "But don't be angry with Dmitri Polikarpovich. The same thing could have happened to anyone."

"There are plenty of people to fly missions. Let politicians handle the work on the ground!" she burst out.

I didn't agree. As I saw it, if the political commissar flew with us, he'd better understand us pilots and our difficult work. For example, sometimes

---

[4] A town in eastern Poland, 32 miles (51 km) north-northeast of Lublin.

when a pilot landed after combat, his heart still pounding from the flight, he might make some insignificant mistake while taxiing in. Maybe he'd even been wounded himself or lost a comrade. Often the *zampolit* would reprimand him and even attempt to instruct him in piloting technique, without the slightest idea what he was talking about.

No, our regiment was lucky to have a *zampolit* who was also a combat pilot.

53
Shot Down

On August 20, 1944, we took a break from combat missions in honor of Air Force Day. We celebrated at Prince Zeltowski's lavish estate in Milanow, near Parczew. The prince had been executed by the Fascists in Warsaw two months before. The servants raved about the prince as if he were a hero. We, frankly, didn't wish to delve deeply into the question of his heroism. He was a *prince*, after all.

Everyone was in high spirits. To me, those pilots were a special breed. It wasn't that they scorned death; fear is universal. But the men suppressed it. They would look death right in the eye, and the next moment, they were joking and singing as if nothing had happened. The laughter and songs somehow protected them.

That day the pilots arranged an amateur performance for the holiday. One of the squadrons performed a song we especially loved. A regimental navigator from the 7th Ground Attack Regiment who used to study at the conservatory composed it when we were fighting on the Taman. The refrain went like this:

> *Hey, "Ilyusha," my dear friend,*
> *Let's attack them yet again!*

Our revelry didn't last long. By midday, division pilots were fending off furious attacks over the Magnuszew bridgehead, on the west bank of the Vistula, south of Warsaw. For Chuikov's guardsmen[1] to resist the enemy onslaught, they would need our Shturmoviks like they needed air.

Our 805th was to fly in echelons, in two groups. Karev, our new Regimental Commander, *Zampolit* Shvidky, and I discussed the mission in the command post. "I'll lead the first formation of fifteen planes," said Karev, "and Yegorova will take off with the other half of the regiment ten minutes

---

[1] Vasily Ivanovich Chuikov (1900–82). A Soviet general (later marshal) who became a national hero leading the defense of Stalingrad. ("We will defend the city or die in the attempt," Chuikov famously said.) Chuikov and his 8th Guards Army (formerly the 62nd Army, promoted to "Guards" status after its success at Stalingrad) spearheaded the advance through Belorussia and Poland and into Berlin. He accepted Germany's surrender and commanded the occupation forces after the war.

later. We'll need all our crews. Which group will you fly with, Dmitri Poli-karpovich, mine or Yegorova's?"

After a long silence, Shvidky declared, "I'm not flying!" We were stunned.

With takeoff time fast approaching, Pyotr Timofeyevich lost his temper. "What kind of commissar are you, if you desert your regimental compatriots at this difficult hour?" he snapped.

We hastily left the dugout and saw the green flare sailing into the air, signaling the first group's departure clearance. Karev sprinted to his plane as Shvidky melted away. I sat down on a stump to think, trying to banish my nasty thoughts by humming a song: *Mishka, Mishka, where is your smile?*

I anxiously awaited the green flare. I hated the waiting. I always wanted to take off right after the mission briefing. It's true what they say: the worst things of all are "hurry up" and "catch up."

I headed to the parking area. In the distance I spotted my tail-gunner Nazarkina in the airplane's rear cabin. I hadn't seen her smiling like that in a long time. Her cheeks were rosy, her eyes shining. *Well*, I thought. *She looks like she's perking up after the shock she had.*

My mechanic Gorobyets made his report, then nodded covertly in Dusya's direction and whispered, "Comrade Senior Lieutenant, Sergeant Nazarkina's been sneaking anti-tank bombs into the rear cabin."

"She's lost her mind!" I blurted. "Clear the cabin at once!" I looked at my watch. We had three minutes before takeoff.

"She won't let me," Gorobyets explained. "She threatened me with her pistol."

I bounded onto the wing and turned to Nazarkina. Dusya scurried to cover something with her hands like a mother hen protecting her chicks. I gently moved her aside and reached toward the floor of the cabin. Bombs! I pulled a one-and-a-half kilo bomb out and handed it to the mechanic.

When I tried to extract another one, Dusya cried frantically, "Comrade Senior Lieutenant! Let me keep them. If these bombs make a direct hit, they'll blast right through any tank—'King Tigers,' 'Panthers,' 'Ferdinands.' Please, let me keep them! I promise to only use them over the target when there aren't any Fascist fighters attacking. I'll drop them with my bare hands. After all, we're supposed to be driving back tanks!"

"Mechanic! Clear the compartment, quickly!" I ordered.

The flare traced a green arc in the air. I threw on my parachute, popped into the cockpit, cranked the engine, and taxied out, checking the radio. Nazarkina's voice sounded unnaturally merry on the intercom. I wondered why. Had Gorobyets managed to pry all the bombs out from under her feet? I took off, with fifteen Shturmoviks following me.

The wide Vistula with its lush islands came into view ahead. Somewhere to our right lay Warsaw, seemingly sheathed in fog. The day before, on our way home from a mission, we had glimpsed the city, engulfed in flames and a dense cloud of smoke. We had lost several pilots in that inferno as they delivered food and arms to the insurgents.

I glanced sadly in the direction of Warsaw. I felt sorry for the poor, deceived Polish people. When the Polish National Liberation Committee[2] was formed, the Polish-London Émigré Government called for a revolt in Warsaw, with the goal of establishing its own rule there before Soviet troops could enter the Polish capital.[3]

---

[2] The Soviets and pro-Soviet Poles created the Polish Committee of National Liberation (PKWN) in Chelm in July 1944, later moving its headquarters to Lublin. According to historian Norman Davies, the "Lublin Committee's" formation coincided with the Red Army's crossing the Bug River into Stalin's future Poland. Davies describes the Committee (in *Rising '44*) as "a ruling political committee which was made up of almost completely unknown politicians, many with false names, which was packed with Russians pretending to be Poles, and which was subordinated to droves of agents, informers, and secret policemen."

Although the Soviet-controlled Lublin Committee's plans were initially quite obscure, its intent was to assert authority over captured Polish territory and ultimately usurp the Polish Government-in-exile, forming a Soviet-sponsored Polish government once the Red Army captured Warsaw. In a *Tribune* article of October 6, 1944 (quoted in *Rising '44*), George Orwell characterizes the Committee's objective as "the reduction of Poland to a vassal state."

[3] The Warsaw Uprising was, indeed, an absolute disaster. The political machinations of both sides—the Polish Government-in-exile in London and the Soviets with their "Lublin Poles"—leading up to the revolt remain controversial, murky, and virtually incoherent. The "London Poles," closely allied with the Polish Underground's Home Army, had debated the possibility of an uprising ever since Poland capitulated in 1939—with the goal of heading off the likely Soviet seizure of Poland by liberating the city just before the Red Army arrived. (No decision was made until the final moment, and when it was made, it was ill timed and based on poor information.) Britain and the U.S. certainly knew of this plan, but it seems they offered neither practical support nor strong opposition.

Miscalculations abounded, resulting both from the London Poles' failure to coordinate the Uprising (politically and militarily) with either Russia or the Western Allies, and from U.S. and British failure to fully comprehend Stalin's predatory tactics. As Rokossovsky's Front swept rapidly toward the Vistula, Radio Moscow and the PKWN Polish language station urged the Poles to "join the struggle." But once the Uprising began on August 1, the Soviets began denouncing the Home Army's revolt as an "adventure" perpetrated by "criminals," and the swift Soviet offensive suddenly stalled just east of Warsaw. Some among the Allies (including Churchill) believed that Stalin was purposely waiting, to allow the anti-communist Home Army to be destroyed; others were satisfied when he countered that the Germans legitimately halted the Soviet advance. All were mystified when Stalin failed to make much effort to supply or support the Uprising from his nearby bases. The RAF made some valiant attempts to supply the insurgents from nearly a thousand miles away, but Stalin withheld permission to land on nearby Soviet-held airfields, and these attempts were dismal failures. However, Churchill had at least tried to bail out his "First Ally," whereas

Thousands of Polish patriots, deceived by the Émigré Government's seemingly noble appeal, took up arms against their German-Fascist occupiers. They started building barricades on August 1, 1944. Tragically, the rebels didn't have nearly enough weapons, and the Hitlerites hurled the full force of their tanks, artillery, and armored vehicles at them. The unequal fight bled the selfless patriots dry, yet they gallantly defended every street, every house... until they could fight no more.

As Warsaw burned, I felt such a sense of loss for the citizens of that ruined city and for its vandalized cultural and historic treasures.

"Four 'Fockes' on the left," came Nazarkina's voice. She was the first to spot the enemy fighters and immediately launched a flare in their direction to warn everyone.

Long-range anti-aircraft guns blocked our path. We maneuvered. Shells exploded, so dangerously near that fragments drummed ominously on the "Il's" armor. Oerlikon tracers whizzed by the airplanes like glowing red marbles, so beautiful that it was hard to believe they brought death.

My wingmen were in position on the right echelon. The gunfire intensified by the minute. If we made a direct approach, we'd find ourselves in an even denser wall of fire. If I turned left, my wingmen would find themselves under merciless fire as well. So I decided to veer to the right, making a gradual bank that I hoped wouldn't be noticed from the ground. The powerful curtain of fire moved away from us. But we were pushing further from the target, and the enemy guns would soon adjust their aim.

We turned back left and maneuvered through the artillery fire. It was time for the attack. I went into a dive. I couldn't see my wingmen, but I knew

---

Roosevelt's indifferent efforts (his attention diverted by Normandy and the Pacific) were confined to a single airlift.

In the end, the 40,000-or-so poorly-armed Home Army fighters were no match for the Germans. Although the resistance held out for an astonishing two months, the Nazis crushed the Uprising and began following Hitler's orders to erase the city from the earth, resulting in more than 200,000 civilian deaths in Warsaw and the nearly complete destruction of the city.

When the Soviets marched into Warsaw soon afterward, their motives became quite clear. The NKVD began systematically disarming and purging the Home Army (and anyone else deemed an opponent of the Lublin Committee), deporting and even executing many of them. The Soviets duly installed their puppet Provisional Government.

At the "Big Three" conferences in Tehran (before the Uprising) and Yalta in 1945, Roosevelt and Churchill acceded to virtually every one of Stalin's demands regarding Poland—including its new eastern frontier (giving the USSR virtually all the territory it had occupied in 1939) and future governance.

If any conclusion could be drawn from this quagmire of deceit and error, it is that Ms. Yegorova's pity for the "poor deceived Polish people" is well-placed. Abandoned by the Western Allies and devoured by the Soviets, the Poles would not enjoy the independent Polish Republic for which so many had sacrificed for another half-century.

they were with me. We unleashed our guided missiles, cannons, and anti-tank bombs against the tanks. The ground beneath us erupted into flames. In the heat of battle, I forgot about the enemy's anti-aircraft guns. I didn't notice the rockets or the machine gun tracer bullets anymore.

Another attack, and another. Suddenly, my plane was shoved upward, as if someone had punched it from below. A second blow came, and then a third. The airplane became harder to control. It wasn't responding. *For God's sake, climb!* I could no longer maneuver.

I tried with all my strength to force the Shturmovik into a dive and open fire. At first, I seemed to have succeeded. I led the group on another pass at the tanks, and my wingmen followed. Then they noticed I'd been hit. Someone shouted over the radio, "Try to make it to our side!"

The plane must be damaged, I thought. Suddenly, I noticed the silence—not a word from Nazarkina. *Is she dead?* flashed through my head. The plane shivered feverishly. Flames licked into the cockpit from the engine. The plane wouldn't obey the control stick at all. I tried to open the canopy, but it was jammed shut. Smoke filled the cabin, choking me.

The blazing plane spun toward the earth, and I burned and tumbled with it.

54
Prisoner of War

When the other pilots returned from the Magnuszew Bridgehead, they reported that my crew had perished near the target. The military sent a death notice to Volodovo, where my mother, Stepanida Vasilyevna Yegorova, lived.

Death retreated from me this time, however. By some miracle, I was thrown from the burning plane. When I opened my eyes, I realized that I had landed without a plane or a parachute canopy. Before I hit the ground—I still don't know how—I had pulled the ring, but the smoldering parachute didn't open completely.

Terrible pain woke me, wracking my entire body. I could not move. My head felt like it was on fire. My spine hurt unbearably, and my arms and legs were burned nearly to the bone. With difficulty, I pried my eyes open and made out a soldier in a grey-green uniform. An awful realization seized me, an idea more unspeakable than the worst of my pain: *A Fascist! I'm in the hands of Fascists!*

It was the thing I feared most of all. Psychological pain is a hundred times worse than fire, bullets, or any kind of physical suffering. My mind pounded feverishly: *I'm a prisoner!* I was powerless to defend myself. I couldn't even move my hand toward my pistol.

The German planted his foot firmly on my chest and yanked on my smashed hand. I passed out.

I came to as I thudded against the ground. The Hitlerites were trying to load me into a truck, but I couldn't stay on my feet. Whenever they stopped supporting me, I would fall again. They brought a stretcher and laid me on it. As if in a dream, I heard Polish being spoken. Hope flashed in my mind. *Could these be Polish partisans?* After all, we were on Polish soil, and we'd been fighting side-by-side with Polish soldiers. But no, again I saw the Hitlerites and heard their harsh German speech.

"*Schnell! Schnell!*" they urged two Polish medics who were hurriedly tending to my wounds as Soviet airplanes roared over us. "*Schwarze Tod! Schwarze Tod!*" they shouted and disappeared somewhere in a panic. Again, a ray of hope flickered. *Our planes are flying over!* I realized. How perfect it would be if they blew the whole place to pieces!

The medics didn't give me any medications, but only bandaged me and furtively hid my awards and Party card under the bandages. When the attack planes flew away, the Fascists again gathered around my stretcher. I summoned all my strength so as not to let out a single moan of pain in front of them.

I recall the Polish medics whispering something about Radomsk Concentration Camp. After a lapse in consciousness, I awoke on the floor of an endlessly long barracks.

"What have they done to you, the barbarians!" I heard a young female voice. "You need ointment."

"Where are we going to get ointment? The Germans don't have any medicine for us, said a man's voice. "And you, Miss, how did you wind up here?"

"I'm a medical instructor," she said. "Yulia Krashchenko. I got here just like you did, captured on the Vistula, at the Magnuszew Bridgehead. A tank collapsed the trench where I was bandaging the wounded, and the Hitlerites captured us there.

"I know you, Little Sister. You're from the 2nd Guards Battalion under Captain Tskaev, my countryman.

"Come a little closer, Medical Instructor Krashchenko. We need to talk," he whispered. "You see, when we examined the female pilot, we found medals under her bandages. We've got to get them out of here and hide them somewhere the Fritzes can't get to them. Otherwise they'll accuse us of God knows what! Can you do it, Sister? It'll be easier for you."

"I see. But where should I hide them?"

"Let's put them in her burned-up boots. The Fascists won't want them anyway. They like everything brand new," suggested a third person.

When I heard my dear mother tongue, my throat constricted with spasms. With a groan, I squeezed out my first word: "Wa-a-a-ter!"

Yulia stayed by my side from then on. The Hitlerites couldn't drag her away from me, no matter how much they swore at her or beat her.

Sometime later, Yulia sat nearby crying, as I lay on a bunk. Three men wearing rubber aprons and gauze bandages on their faces came in. They tore the bandages off my burned arms and legs, sprinkled some kind of powder all over me, and left.

As Yulia would tell me later, I thrashed around wildly from the pain, hitting my head, screaming, and falling in and out of consciousness. The Polish inmates, who'd landed in the Radomsk camp after the Warsaw Uprising, would have none of it. They started smashing the windows and tearing everything up, demanding that the Germans stop tormenting the Russian female pilot.

The three German "doctors" came back and washed off the powder they had sprinkled on me before.

The next day, they loaded us onto a cargo train and transported us somewhere. It was September 1944—obviously, the front was drawing closer.

Yulia was there with me in the train car, and two other prisoners traveled with us: a soldier from a penalty battalion who was barely alive and a perfectly healthy captain—a battalion *zampolit*. The captain kept plotting to escape, but no opportunity presented itself. Meanwhile, he attended to the dying soldier with fatherly concern.

We prisoners lay on the floor in one half of the car. In the other half, two German soldiers and three Ukrainian policemen slept, ate, drank schnapps, played cards, sang, and told jokes. The Germans basically kept to themselves, but the Ukrainians were completely devoid of mercy for us, their compatriots.

Fortunately, Yulia was with me. I tossed and turned deliriously. In my mind, I was back in the burning plane, tumbling, the flames licking at me. I had to somehow loosen the hot vise tightening around my head...

Each time I regained consciousness, I saw Yulia sitting beside me. "Be patient, dearest. When we get there, we'll find you some medicine. Of course we will," she said through her tears.

The SS drove us through Germany for five days. At the stations, the freight car door would open with a crash. At one stop, an SS man shouted, "Look!" and many eyes fell on the two wounded—me and the half-dead soldier—lying on the floor. Some of the eyes betrayed malice, others compassion, and some were merely indifferent.

I was desperately thirsty. But how could I drink when instead of a face I had this dreadful burned mask and lips that seemed permanently glued together? But Yulia found a way, inserting a straw into the parched slit between my lips.

It was suffocatingly hot, and my burns were starting to fester. It was five days of utter hell. I just wanted the torture to end.

At last, we arrived. Escorted by numerous guards, a column of prisoners marched through the gates of the Hitlerite camp, "III-C." Our comrades in misfortune carried me in on a stretcher, like a coffin into a graveyard. The gates closed behind us.

When the prisoners set my stretcher on the ground, lots of Germans rushed toward me to gape at the Russian captive. I lay there, helpless, burned, broken, and dying.

Later I learned that news of my arrival ripped through the astonished camp like a bomb blast—a female Russian pilot! A group of Germans gathered around me, arguing loudly. I only understood one thing—isolation cell.

Again, my stretcher was carried along a narrow corridor of barbed wire. Through the fence I could see towers manned by submachine gunners. From behind the wire on both sides I heard a low murmuring, and then something flew in my direction. Apparently, the French, Italian, and English inmates of the Küstrin[1] camp were throwing me pieces of bread and bits of sugar, in a quiet show of support and solidarity. Yulia, following along behind the

---

[1] Küstrin (or Kostrzyn, in Polish) is a town in western Poland on the Oder River, about 60 miles east of Berlin. The German POW camp "Stalag III-C Alt-Drewitz," for Allied soldiers (including Italian, French, English, Polish, Yugoslav, Belgian and Soviet prisoners) was just outside of the town, in a village called Alt-Drewitz (Pol. *Drzewice*).

stretcher, picked up the morsels and gathered them in the lap of her army skirt.

Yulia and I were placed into a stone isolation box with smooth concrete walls and two tiny windows with double iron bars over them. The room had evidently served as a prison punishment cell before. A lamp hung from a wooden crossbeam across the low cement ceiling. A two-bed bunk stood by one wall. They put me in the bottom one.

Yulia turned over her skirt and poured out the collection of morsels at my feet. Just then a tremendously tall Gestapo officer came in with two German soldiers.

"Everysing vill be fine here," he said in quite decent Russian. "Vat's all zis garbage?" he pointed with his lash to the bread scattered across the bunk.

"Clean it up!" he ordered the two soldiers. They swept everything up, leaving not even a crumb. Yulia pled with them to leave some bread and sugar, but the Gestapo officer ignored her. The three left.

A Hitlerite with a face carved of wood and a machine gun slung over his shoulder stood frozen behind the door. Yulia hid my Party membership card, my two Orders of the Red Banner, and my medal "For Bravery" in my charred boots under the bed.

For me, a new life was just beginning, a nightmare existence, full of utter physical and spiritual suffering, at the Fascist camp "III-C."

55
The Russian Doctor

The Hitlerites seemed to think that the best thing to do with me was to just leave me in that basement cell, dangling between life and death. They didn't torture me. They just tossed me into that damp concrete box and left me to the mercy of fate. They didn't kill me on the spot, but simply left me to rot, without medical care, most likely dying slowly in agony. It was so like the Nazis— the cold, detached cruelty of it.

Somewhere along my path to death, human compassion stepped in. The very day I went into that solitary confinement cell, dozens, even hundreds of prisoners, good-hearted people of many nationalities, began the battle for the Russian pilot's life. What kindness and solidarity they showed me! What goodwill!

By that time, a deeply-rooted underground resistance organization existed at the Küstrin camp. The underground kept people informed of the news from the front, coordinated acts of sabotage, exposed traitors, and treated the sick and wounded.

Unwittingly, I came to the attention of the organization as soon as I arrived. One of the group's leaders, Dr. Sinyakov, or "the Russian doctor," as everyone called him, took a special interest in me. He was worried. For an experienced doctor like him, a quick glance at me as I was carried by was enough to confirm that I was in critical condition. He knew I would need immediate medical help if I were to survive.

The underground charged Sinyakov and Pavle Trpinac, a former professor from Belgrade University, with the task of asking the camp administrators for permission to treat me. Sinyakov went straight to the camp commandant's office.

When you saw Dr. Sinyakov for the first time, you couldn't tell from his appearance how strong and steadfast the man was. Not particularly tall, his emaciated frame moved slowly and deliberately, and a shock of unruly graying hair crowned his head. He spoke an unhurried German. But with each word, his voice was all metal, quite certain of its rightness.

There's a severely wounded Russian female pilot in the camp," he said.

"And?" said the Fascist. "We receive new groups of prisoners every day. The Reich needs a labor force."

"She's not like the others. She's maimed and burned. She's been here ten days without medical care."

"This is not a hospital."

"I demand, in the name of all camp inmates, that you let me and Dr. Trpinac treat her," said Sinyakov.

"You *demand*?" spat the Gestapo officer, flushing crimson. "For this word alone I could simply…"

It was true. In the camp, he could simply do anything to anyone. Every day, death claimed a new victim. Disobedience—a bullet. Refusing to work—a bullet. Any guard could judge you and carry out your sentence. It was as simple as the Stone Age. Sinyakov knew all that, but he looked straight into the Hitlerite's rabid eyes all the same. Sinyakov's hands protected him from the Nazi's rage. His skilled, strong, able surgeon's hands.

When Georgi Fyodorovich first arrived at the Küstrin camp, the Germans ordered him to perform surgery on a sick inmate's stomach. The German camp surgeon, Dr. Koshel, brought his German medical staff to watch, along with French, English, and Yugoslav specialists from among the prisoners. *Let's see what kind of doctors these Russians have got,* was Koshel's tacit message to the spectators.

Sinyakov's assistants laid the patient on the table. Their hands were shaking with nervousness. One of the Fascists declared that even the best Russian doctor was still worse than a bad German orderly. But Dr. Sinyakov, barely able to stay on his feet, pale, barefoot, clothes in tatters, performed a brilliant stomach resection with a sure, accurate touch. Everyone who watched understood at once that the surgeon didn't need to be tested.

After Georgi Fyodorovich finished, the Germans withdrew quietly. But the French, Yugoslav, and English doctors stayed to congratulate Dr. Sinyakov on his victory. "You only need to look a little better, my friend," remarked the Yugoslav, Dr. Bruk.

"Comrade…" said Pavle Trpinac, shaking Sinyakov's hand. It was the only Russian word Trpinac knew.

Dr. Trpinac, like a political agitator, started spreading the word about the Russian doctor. Inmates streamed to him from all over the camp to be healed. *He raises people from the dead!* they whispered of him. Sinyakov treated perforated ulcers, pleurisy, and osteomyelitis. He operated on cancers and thyroid glands. Every day he did around five surgeries and bandaged at least fifty people. He was exhausted, but he would not rest when there were more than fifteen hundred wounded and sick prisoners who needed his help.

Once, a panicked guard turned up suddenly with a translator from among the prisoners, and shouted at Georgi Fyodorovich, "To the commandant, immediately!"

It turned out that the young son of one of the Gestapo officers had gotten some object lodged in his trachea. The little boy was choking, his life fading fast. He desperately needed medical help, but the German doctors waved away the suggestion. It was futile, they said. Then the Gestapo officer remembered the Russian doctor, a miracle worker who healed people in squalid camp conditions, without medical instruments or assistants. Sure, he was of an "inferior race," but what choice did they have?

What choice did Dr. Sinyakov have? The Gestapo officer stated quite clearly that if his son died, the doctor would be killed. If Sinyakov had been ordered to operate on the evil, sadistic father, he certainly would have refused. But this was a child. He was innocent of his father's crimes. Sinyakov agreed to do the surgery.

He hurried to the operating table. By some miracle, this man, staggering from malnutrition and suffering, brought to bear his intellect and his art and saved the boy. And once he had fended off death, another miracle occurred. The baby's mother, a haughty, "pure-blooded Aryan," knelt in front of him and kissed the hand that had held the scalpel.

Since that time, he gained a certain measure of independence and, occasionally, the right to make a request. That's why the Germans allowed him and Dr. Trpinac to treat me.

And so when Sinyakov stood there before the commandant, the doctor ignored the Gestapo officer's threat and repeated his demand. Finally, the Gestapo man agreed.

Twilight. The door creaked open, and a German sergeant materialized, like an apparition. "Whoo! It smells like dead people in here," he said, puffing on his cigarette.

He bent over my bunk and exclaimed, "A thousand devils! These Russian witches just won't die. She's still breathing! There's not a spot on her that's alive."

I really did smell like a corpse. I had severe burns on my face, and pus covered my arms and legs. That's probably what saved me from having terrible burn scars later.

"Come in!" the sergeant ordered the man standing at the door. It was Georgi Fyodorovich Sinyakov, the "Russian doctor."

I didn't know who the men were, but I immediately sensed that they were on my side. Georgi Fyodorovich and Pavle Trpinac got all the medications I needed from English, French, and American inmates. All the prisoners received packages of food and medicine from the International Red Cross, everyone except for the Russians, that is. The Soviet Union withdrew from the organization. According to Stalin's reasoning, "We don't have prisoners of war. We have traitors."

Sinyakov and Trpinac also shared their meager bread ration with me. I'll never forget their generosity. I still recall Trpinac bringing me a cracker, or sending Zhiva Lazin, a peasant from Banat,[1] with a bowl of beans.

Whenever Trpinac got any reports from Sovinformbureau, he would throw on his medical gown and slip a pack of cigarettes to the sentry, who'd

---

[1] An agrarian region of Central Europe that comprises parts of Romania, Serbia, and Hungary.

then let him into my cell. He'd tell me the news, in a kind of half-Russian, half-Serbian dialect: "Oh, good news I have for you! The Scarlet Army is advancing most wonderfully westward..."

Once he brought me a topographic map. He had marked the Soviet troops' advance to the Oder in red pencil. Pavle knelt beside me, his back to the door, and showed me the red arrow pointing toward Berlin. "They will be here soon!" he said.

The German sergeant suddenly burst in, cursing. Dr. Trpinac somehow managed to hide the map and pretend to bandage me. The sergeant left.

Another time, Professor Trpinac brought me a scrap of the *Pravda* newspaper with information about the heroic deeds of a Colonel Yegorov. "Happy news is good medicine!" he said, assuming the colonel was my husband or a relative. Dear Pavle had no idea that Yegorov was a very common name in Russia, like Stepanov or Ivanov!

Professor Trpinac often told me about his beautiful homeland of Yugoslavia. He sighed sadly when he talked about his sister Melka, whom the Fascists had hanged in 1941. His sister Yelena had joined the partisans with her daughter (Mira Aleckovic, who would later become a famous Serb poetess). The Fascists arrested Trpinac right from the lectern where he was addressing a biochemistry class at Belgrade University.

He and Dr. Sinyakov did everything they could to fight against Fascism in the camp, often risking their lives. Sinyakov helped the underground arrange for Russian prisoners of war to escape. He would feed them, prepare dried bread for their journey, find them a watch or a compass. Once he saved a seriously injured pilot by treating his wounds and then telling the Germans the man had died. He then replaced him with a dead soldier so the Germans wouldn't realize he was missing. Another victory for the Russian doctor against the Fascists!

56
Help Me, Sister!

Little by little I began to get better. All sorts of traitors and provocateurs began frequenting my cell. One day a high-ranking SS officer who spoke Russian came to see me.

"So, we're rotting nicely, are we?" he asked with an arrogant sneer. I silently turned toward the wall. He rapped me on the shoulder with the rubber handle of his lash.

"Don't worry, Girl. I'm not angry! We respect strength," he said, after a pause adding, "A single word from you, and tomorrow you'll be in the best hospital in Berlin. The day after tomorrow, all the newspapers of the Reich will trumpet your name. So?"

"You beasts!" Yulia's voice rang out. "She's on the verge of death, and you only have one thing on your mind!"

"Shut up, Russian swine!" the officer erupted.

"You are the swine! German swine!"

"You'll rot next!" the Hitlerite screamed and rushed out of the cell.

When Georgi Fyodorovich visited us later, I told him about our visit from the SS. "Do you not grasp the situation?" he pled with Yulia. "You're being foolish! You've got to outsmart these people.

"I won't lie to you," he added. "This does not bode well for you."

"My Party card and medals are hidden in my boots," I told Sinyakov. "Please take them. If you make it to the motherland, would you get them to my people?"

Sinyakov agreed and left us. We sat quietly for a long while, anxiously listening to every sound, every rustle, lost in our private thoughts. Finally, I broke the silence. I asked Yulia how she found herself at the front.

"It's simple," she began. "I'd just finished the seventh grade in my village school in Novo-Chervonnoye, in the Lugansk Region, when the war broke out. My four brothers left for the front. Hitlerites occupied our village. What a horrible time! They chased Mama and me out of our hut, and we lived in a shed for a long time.

"When our troops came back through, I ran first thing to the commander with the 'Ready for Medical Defense Work' badge I'd earned at school and asked to be sent to the front."

"How old were you then?"

"Seventeen."

And that's how a seventeen-year-old Ukrainian student named Yulia Krashchenko became a soldier-medical instructor.

Who can forget his first taste of combat? Yulia rushed about the battlefield, answering every moan, every call: "Sister, help me!"

The tiny girl wasn't strong enough to carry a heavy man off the field. She was terrified of wounds and of men's furtive tears. "You'll destroy yourself. You won't be able to handle it," a wounded soldier wheezed, watching her.

"Don't you worry about a thing, Uncle. Everything's going to be OK," the words poured out, as Yulia summoned her reserves. "I've hauled out fellows heavier than you."

Never mind that he was the first wounded man she'd ever carried, and this, her very first battlefield. But the lie soothed him. One step, two, ten—to safety! Then another call: "Sister, help me!" The cries kept coming.

Yulia was with the soldiers the night they forced the Vistula and seized the Magnuszew Bridgehead on the opposite bank. German artillery ceaselessly shelled their position, but they held on. They had vowed to retain the bridgehead at any cost.

Columns of German tanks advanced toward the Vistula, while I flew my unlucky sortie above them, and right over my dear Yulia. The Fascist tanks rolled over the trench where Yulia was dressing the men's wounds, trapping her in the enemy's rear.

Later that night, after our argument with the SS officer, two huge Germans burst in and, pointing at Yulia, said, "*Kommen. Schnell, schnell.*"

I asked the Hitlerites where they were taking the girl, and why. One of them pressed his finger to his temple, emitted the sounds, "Piff! Paff!" and left.

I was locked in, alone. Silence. How unbearable silence can be!

57
Liberation

Grief drained away my strength. I wanted to close my eyes and never open them again. I fell into a state of complete apathy, which wound my will and stamina into a tight, hard knot.

Sinyakov and Trpinac weren't allowed to see me anymore. Some traitor with deceitful black eyes was now changing my dressings. But my comrades in misfortune didn't abandon me.

I don't know what would have happened to me without them. My fellow prisoners found countless ways to show me compassion, as if their brotherly, helping hands could reach right through the walls of my cell. The English inmates gave me an overcoat. The Poles re-tailored it into a jacket in the latest fashion. The Yugoslavs sent me a warm scarf, and my own Russians stitched me a pair of woolen slippers with red stars on the toes. If the camp administrators had gotten wind of these gifts, they would surely have punished those generous souls. But for me, what was a firing squad in the face of such human kindness and solidarity?

Once, by some miracle, they even managed to deliver a ration of bread with a note inside that said, "Hold on, Sister!"

That unforgettable piece of bread... I can't explain what that meager slice meant to me just then. Anyone who has ever known hunger understands already, and those who haven't—well, God save them from it!

Two hundred grams of the worst bread and a liter of yeasty soup made from a dirty rutabaga, that was a Russian soldier's daily ration in the "III-C" camp. When a man wasting away from starvation sends you his only slice of bread...

On one of those dreadful days of solitary confinement, I noticed a tall, skinny sentry not more than seventeen years old casting furtive glances at me. He had served on guard duty for several days, and his curiosity about the "flying witch" seemed to be getting the better of him.

I realized that the guard wanted to say something to me, but he was hesitant. Finally, looking around, he pulled a package out of his pocket, unwrapped a piece of pie, strode to my bunk, and placed it on my chest with a smile.

"*Bitte, essen, Russische Frau!*" he said very amiably and returned to his place. "*Bitte!*"

I gestured to him that I didn't want anything from him, that he should take the pie away.

"Nein, nein! Ich bin Faschisten nicht!" the guard exclaimed, hurriedly explaining that his mother had brought him the treats from her village.

One day the SS began chasing anyone who could stand up out of the barracks. They lined the prisoners up in columns and marched them toward the west with German Shepherds at their heels. Only the dying inmates remained in the camp, with a few doctors and orderlies headed by Dr. Sinyakov. The doctors had surreptitiously dug a deep hole under the operating room and hidden many people there until the camp was liberated.

Through the bars over my windows, I watched a Gestapo officer and two submachine gunners rush into the Frenchmen's barracks and open fire. They seemed to be finishing off anyone who couldn't walk out.

The roar of distant gunfire drew closer and closer, like a thunderstorm. And then it was upon us, shells exploding to the right, then to the left of my cell, which was still locked from the outside. But my sentry had gone.

Suddenly all fell silent. The door flew open, and our tankists appeared on the threshold. It was the last day of January 1945, and the 5th Attack Army had come to liberate the cursed "III-C" camp.

Major Ilyin, the tank brigade commander, offered to send me to the hospital along with his wounded tankists, but I refused: "I have to find my regiment," I said. "They must be here somewhere on this part of the front."

I immediately had the tankists send a letter for me to Mama in Volodovo and another one to the regiment through the field mail. I slid joyously into the red-starred slippers my unknown friends had sewn for me, gripped the edge of my bunk, and took a step forward. My legs wobbled like strings, the wasted muscles refusing to obey. The new skin that had just grown over my burns immediately cracked and started bleeding.

Stop. Sit down a minute. Take a break, I told myself.

I slid my feet gingerly onto the floor again and ventured a tiny step. I staggered but did not fall this time. I groped my way along the wall, taking small steps. I was walking!

Any former inmates of the Küstrin camp who could hold a weapon climbed aboard the tanks and headed off to join the fight at Küstrin.

The tankists asked Dr. Sinyakov to set up a field hospital in the rear, which had lagged far behind our army's rapid advance. For several days, Georgi Fyodorovich operated on more than seventy tankists. He returned my Party membership card and awards to me right after we were liberated, just as he had promised.

58
SMERSH[1]

Memory. These memories... For some strange reason, they awoke of their own accord and brought to light such things... God forbid, such things! One day it suddenly stirred, dug deep, and exhumed such distant times, events, and people, some living today and some long dead.

I'm wary with my memories. I generally try not to lose myself in recollections. What use is it? Still, I must tell my grandchildren and great-grandchildren the truth. I must tell them what happened after the battle at Küstrin abated, when the rear caught up with us, and all former prisoners of Küstrin were ordered to the town of Landsberg to be "checked."

I could not walk. A soldier passed by in a cart, and Dr. Sinyakov persuaded him to take me in the cart to the nearest town. Georgi Fyodorovich arranged for me to wait for him by the first house at the outskirts of town. I didn't have to wait long. I had just gotten settled on a small bench when an officer and two soldiers with submachine guns approached and ordered me to follow them. I hobbled along behind the officer to the other side of town with an armed soldier on either side of me.

I wore the jacket the English had given me and the Poles had altered "in the latest Warsaw fashion." I carried my Party membership card in the breast pocket and my awards pinned to my chest. My burned scalp had just begun to grow hair again, and so I wound the scarf the Yugoslav peasant Zhiva Lazin had given me around my head. On my feet I wore the slippers my

---

[1] The successor to the NKVD Special Sections, *SMERSH* was a Soviet counterintelligence organ whose stated aim was to root out saboteurs, spies, collaborators, and traitors in the armed forces and occupied territories. (The word is an acronym for *SMERt SHpionam*, or "Death to Spies.") The existence of numerous "Hiwis" (a German abbreviation for *Hilfswillige*, or "volunteer helper" —Soviet prisoners and defectors who assisted the Germans with labor or combat duties) and "Vlasovites" (a force of Russian turncoats called the "Russian Liberation Army" fought for Germany under former Red Army General Vlasov; the term later came to refer to any turncoat or collaborator) certainly prompted a need for counterintelligence. But SMERSH cast a far wider net, taking Stalin at his word—that all Soviet POWs were traitors—and subjected any Soviet soldier liberated from POW or forced labor camps to interrogation at best, and internment or even execution at worst. "The fear of SMERSH..." writes a soldier named David Samoilov, quoted in Merridale's *Ivan's War*, "corrupted the lofty notion of a people struggling against the invader...." (231).

Russian friends had fashioned for me from an old woolen overcoat—the slippers with red stars on the toes.

They brought me straight to the commandant himself. He didn't think twice, didn't even question me, the "suspicious personage"—just sent me under guard directly to the SMERSH Counterintelligence Department, 32nd Infantry Corps, 5th Attack Army. They "quartered" me on a plank bunk bed in a sentry-room. They housed German prisoners below me in the basement. Thank God I was above them instead of among them.

The first night, two soldiers with submachine guns escorted me to the interrogation. I struggled to climb to the second floor. My legs kept failing me, and the thin skin just beginning to grow over my burns kept cracking. My arms and legs stung and bled at the joints. Whenever I stopped to rest, a soldier would jab me in the spine with his weapon.

They brought me into a brightly-lit room with pictures on the walls and a large carpet on the floor. A major sat behind the desk. He had a friendly look, but...

First, he confiscated my Party card and the awards. He scrutinized them for a long while under a magnifying glass. I was not allowed to sit down. I felt sure I would collapse, but I somehow managed to remain on my feet. Finally, the major let me sit. I thought that no force on earth could tear me off of that chair, but I was wrong—when the major barked, "Stand up!" I rose as quickly as I could.

"Where did you get the awards and the Party membership card?

"Why did you allow yourself to be taken prisoner?

"What was your assignment?

"Who gave you that assignment?

"Where were you born?

"Whom are you supposed to contact?"

The major bombarded me with these and other questions all night long, repeating the same ones over and over again, nearly until dawn. No matter what I said, he shouted, "You're lying, you German dog!"

One night bled into many. Soldiers escorted me to the toilet. They brought food to me once a day at my little sentry-room bunk. They insulted me, calling me all sorts of filthy names. My name was forgotten. I was simply "Fascist Bitch."

After the war, I confided in our former regimental commander Pyotr Karev about my time with SMERSH. I was crying hysterically. Suddenly, he broke in.

"What's wrong with you?" he shouted in a fury. "Why didn't you remind him of '41, when you flew reconnaissance missions in a defenseless U-2? Or in '42 when you, Anya Yegorova, were shot down by Fascist fighters and burned terribly in that same U-2 and still managed to deliver the orders to our troops? After everything you've been through! Did you forget who you are? Look back, Anya Yegorova! No! *No!* No one can take it away from us. An attack pilot! A shturmovik! Do you know what that means?

"We took Novorossisk, Kovel, Lutsk, Warsaw! Took them! All that and more! Who did he think you were? *No!* Why didn't you throw it back in that bastard's face? Sitting back in the rear while we're fighting.

"Let's drink, Anya Yegorova. Let's drink our 100-gram front ration one more time," said Karev.

"You know I don't drink," I smiled. "I always gave my combat ration away to my mechanic..."

On the tenth day of my confinement, my patience snapped.

I stood up from the bunk and headed silently for the door, then up the narrow staircase and straight to the major's office. "Freeze, Bitch, or I'll shoot!" shouted the soldier as he hurried along behind me. But I continued climbing the stairs, nearly at a run. I don't know where I found the strength. "Beware the fury of a patient man," a seventeenth-century Englishman named John Dryden once said.

I threw open the door and shouted (or it seemed to me that I shouted) right from the doorway: "When are you going to stop tormenting me? Kill me if you like, but I won't let you torment me any more."

I regained consciousness, lying on a thick carpet, a glass of water next to me. I was alone in the room. I got up slowly, gulped some water, and sat down on a divan. The door soon opened, and the major—Major Fyodorov was his name—came in.

"Are you OK?" he asked me courteously.

I couldn't answer.

"About nine days ago, some doctors who were inmates of the Küstrin "III-C" camp were trying to find you," he told me. "They wrote down everything they knew about you: how you were captured, how you behaved in the camp, and how they treated your wounds. They asked if we would allow you to go to the Landsberg camp with them for the "check," but we could not do that. You see, it was all very suspicious for you to have saved your awards and above all, your Party card, in that infernal place. To make a long story short, we are releasing you. We've checked you out thoroughly. But if you want, you can stay with us and work."

"No, no," I said hurriedly. "I want to find my regiment. They're fighting somewhere nearby—"

"You are free to go wherever you like," the major cut me short.

"And how do you expect me to go anywhere without my ID? They'll just arrest me again right away and put me away."

"We don't issue ID's!" the major said. "If you want to get to your regiment, then I would advise you to stop by the checkpoint on the road and ask them to give you a lift."

"You have been tormenting me, Major, and now you are mocking me. You see that I can hardly walk. And who is going to give me a lift if I have no papers? Please, for heaven's sake, give me my ID and take me to the check-point, I beg you!"

The major took pity on me. He gave me documents stating that I had been checked and ordered a soldier to take me to the checkpoint in a cart. There they told me where 16th Air Force headquarters were and put me in a car headed in that direction. When I arrived, the army personnel unit immediately "filtered" me into the army SMERSH unit.

"We're going to send an inquiry to the 34th Infantry Corps of the 5th Attack Army, where you were checked," they told me and set me up in a very comfortable room with access to the officers' mess. The SMERSH chief's wife brought me magazines and books to read.

Many people came to visit me—officers from headquarters, pilots, various women. They brought me piles of gifts and congratulated me on my return. "You have been to hell, Comrade Yegorova," some of them joked. "Now paradise awaits you."

A Captain Tsekhonya, who had formerly been an aide in our regiment, came by. I used to reprimand him for all sorts of trifles, but he didn't seem to resent that now. He gave me some beautiful dresses and said, "I put together a parcel for my wife, but when I found out you were alive, I brought them to you instead."

"What am I going to do with dresses?" I asked him. "I'm sure they'll give me a soldier's blouse and shirt."

"You need medical treatment, Annochka," he said kindly, rummaging in his pocket for a handkerchief.

The regiment received my letter and passed it on to the division. Colonel V. A. Timofeyev, division commander, ordered *zampolit* Shvidky to initiate a search for me.

I waited on a bench. A small crutch lay next to me, along with a straw bag the pilots interned at the Küstrin camp made for me. They decorated the bag with the Air Force emblem and my initials—"A.Ye." (Today you'll find that gift at the Central USSR Armed Forces Museum.)

Shvidky spotted me first. He jumped out of the car and rushed to me with his arms outstretched. I didn't recognize him at first. The diminutive *zampolit* looked like a bear cub in his fur overalls, boots, and *shapka-ushanka*. Shvidky's surname (which sounds like "speedy") suited his character perfectly. He quickly kissed me, sniffled, and rushed to validate my documents so that we could leave right away for the regiment.

A group of gunners who accompanied Shvidky greeted me noisily, interrupting each other as news of the regiment tumbled out. Only one of them stood to the side, unable to hide his grief. He wept freely and kept repeating, "Dusya is dead!" I looked carefully at him and realized it was her Seryozha, the tail-gunner for whom she'd grieved so piteously that day at the revetments. For him she'd secretly filled her cabin with anti-tank bombs, hoping to avenge his death, on our final flight together.

59
The Colonel's Courtship

When Major Shvidky found me at 16th Air Force headquarters, he gave me a letter. It began in an unusual way:

Dear Annushka!
I am very sick, and I'm writing to you in bed. But I am so happy to be writing to you.

When we lost you, I couldn't overcome my grief for a long time. Do you understand this feeling? I scarcely understand it myself, but I know for sure that you are very dear to me. Maybe this isn't the right time to write to you about this. You probably have other worries right now.

I am doing everything I can for you, and even a little more. Try to stay composed, but be persistent. I hope that Major Shvidky brings you back to the regiment! Please come to see me at once, or I'll be hurt.

Everyone is waiting for you at the regiment. If they don't let you come back, be patient and remember that I am always thinking about you and that I will be constantly pestering the authorities. I so want to believe that you will come back…

I wish you all the best and offer you a friendly embrace.
With deepest respect,

V. Timofeyev
02/21/45

Colonel V. A. Timofeyev was the commander of our 197th Attack Air Force Division.

His letter surprised me and made me happy. But it also set me to thinking. Why had he written such things to me? I barely knew him. Besides, I have always felt wary of authority figures. The pilots in the regiment joked, "Yegorova always ignores the bosses, which is why she's still a lieutenant, doing the job of a lieutenant colonel."

I had even clashed with Colonel Timofeyev once. The regiment was redeployed to Dys, near Lublin, and I was to fly to the new base with the last group. I was chatting with some of the pilots when the commander suddenly appeared. I made my official report to him that in a few minutes the planes would be out of the shop and that we'd soon take off.

"Take me with you!" the colonel said jovially, but, it seemed to me, only half-jokingly.

"What do you mean, 'Take me with you'? Please, let's fly together. But you're my senior, so you'll be the flight leader," I answered.

"No, I don't want to be the flight leader. I'd rather be somewhere in the tail of your group," said the colonel, rather overdoing the whole scene.

"I don't like it when leaders hang around our tails!" I pronounced without a second thought. The colonel looked hurt, turned, and left without a word.

He avoided me after that, which suited me just fine. The further I was from our commanders' scrutiny, the better.

Still, it was wonderful to know that there was a person in the world who was thinking of me, who cared enough to try to ease my burdens.

The division commander asked Major Shvidky to drop by division headquarters with me on our way back, which we did. The commander seemed overjoyed to see me. He held my hands in his for a long time, gazing at the burn scars, then suddenly kissed them. I pulled my hands away, blushing.

Timofeyev invited Shvidky and me to have lunch with him. He called his orderly and asked him to bring three lunches from the mess. He produced a bottle of wine from somewhere. After lunch, he said, "Now, Annushka, you need to go to the field hospital for proper treatment. When the doctors pronounce you fit and you feel up to it, then we'll decide how you'll proceed with your military service."

They didn't keep me long in the army hospital. I was sent to the Air Force Personnel Department in Moscow, where they would decide whether I could continue as regimental navigator. General Shadsky, the personnel head, referred me to the Serpukhov Military Commissariat to discuss my further service.

A young lieutenant wearing aviation insignia picked me up the next morning, and we took the *elektrichka* to Serpukhov.[1] When we arrived at the military commissariat, he delivered a sealed packet to the officer on duty. The officer opened the packet, only to find another envelope inside it with a wax seal. "You'll have to go to the school building next door," said the officer. "You'll see it. It's the one behind the barbed wire. The entrance is on the other side."

When the lieutenant showed the envelope to the guard at the entrance, the guard let us inside and told us how to get to the chief's office. I still didn't fully realize where I was. The lieutenant said suddenly, "You sit here in the waiting room, and I'll go into the office first."

When the lieutenant went inside, I heard someone swear loudly at him and shout, "Why are you escorting the criminal unarmed?"

---

[1] An ancient city on the Oka River 60 miles (97 km) south of Moscow. *Elektrichka* is a common nickname for the *elektropoyezd,* an electrically-propelled suburban and commuter passenger train.

The lieutenant answered quietly. "Comrade General, she is wounded," he said. "She's wearing a uniform with her awards, and here's a certificate that says she was awarded the 'Hero of the Soviet Union'... posthumously." Again, obscenities flew, and the lieutenant shot out of the office like a bullet.

"Let's get out of here. These Air Force guys are a bunch of pigs. They're sending you to be 'checked' again!"

We rode the train back in silence. I went to pieces. With the lieutenant's help, I somehow made it to Arbat Street. I never saw him again.

After I pulled myself together under the vigilant eye of Yekaterina Vasilyevna, my brother's wife, I went to the Air Force Personnel Department alone, right to General Shadsky's office. I planned to spit in his face. But he wouldn't receive me. It was almost as if he knew my intentions. I hadn't seen the last of these interrogations.

The doctors at the medical department deemed me unfit for combat flying service and classified me as an invalid of the second degree. I received a voucher for a sanatorium. It all came as a great shock.

I was young then, and by nature an optimist. And so I slowly recovered, taking my medical treatment there in Moscow, on Arbat Street with my brother's family, near my beloved Metrostroy.

Soon the war ended. Vyacheslav Arsenyevich Timofeyev came from Germany on leave and found me on the Arbat. He asked for my "hand and heart," as they used to say in olden days.

His proposal surprised and frightened me. Here was a man at least twenty years older than I was, who hardly knew me at all, asking for the hand of a young woman who'd been maimed in the war... and I still grieved for Viktor Kutov.

"Are you joking?" I asked him.

"I'm in no mood for jokes," he said. "This is a serious step in my life."

"And how many such steps have you already made in your life?" I asked him impertinently. "The pilots who studied under you at the flying schools said you'd taken a number of these 'steps.'"

The colonel blushed and said that he had had a wife and daughter, but when he went to prison in Chita as an 'enemy of the people,' his wife left him and married someone else.

"I remarried after I was rehabilitated," he explained. "after they returned my awards and rank to me. But she and I split in 1942. We didn't have a family. Now I am a bachelor."

Perhaps Yekaterina Vasilyevna was thinking of her own husband, my brother Vasya, who was still in Norilsk serving his ten-year sentence. But something made her snap. "Don't be stupid," she said curtly. "He loves you. He worries about you, protects you, and helps you. You can see that he's a good man. Go, Nyurochka. Marry him and put the past behind you. You've got to go on living!"

We didn't have a wedding ceremony as such. We simply registered at the Acts of Civil Status office in the Kievsky district of Moscow and had dinner at the Moscow Hotel, where Timofeyev was staying.

We used our Air Force clinic vouchers at a sanatorium in the Caucasus. We spent a month together on the Black Sea coast. When we returned to Moscow, we decided to visit my mother in Volodovo. Mama was so happy and cheerful. I had no idea it was the last time I would see her.

60
A Reliable Fortuneteller

When my mother received the letter from me, sent from the camp by the tankists who liberated us, she thought she had gone mad. She read it several times, crossed herself, and went to see the woman next door. "Tolyushka, read this! I think I've lost my mind."

Mama had fallen ill with grief when she received the notice of my death. She refused to believe that I was really gone. Someone from the village told her confidentially that there was a very reliable fortune-teller who foretold only the truth. "But she's very expensive," the villager warned.

Mama collected all her valuables and some money and wrote to her eldest daughter in Kuvshinovo. "Mashyushka! I need you to come and see me for a day. Ask for permission from work."

Mariya arrived in Volodovo late at night. "Please, go to Spas-Yasinovichi," Mama begged. "The fortune-teller is my only hope. Whatever she says, so be it."

Masha set off early the next morning on foot, thirty kilometers one way, to fulfill her mother's request. The fortune-teller said to tell Mama that I was not among the living.

Obviously, Mama hadn't paid her enough. Usually, a fortune-teller wouldn't give bad news without leaving any hope.

When my sister Mariya revealed the fortune-teller's "truth," Mother fell seriously ill again. Soon after that, the Kalinin Military Commissariat awarded Mama a bereavement pension in lieu of the money she regularly received from me. That destroyed her hope altogether.

She lay sick for a month. Then one day she got up, made her way to the village church, and asked the priest to hold a prayer service for me. In my writing desk, I still keep the little book with a cross on the cover, in which the priest registered deaths in the village. The last column reads "Warrior Anna," angrily crossed out in different ink (presumably by my mother).

When Mama received my letter (and once her neighbor read it and assured her I was indeed alive), she dressed up in her holiday finery and headed for the local military commissariat. Many years later, the chief there told me about it. "An old woman—very agitated—came into my office," he said. "She walked right up to me and said, 'Son, take this cursed pension away from me!'"

He finally got her settled down enough to have a cup of tea and explain who she was and what pension she was talking about. She left feeling reassured, but she never stopped insisting, "Take the pension away from me, that's it."

About five years after the war, the military commissariat where I lived summoned me. They alleged that my mother had received a pension for five months illegally and that I had to pay back three thousand rubles or face a judge.

"I'm not paying," I told the officer. "Why don't you have the Air Force reimburse me for all the combat flights they never paid me for? That would be a much bigger sum!"

"Write a report!" he said. So I wrote one. So far, I have not received an answer.

After all my troubles, I finally came home to Volodovo to see my mother. I sat at the table with Anisya, my mother's lively and talkative sister. As Mama brought in plate after plate of food, Aunt Anisya told me about how the old women gathered for a commemorative feast in the village after my funeral. There were no young people left, she explained.

"Little Niece, you should have seen the feast your mother had for you!" Anisya said loudly, so my mother would hear.

"I won't lie to you," my aunt went on. "There was an enormous amount of food on the table, and wine glasses all around. But then your mama fetched a decanter from the cabinet, poured each of us a glass, then put the decanter back into the cabinet and locked it!"

"Please! That's not true, Anusushka!" Mama pleaded.

Anisya winked at me and said, "Not true? What do you mean? It's as true as clean water!" Mama looked distressed, not appreciating the joke, but Anisya pressed on merrily.

Water bubbled in the medium-sized samovar, polished to a brilliant luster. My mother's uncle, Gavril the priest, had given us three samovars. Mama always boiled water in the medium-sized one early in the morning for tea. We'd heat the biggest one with coal when the whole family got together. It was especially nice on Saturdays, when we boiled water for baths. The men washed first, when the water was still very hot. Then our turn came.

After the baths, we would all drink tea until we broke a sweat. The table would be loaded with plates of soaked cowberries, cranberries, blueberries...

Amid these recollections, I sat arm-in-arm with Aunt Anisya. The table was covered with our old white hand-woven festival cloth with tassels, the samovar shone like gold, and Mama crossed the threshold with yet another dishful of steaming food. It was 1945, the war was over, and we celebrated my "resurrection" together at home, in Volodovo. Just at that moment, it was all just as I remembered it.

61
Epilogue
(The Survivors Can't Believe They Are Alive)

When his leave ended, my husband had to return to Germany. He came to fetch me at Volodovo in a small car. Since I had no military documents, traveling was a bit tricky, but we made it as far as Warsaw. The Air Force commander in Poland lent us a two-seater U-2, and we squeezed into the rear cabin behind the pilot.

The plane ran out of fuel near the Oder River. When the engine went quiet, the young pilot panicked and headed for a woody bank. Fortunately, we had plenty of altitude, and Timofeyev leaned forward, grabbed the controls from the pilot, and put the plane down in a field. My husband's Air Force cap blew off in the process. We finally found it hanging in a tree by the river. We walked to Frankfurt-on-the-Oder on foot and took a car to Kottbus, where my husband was stationed.

In Kottbus, I gave birth to my son, Pyotr, despite the doctors' warnings. I was sick and unable to walk for a long time afterward. Apparently, my unfortunate landing with a half-opened parachute had not done me any good. We were very relieved that our son was healthy.

A year later, my husband was recalled to Moscow, and we took a train back to the Soviet Union. Timofeyev was promoted and appointed commander of an air corps in Kamchatka. He refused to go because of my health. "We cannot offer you anything else," said Personnel Chief Shadsky curtly.

Because of Timofeyev's wounds in the Civil War and my more recent injuries, we both became disabled pensioners. We had nowhere to live. After a great deal of trouble, we finally settled in a small town just outside of Moscow called Obukhovo, near the Monino Air Force Base. We wanted at least to hear the roar of airplanes.

There I gave birth to Igor, my second "contraband" son—the doctors had strictly forbidden me to give birth because of my spine and pelvic trauma, so I didn't go to see them until my first labor pains came. Fearing for Igor's life, I asked to be placed in a maternity home in Electrostal. They saved our lives there.

My political problems didn't end after the war. I continued to be denied my Party membership because of my time in the Küstrin camp. On arriving in Moscow, I visited the Chief Political Directorate of the Soviet Army to try and recover my Party card. They couldn't find it there and advised me to search for it in the political directorates of the various armies and air forces. I mailed countless letters and finally located it in some warehouse at the Moscow garrison, near the Manezh. I arrived wearing my uniform and awards and walking with a cane, showed my ID from the 197th Attack Air Division, and was received in a friendly way.

"Yes, your Party membership card is with us. I'll get it for you now," said the political officer and headed for the safe. "By the way, in what hospital were you treated?"

"I was a prisoner-of-war," I said.

The officer's face darkened. He slowly opened and then closed the safe. "We're not giving you your card. Go to the Party commission."

"Which one? Why?" I asked.

"We have no prisoners-of-war. We have traitors. That's what Comrade Stalin said. Leave the premises at once," he said.

I left feeling angry and bitter. I walked along the Kremlin wall, with a clamorous ringing in my head, my eyes unseeing. I sat for a while on a bench in Alexander Garden. I had calmed down a bit, but I could still not stop the tears that streamed down my cheeks, nor my feverish shivering and chattering teeth.

A policeman came up to me and asked what was wrong, if I needed an ambulance. "No, no." I told him. "Just help me get home." He accompanied me to Arbat 35, where Yekaterina Vasilyevna gave me some pills and put me to bed.

Two days later I received a phone call summoning me to the Air Force office of the Moscow Military District, commanded by Vasily Stalin[1] himself. Vasily Yosifovich had received my letter and had written a note across it in his own hand, "It seems to me that Yegorova is right."

Still, there was no resolution at the Moscow Military District, and none at the Party commission.

Finally, I was called to the Party Collegium at the CPSU[2] Central Committee. The Party investigator declared, right in front of me and the whole commission, that I had parachuted out of the airplane with some kind of special mission for the Germans!

I stood up and pronounced, "That's a lie!" They all looked at me as if I were their sworn enemy. I asked myself, *Who are these people who are judging me?*

They refused to restore my Communist Party membership. I was relieved. They could have thrown me in prison, and me with two small children. But I kept writing letters to the Central Committee, despite my husband's and friends' advice. "What do you need it for?" Vyacheslav

---

[1] Joseph Stalin's son.

[2] Communist Party of the Soviet Union.

Arsenyevich reasoned. "What you need is your health, so you can raise your sons!"

A year later I was summoned again to the Central Committee and investigated by a KGB colonel. He asked me politely to sit with him on a sofa, showed me photographs of his two daughters, and asked about my family. Then he asked me how I found myself in German captivity.

"Is it really all true?" he asked in amazement when I finished. "Just yesterday, I had a pilot sitting right here, swearing that he was clean as a windowpane, and all the while I had evidence in my desk proving he was lying."

"I'm quite sure, Comrade Colonel, that you'll find no evidence in your desk that discredits my name," I told him sharply.

"OK, you may go. You'll be summoned again to the Party Collegium."

At about that time, my Polish combat friends delivered my Silver Cross of Merit that I had won in May of 1945, and the Ministry of Defense also awarded me the Order of the Great Patriotic War, First Degree.

In the end, the Central Committee rehabilitated me. After so many hellish trials, I hesitated to appear again before the Collegium. But they insisted that this time would be a mere formality.

When I arrived, I recognized Ivan Dyachenko, the former chief of the 197th Division's political department. He had initially given the order to confiscate my Party card right after I was liberated. For some reason, Dyachenko's arms and legs were shaking. I tried to calm him as best I could while we waited.

When the Collegium called us in, the chairman asked Dyachenko how it was that Yegorova had "managed to save her Party card in that Hitlerite hell," only for him to "snatch it away from her." Ivan Mironovich stood up nervously and murmured something incoherent about a combat assignment and fifteen attack planes.

The chairman cut him off and dismissed him, then addressed the Collegium. "Marshall S. I. Rudenko, commander of the air force where Anna Yegorova flew before the tragedy, told me that 'Yegorova was an honest fighter.'"

"And so, Comrade Yegorova," he continued, "We rehabilitate you in the Party's ranks. You will start paying your dues as soon as the regional party commission issues your new Party card. Unfortunately, we won't have it to you in time for the anniversary of the October Revolution. It's only five days away."

Pilots from our disbanded 805th sometimes came to visit us and pass on news of our comrades, alive and dead. They would listen, enthralled, as I told them the saga of my Party card and my many trials. "OK, guys, let's drop the subject," my husband would break in, trying to calm me. "Anna gets excited when she talks about this."

"You're right, Vyacheslav Arsenyevich," a combat friend of mine named Lyova Kabishcher once said. "But it's hard not to get upset! It's just so unfair to Anna! How humiliating! Besides, I think it's important to know about these 'twists' in our system."

"System? What does our system have to do with it, Lyova? It's just politics," I said.

My children grew, strong and healthy, but my health improved little. My little men learned to help around the house. Igor did the shopping, and Petya cleaned and cooked. Vyacheslav wrote several books about attack pilots.

Over the years I received many letters from my regimental comrades, and occasionally we got together to reminisce. I regularly corresponded with our old political commissar, Dmitri Shvidsky. He was working at a tractor manufacturing plant in Kharkov. He said that he and Colonel Tupanov, the political officer who chose me for the 805th all those years ago, were hunting for my awards records. They needed the records so they could apply for a Hero of the Soviet Union title for me.

Shvidsky, along with many other combat friends, wrote to me urging me to see the film *Clear Skies*.[3] He insisted I see the film "about your fate and the fates of many others like you." *Could a movie really make me feel better?* I wondered. Finally, I went.

Tears streamed down my cheeks as I stared at the screen. My sons sat on either side of me, whispering, "Mamochka! Don't cry! It's just a movie. They're just actors."

Soon after that, my Metrostroy friends found me. I hadn't returned from the war like a victorious knight on his horse, but amid shame and accusations. And so I had been afraid to visit them, afraid they had forgotten me. But an essay about me entitled "Yegorushka" appeared in the newspaper, and my old Metrostroy "team" found me soon thereafter. I was boundlessly happy to see them, and very grateful to them. Thanks to them, I finally received an apartment in Moscow.

I also received a letter from a Polish writer that contained photocopies from a West German magazine dated 1961. In the article, a Hitlerite officer, a former parachutist, reminisced about his experiences on the Eastern Front:

Our division was transferred from sunny Italy to that accursed hell in the East. The Russian Air Force was attacking us. I went to the field-dressing station for something. When I got there, I saw some soldiers bringing a Russian pilot back from the front lines. He looked pretty badly maimed. His flight suit was burned and torn up, and his face was covered with blood and

---

[3] A 1961 film (made during a brief period during the "Khrushchev Thaw" when criticism of Stalin's policies was tolerated) about a test pilot in the Soviet Air Force during World War II who is shot down over Germany and taken prisoner, awarded posthumously, and then stripped of his honors and livelihood upon his return to the USSR.

oil. The soldiers said the pilot had bailed out of a burning airplane and had landed near their position.

When the orderlies took off his helmet and overalls, they were stunned. The pilot was a girl! Everyone was even more astonished by the female pilot's behavior. The orderlies were removing pieces of her burned skin, and she didn't utter a single sound! How was it possible for a woman to maintain such inhuman self-control?

I received many letters over the years from former soldiers. One from a college professor in Tashkent said:

Thank you, Russian woman! Our 8th Guards Army was having a terrible time of it at the Vistula Bridgehead. We took it especially hard on that tragic day when you were shot down. To us at the bridgehead, attack pilots were heroes. Whenever the Il-2s appeared, the Fritzes' attacks would bog down. I always wanted to kiss you pilot-shturmoviks! Now I find out that there were lovely Russian women among our saviors. I've seen many battles and won many medals, but I bow my head to you...

Our 805th Attack Aviation Regiment, awarded the Order of Suvorov, fought with General Vershinin's 4th Air Force in the Kuban and in Taman, with General Polynin's 6th Air Force near Kovel and Lutsk, and with General Rudenko's 16th on the approaches to Berlin. My regiment-mates would converge from all corners of the Soviet Union whenever there was a reunion of the aforementioned air forces. Every time we met, some names were missing at roll-call, more friends had fallen ill or passed away. I always thought of Konstantin Simonov's[4] poem:

That longest day of the year
With its cloudless weather
Brought us universal disaster,
For four long years.
  It has gouged such a scar
  And cast so many into the dirt
  That for twenty and thirty years
  The survivors can't believe they are alive.
    Relatives come to visit the dead
    And time adds to the lists
    Still more names of those gone
    And keeps erecting obelisks...

---

[4] Konstantin Mikhailovich Simonov (1915–79). A popular Soviet author who wrote several war novels and a number of well-known war poems.

When we still lived near the Monino aerodrome, where some of the reunions were held, my regimental comrades would stop by our house on the way to the airfield. Once Pyotr Karev came by, as always a jovial and noisy "worker-airman" who seemed to really enjoy the reunion circuit. "I flew in the North after the war, but now I'm tossed aside," he joked with a sadness uncharacteristic of him. "I thought my health would last, but this cursed war seems to have finished me off."

"Do you remember? Do you?" he liked to ask me. *Yes, of course I do.*

A year later, Karev was gone. I went to his funeral, to see him off on his last "flight."

Vakhramov, our "magician," was living in Kiev. He and his wife raised three children. "I thought when my kids grew up, Katya and I would have a break. She was at the front, too, after all. But then the kids unloaded the grandchildren on us," Valentin confessed seriously, but his eyes twinkled with laughter.

Do you remember the story about Ivan Sukhorukov, who borrowed my gray greatcoat to propose to his girl? He got his wish. He and Tamara brought up two children, and Colonel Sukhorukov trained hundreds of young pilots at the flying school where he instructed.

Mikhail Berdashkevich came to the first 6th Air Force reunion, escorted by his two daughters. Their mother had "mobilized" the young university students to assist their father after his heart attack. Years of skin-transplant surgeries had smoothed the burn scars on his face and hands. His eyes, blue as the lakes of his native Belorussia, seemed more cheerful than they had during the war. His daughters resembled him like two water droplets. They worshipped him and tended to him with great tenderness. I was happy that Misha had such a loving family, after all he had suffered at the front.

Misha Zubov was shot down over Berlin and held prisoner for five days. On Victory Day[5] he was sent to the Urals and interrogated for four months. He told us how hard it had been for him to find a job after the "check." Everyone refused him work as soon as they learned he had been a prisoner-of-war.

Spending even a day in German captivity stamped you with a mark that could never be washed clean. It didn't matter if you'd fought since the war's opening shots. None of it mattered to the bureaucrats. You had been with the Fascists. You were an enemy. Thank God that most of us, by now, have been rehabilitated.

Still, there's always some vigilant, flunky politician who feels the need to remind you that you are "marked," and you'd better keep a low profile.

Yulia Krashchenko returned to her native town, Novochervonoye, near Lugansk, and raised three daughters. When the Gestapo took her away, they spread the rumor that she had been executed. In fact, they sent her to a penal

---

[5] May 9, 1945. Victory Day is still a major Russian holiday.

camp called Schvaidek, where she was beaten repeatedly and her head was shaved. From there, she went to Ravensbrück, a concentration camp for women. She was forced to work in a munitions factory. She couldn't bear to help the Fascists, so she began stuffing the bombs with sand. For that, the Nazis beat her and left her for dead in a penal block.

Soon afterward, the block was bombed. She somehow survived the building's collapse and escaped out a hole in the wall.

Pavle Trpinac wrote to me in 1963 to tell me he was alive and well and was head of the biochemistry department at Belgrade University. Three years later, I read a decree of the Supreme Soviet awarding him an Order of the Patriotic War—"for courage and bravery in saving the lives of Soviet prisoners-of-war."

Dr. Sinyakov found me through a newspaper article. He taught at a medical school and worked as head of surgery in a hospital in Chelyabinsk.[6] Not long after Trpinac received his award, Sinyakov and Trpinac flew to Moscow for a reunion, along with many other former prisoners. There was no end to the reminiscing. A fighter pilot and former inmate named Alexander Kashirin told Dr. Sinyakov, "It wasn't just our wounds you treated. You also healed our souls..."

The Soviet government never gave Georgi Fyodorovich any awards. But we knew...

My nephew Yurka finally saw his father again, many years after the war. After serving his ten-year sentence in the Gulag, Vasya was exiled. He and many other political prisoners survived thanks to the kindness of a construction chief in Norilsk[7] named Zavenyagin. To provide top experts for the construction projects there, he recruited specialists from the ranks of political prisoners, thus easing their daily hardships. Apparently, they flew my brother secretly to Moscow many times on aircraft convoys to approve construction plans. They secreted him away in the KGB hotel in Mayakovsky Square and never once let him visit his family on the Arbat. He wasn't even allowed to telephone them.

I often call Vasily's wife Katya a "Decembrist wife."[8] She undertook the long, dangerous journey to Norilsk to see her husband. For three months, she

---

[6] An industrial center in the southern Ural Mountains, 1,192 miles (1,919 km) east of Moscow, and a stop on the Trans-Siberian Railroad.

[7] The world's second-largest city above the Arctic Circle (after Murmansk), in Siberia's far north. Founded in 1935 as a major metallurgical mining complex, Norilsk was also the site of numerous Stalin-era forced labor camps.

[8] To call someone a "Decembrist wife" is to say that she is an exceptionally devoted wife. The expression comes from the 19th century, when the Decembrists (a group of several thousand Russian soldiers who revolted against the tsarist regime, demanding a constitution, in 1825) were exiled to Siberia, and many of their wives followed them into exile.

and Yurka made their way east by boat, the cheapest mode of transport. They suffered terribly, but the reunion gave the family much hope and happiness.

In 1953, Vasily was rehabilitated and released, but he and his family chose to stay in Norilsk. He was appointed deputy director of the metallurgical mining plant which Zavenyagin had founded. Katya worked in a tailor's shop, and Yuri continued school.

When the World Youth Festival came to Moscow in 1957, Vasya found himself longing to see the capital once again. He was offered a high position in the Ministry of Trade, the very place where he had worked in 1937. The ministry had transferred him to Stalino, in the Donbass—where he was arrested soon thereafter. Such ironies of fate...

My brother retired when he was seventy-five, and his son Yuri Vasilevich worked at the Norilsk Power Plant for many years. Now the third generation of Yegorovs works there—Vasily's grandsons Viktor and Andrey, who graduated from the Moscow Institute of Energy. They are raising Vasily's four great-grandchildren Antoshka, Danilka, Masha, and Sasha. Life goes on.

☆ ☆ ☆

On May 7, 1965, the telephone buzzed bright and early in our apartment. I picked up the phone and said "Hello?" softly, so I wouldn't wake the boys. "Hurrah! Hurrah! Hurrah!" came the excited voice of my friend Gilyardi, the poet.

"Why are you rejoicing so early in the morning, Nikodim Fyodorovich?" I asked, laughing.

"Turn the radio on, Annushka! They're giving you the 'Hero' award!"

Many more calls came that day, and throughout the month, from combat friends, newspaper and magazine editors, schools, and all sorts of other people. Generals Vershinin, Rudenko, and Polynin all sent letters of congratulations.

I'll always remember the decree from the Supreme Soviet of the USSR awarding me the Hero of the Soviet Union: "For exemplary fulfillment of combat missions at the front against the German-Fascist invaders in the years of the Great Patriotic War, and for displaying courage and heroism...."

As I read the words of this solemn document, I saw the faces of my regimental comrades, who had ascended into the flaming heights, never to return. I heard the formations of Shturmoviks, roaring evermore into the troubled skies of my youth.

"Why are they drafting girls to the war?" I heard Boris Strakhov's voice. There he was, standing in front of me at the aerodrome with an armful of wildflowers, his smile all youthful shyness, full of happiness and light. Behind him stood attack-pilots Pashkov, Andryanov, Usov, Stepochkin, Zinoviev, Tasyets, Podynenogin, Pokrovsky, Rzhevsky, Mkrtumov, Grudnyak, Balyabin...

Those terrible war years passed long ago. My children and grandchildren have grown up. How time flies... When I think of past battles and my combat friends, I recall their courage and nobility, their towering sense of duty and scorn for death, and most of all their deep feeling of front comradeship.

Russian literature boasts of our proud Slavic women, who can "curb a galloping horse" or "walk into a burning hut." Those are big shoes to fill. But I think the war showed the whole world who these "women in Russian villages" are and how their hearts can soar in the name of their motherland.

In those mournful war years, heroism wasn't any one person's lot but the destiny of our generation. But how much sorrow can the Russian woman endure? And why must she? I doubt whether anyone could bear more.

And may no one on earth ever suffer such a fate again.